A Year at the Shore

Philip Henry Gosse
F.R.S.

Coachwhip Publications
Landisville, Pennsylvania

A Year at the Shore, by Philip Henry Gosse (1810-1888)
Reprint of 1870 London edition, first published 1865.
Coachwhip Publications. 2008. All rights reserved.
CoachwhipBooks.com

ISBN 1-930585-51-9
ISBN-13 978-1-930585-51-5

QL122 .G6
591.92

Contents

January	5
February	19
March	35
April	49
May	63
June	77
July	93
August	107
September	121
October	135
November	149
December	163
Footnotes	177

Plate I

Dog-Whelk. Pelican's Foot. Top. Cowry.

I.
January

How grandly those heavy waves are rolling in upon this long shingle-beach! Onward they come, with an even deliberate march that tells of power, out of that lowering sky that broods over the southern horizon; onward they come, onward! onward!—each following its precursor in serried ranks, ever coming nearer and nearer, ever looming larger and larger, like the resistless legions of a great invading army, sternly proud in its conscious strength; and ever and anon, as one and another dark billow breaks in a crest of foam, we may fancy we see the standards and ensigns of the threatening host waving here and there above the mass.

Still they drive in; and each in turn curls over its green head, and rushes up the sloping beach in a long-drawn sheet of the purest, whitest foam. The drifted snow itself is not more purely, spotlessly white than is that sheet of foaming water. How it seethes and sparkles! how it boils and bubbles! how it rings and hisses! The wind sings shrilly out of the driving clouds, now sinking to a moan, now rising to a roar; but we cannot hear it, for its tones are drowned in the ceaseless rushing of the mighty waves upon the beach and the rattle of the recoiling pebbles. Along the curvature of the shore the shrill hoarse voice runs, becoming softer and mellower as it recedes; while the echo of the bounding cliffs confines and repeats it, and mingles it with the succeeding ones, till all are blended on the ear in one deafening roar.

But let us climb these slippery rocks, and picking our way cautiously over yonder craggy ledges, leaping the chasms that yawn between and reveal the hissing waters below, let us strive to attain the vantage-ground of that ridge that we see some fifty feet above the beach. It is perilous work, this scrambling over rocks, alternately slimy with treacherous sea-weed, and bristling with sharp needle-points of honey-combed limestone now climbing a precipice, with the hands clutching these same rough points, and the toes finding a precarious hold in their interstices; now descending to a ledge awfully overhung; now creeping along a narrow shelf, by working each foot on, a few inches at a time; while the fingers nervously cling to the stony precipice, and the mind strives to forget the rugged depths below, and what would happen if—(ah! that "if!" let us cast it to the winds): another long stride across a gulf, a bound upward, and here we are.

Yes, here we stand, on the bluff, looking out to seaward in the very eye of the wind. We might have supposed it a tolerably smooth slope of stone when we looked at the point from the sea, or from the various parts of the shore whence we can see this promontory. But very different is it on a close acquaintance. It is a wilderness of craggy points and huge castellated masses of compact limestone marble, piled one on another in the wildest and most magnificent confusion. We have secured a comfortable berth, where, wedged in between two of these masses, we can without danger lean on one breast-high, and gaze over it down upon the very theatre of the elemental war. Is not this a sight worth the toil and trouble and peril of the ascent? The rock below is fringed with great insular peaks and blocks, bristling up amidst the sea, of various sizes and of the most fantastic and singular forms, which the sea at high-water would mostly cover; though now the far-receding tide exposes their horrid points, and the brown leprous coating of barnacles with which their lower sides are covered is broadly seen between the swelling seas.

Heavily rolls in the long deep swell of the ocean from the south-west; and as it approaches with its huge undulations driven up into foaming crests before the howling bale, each mighty wave breasts up against these rocks, as when an army of veteran legions assaults an impregnable fortress. Impregnable indeed! for having spent its fury in a rising wall of mingled water and foam, it shoots up perpendicularly to an immense elevation, as if it would scale the heights it could not overthrow, only to lie the next moment a broken ruin of water, murmuring and shrieking in the moats below. The insular peaks and blocks receive the incoming surge in an overwhelming flood, which, immediately, as the spent wave recedes, pours off through the interstices in a hundred beautiful jets and cascades; while in the narrow straits and passages the rushing sea boils and whirls about in curling sheets of snowy whiteness, curdling the surface; or, where it breaks away, of the most delicate pea-green hue, the tint produced by the bubbles seen through the water as they crowd to the air from the depths where they were formed,—the evidence of the unseen combat fiercely raging between earth and sea far below.

The shrieking gusts, as the gale rises yet higher and more furious, whip off the crests of the breaking billows, and bear the spray like a shower of salt sleet to the height where we stand; while the foam, as it forms and accumulates around the base of the headland, is seized by the same power in broad masses, and carried against the sides of the projecting rocks; flying hither and thither like fleeces of wool, and adhering like so much mortar to the face of the precipice, till it covers great spaces, to the height of many fathoms above the highest range of the tide. The gulls flit wailing through the storm, now breasting the wind, and beating the air with their long wings as they make slow headway; then, yielding the vain essay, they turn and are whirled away, till, recovering themselves, they come up again with a sweep, only again to be discomfited. Their white forms, now seen against the leaden-grey sky, now lost amidst the snowy foam, then coming into strong relief against the black rocks; their piping screams, now sounding close against the ear, then blending with the sounds of the elements, combine to add a wildness to the scene which was already sufficiently savage.

But the springy-tide is nearly at its lowest; a rocky path leads clown from our eminence to a recess in the precipice, whence in these conditions access may be obtained to a sea-cavern, that we may possibly find entertainment in exploring.

We reluctantly turn our backs upon the magnificent battle of sea and land, and following this sheep-track, scramble down, holding fast by the tufts of thrift, round and soft and yielding, but sufficiently firm to present some resistance, or by the tussocks of wiry grass, till we leap down on the great piled masses of marble that past ages have thrown from the cliffs upon the beach. Among these we find many basins and pools of still water, for we are in a deep recess of the promontory, whose shelter renders us almost unconscious of the fury of the winter wind without; and the masses of rock that lie piled about so curb and break the force of the incoming sea, that it percolates rather than rushes into these secluded nooks. Tall walls of stone, too, shut out much of the light of day; and as to the sun, only his most slant evening rays ever reach this spot: it is enshrouded in an obscurity which is most congenial to both the plants and the animals which resort to our shores; and here, doubtless, though the season is still midwinter, we shall find our searchings rewarded by not a few of those creatures, beautiful and wondrous, in which the devout naturalist delights to trace the handiwork of the God of glory.

At the very first glance into this little rock-hollow, all fringed with crimson and purple weed, lined with scales of lilac coralline, and partly shadowed by the olive fronds of the leathery tangle, we discern many forms of animal life. Here, for instance, is a fine handsome shelled mollusk, the Purple-spotted Top.[1] Before we take him up, let us notice for a moment with what an easy even movement he glides along over the leaves of the sea-weed, now over the stony projections of the pool, now on the broad weeds again. On lifting the shell, we find that the fine, fleshy, apricot-coloured animal clings with considerable force to the weed; and on transferring it to a glass bottle, we get a better sight of the organ by which it maintains both its stability and its movements. The under-surface of the creature, then, forms a long, nearly parallel-sided sole, abruptly pointed behind, where it stretches to a considerable distance in the rear of the shell, and bounded in front by a slightly-thickened transverse rim, a little arched, and projecting on each side. This organ is the foot, and it is composed of muscular fibres elaborately interwoven, much as in the human tongue, whereby great versatility and power of motion are communicated to it; indeed, when in motion, it strongly reminds one of the human tongue.

The sensitive and muscular foot of our captive has already taken hold of the glass side of its prison, and it is now smoothly mounting up it. With a lens you may see that though it is one undivided area, yet in the arrangement of its muscles, it is separated into two portions by a line which runs down the middle; any that these two sides move alternately.

The muscles of the right half, for example, are moved a little onward, and take a fresh hold of the ground, while those of the left remain clinging; then the right half clings, while the left relaxes and advances a little beyond the right, and again clings, when the right makes its forward move. So that the effect is exactly that of two feet advancing by alternate steps; and if your own two feet were enclosed in one elastic stocking, your own progress would appear very much like that of the *Trochus*. Indeed, some shell-fishes not distantly allied to this, as the pretty little Pheasant-shell,[2] which I occasionally find among these rocks, really have the foot divided into two distinct and separate halves, in which this alternate motion is, of course, more obvious.

Looked at from above, we discern that this foot thickens towards the middle, where it is overlapped by a broad wing-like expansion on each side. This, for manifest reasons, is known by the name of the cloak or mantle. In all cases it performs important offices in the economy of the animal, as I shall presently describe; and in this instance we see it is adorned along its edges with certain lappets and long fleshy taper threads (called *cirri*), which wave vivaciously to and fro as the creature crawls. These are probably the seats of a delicate sense; perhaps receiving impressions analogous to those of touch, from the strokes they continually make on the surrounding fluid.

In front we see a distinct head, with a broad flat muzzle not altogether unlike that of an ox. On each side of the back part of this head, there is another long taper thread: these are called tentacles, but neither in form nor in structure can we discern any difference between these and the *cirri* that fringe the mantle. In all probability they are alike organs of a highly delicate sense of touch.

Immediately behind each of these head-tentacles you see a little wart, which has a black bead set as it were in its substance. You have often, doubtless, observed the similar black points that are placed at the tips of the upper pair of the horns (tentacles) of the common garden snail; and I daresay, when a child, you have amused yourself by touching them, and noticing how instantaneously the sensitive creature would roll them in, so to speak, concealing them far in the interior of the inturned horns. And every child is taught that these black spots are the snail's *eyes*; and so, indeed, they are; and these spots on our Top's warts are its eyes too, notwithstanding that some learned naturalists, apparently from the mere love of paradox, have affected to doubt the fact that such is their function. If you could dissect out one of these points, and submit it to careful examination with a good microscope, you would find all the parts essential to an organ of vision; there is a sclerotic coat, a distinct little pupil and iris, a cornea in front, and a dark pigment layer within, with vitreous and aqueous humours, and even a crystalline lens for the condensation of the rays of light. Minute these parts are, to be sure, but not less exquisitely finished for that. Indeed, the more skill they require in the demonstrator, the more they reflect the inimitable skill of the Creator. Swammerdam, the Dutch physiologist, who so beautifully showed the structure of the snail's eye, seems to have feared the doubts of his conclusions that would ensue from the difficulty of repeating his investigations. "But who will credit this?" he says; "for does it not seem impossible that on a point not larger than the nib of the pen with which I write, such exquisite art and so many miracles should be displayed?"

Now, leaving the animal, though we might devote a few moments to the admiration of its rich colours, adorned as is its deep yellow hue with lines and clouds of deeper brown, let us look at the shell, the solid house of stone, which our friend Trochus has himself built up to cover his head in the hour of danger. How well has he combined the *utile cum dulci!*— the comfortable with the ornamental! Its general form is that of a cone of much regularity, but with an oblique base, and perhaps you may be surprised to learn that this conical form is but the result of the winding of a very long cone upon itself in a spire. But if you examine a dead shell with care, you will see that it is so. Supposing you had a very long and slender hollow cone of plastic material, and, beginning with the acute point, you twined the whole upon itself, descending in a spiral form, you would have the representation of a turbinate shell, which, by a little gentle pressure of the fingers, might be moulded, without at all losing its essential character, into the exact shape of our *Trochus*, in which the progress of the spire can without difficulty be followed as well by slight inequalities of surface as by the arrangement of the colours.

It is one of our showy shells. This specimen before us has for its ground colour a chaste, cool grey, occasionally varied with tints of reddish buff, but most conspicuously adorned with a series of large and regular spots of purplish crimson running along the lower angle of the spire from the base to the summit. Each of these spots passes off into an oblique line above, the repetition of which augments the beauty of the pattern.

The interior of the shell has a glory of quite another character. It is covered with a coat of nacre or pearl, of exceedingly brilliant and rich lustre, and the presence of this inward pearliness is quite characteristic of this genus, and of most of the others belonging to the same family, the *Turbinidæ*. Many of the fine large tropical species are specially conspicuous for this adornment, as I have seen in those that lie along the dazzling beach of coral-sand in lovely Jamaica. The pearl of these shells is used in the arts. De Montfort mentions a necklace which he had seen, that was made out of the nacred part of the shell of the *Turbo smaragdus*, and which was *much more brilliant and beautiful* than any of the finest orient pearls.[3] And Chenu observes:— "Les grandes espèces fournissent une fort belle nacre, employée pour les ouvrages de marqueterie. Quelques espèces ont reçu des noms sous lesquels les marchands les distinguent: il y a le Burgau ou Nacré; la Veuve Perlée, dont les tubercles extérieurs usés ressemblent à des perles; la Bouche-d'Or, dont la nacre est d'un beau jaune doré; la Bouche-d'Argent; le Perroquet, ou Turbo Impérial," etc.[4]

At another time we may examine the structure of shell, and inquire by what instruments and with what materials the ingenious animal

Plate II

Scallops.

contrives to construct so strong and so elegant a dwelling. For the present, however, as the month is January, we shall, if we sit still longer, run the risk of "catching a cold," if we catch nothing else, though the wind *is* in the south, and the temperature is so mild for the season.

Therefore, we will move about and pursue our researches among the rocks and under the loose stones. Well, we are rewarded with other specimens: here are several neat little shells, with a lengthened spire, and with a remarkably thickened lip. This is the little Thick-lipped Dog-whelk,[5] a very common mollusk with us under such stones as these at low watermark. And here is another species of the same genus, the Netted Dog-whelk,[6] which is a much larger shell, being nearly twice as long as the former, and marked with close transverse furrows, which, crossing the longitudinal ribs at right angles, give a peculiar reticulate surface, on which the specific name is founded.

Comparing these shells with the *Trochus*, we see that they have a deep notch cut in the front part, of which no sign appears in the latter; and this mark, trivial as it may seem, is an important indication of the habits of the animal. The inhabitants of all shells which have this notch are carnivorous, while those with simple lips are herbivorous. The *Trochus* gnaws or rather rasps away the tender growth of marine vegetation, or the fronds of the grown *Algæ*, with its remarkable palate-ribbon, all studded with reversed points, of which I may find another opportunity to speak. The Dog-whelk, on the other hand, acts the part of a cannibal ogre, feeding on his simpler brethren of the bivalve shells; storming their stony castles, in which they seem so secure, by, open violence.

Look at this old valve of a *Mactra*. Like hundred more that you may pick up at high water-mark, it is perforated by a tiny hole near the hinge, so smooth an so perfectly circular, that you would suppose a clever artisan had been at work drilling the massive stony shell with his steel wimble. No such thing: the Dog-whelk has done it: this is the breach which he so scientifically effected in the fortress; and hence he sucked out the soft and juicy and savoury flesh of his miserable victim.

In order to understand his plan of operations, let us put down our captive, and see him crawl. He is not long before he begins to march, on his broad oblong foot, which, as you observe, is cream-coloured, elegantly splashed and speckled with dark-brown. But before he moves he thrusts out a long cylindrical proboscis from the front of his head, which he carries high aloft and waves to and fro; and this organ, we see, fits into the deep notch in front of the shell. This proboscis is his drilling-wimble.

This organ is itself a study. Long as it is when extended, it can be thoroughly drawn within the body and there it forms two fleshy cylinders, one within the other, exactly like a stocking half turned on itself. There are proper muscles attached to its walls, and to the interior of the head, by extremities which are branched in a fan-shape, so as greatly to strengthen their insertions; and these, by contraction, draw the one portion within the other. Then there is a broad hoop of muscle, which, passing round the inner cylinder, by contracting pushes it out, and lengthens it. Within the interior of this latter there is a long narrow ribbon of cartilage, which is armed with rows of sharp flinty points, turned backwards; and this tongue or palate, as it is variously called, is the Dog-whelk's weapon.

We cannot induce the Whelk to attack his prey just when we please; but he has been detected in the operation, and I will describe it. With his broad muscular foot he secures a good hold of the bivalve, and having selected his point of attack, in general near the hinge—a selection which probably looks more at the superiority of the meat within than at any peculiar facility in the perforation—he brings the tip of his extended proboscis to the point, so that the silicious teeth can act on the shell. Hard as is the calcareous shell, it is not proof against the flint; for, without any solvent excretion, the aid of which some physiologists have been ready to suppose, these glassy points, grating round and round as on a pivot, soon wear away the substance, and gradually bore the tiny aperture which exposes the sapid morsel.

Continuing our researches, we find, deep in a rocky pool under a tuft of weed, a shell of a peculiar form, because of the enormous expansion of its outer lip. It is known as the Pelican's-foot,[7] from the resemblance which this lip with its diverging ribs bears to the webbed toes of a water-fowl. This, too, is a carnivorous species; and though it is somewhat rare to detect the animal moving, even though kept alive in captivity, yet by carefully examining this one in its deep pool, before we disturb its equanimity, we can just see the proboscis protruding from the wide square notch in the shell, and discern that it is rather prettily coloured, being marked with spots of opaque white on a rose-coloured ground.

This species is interesting from the changes of figure which it undergoes in its progress from youth to maturity. While young the shell is simple, with no trace of the expanded lip; and it is only at mature age, and rather suddenly, that the shell makes its remarkable growth into these far-projecting points and angles, the augmented thickness of which is, moreover, at least equally conspicuous with the expanse.

But far more remarkable changes take place in the growth of the shell in a family of signal beauty, of which I discern a specimen in yonder cavernous hollow. The family I speak of is that of the Cowries; and this individual represents the only species that is indigenous to our seas—the little Furrowed Cowry.[8] Let us pause awhile to admire it, for it is one of the very loveliest of our marine animals.

The shell itself is doubtless familiar to most of my readers, for it is to be picked up on every sandy beach. It varies in size from that of a split pea to that of a large horsebean. It is elegantly marked all over with transverse ridges. These ridges are porcellaneous white, and the alternate furrows between are purplish, or flesh-coloured. The larger specimens commonly display three spots of dark brown, arranged lengthwise. But probably few are aware how very elegant a creature it is when tenanted by its living inhabitant, and crawling at ease in clear water. The foot, on which it glides with a slow but smooth motion over the surface of the rock on which it habitually dwells, or, if you please, on the bottom of the saucer of sea-water in which you are examining it, is a broad expansion spreading out to twice the superficies of the base of the shell. Above this is the fleshy mantle, which is so turned up as closely to invest the shell, conforming to its shape, and even fitting into the grooves between the ridges. This mantle can be protruded, at the will of the animal, so far that the two sides meet along the top of the shell, and completely cover it, or it can be completely retracted within the wrinkled lips beneath; and it is capable of all gradations of extension between these limits. From the front of the shell protrudes the head armed with two straight and lengthened tentacles, answering in function and appearance to the upper pair of horns in a snail; except that the little black points which constitute the visual organs are not, in this case placed at the tips, but on a little prominence on the outside of the base of each tentacle. Above and between these, which diverge at a considerable angle, projects the proboscis, a rather thick fleshy tube; formed by a flat lamina, with its edges bent round so as to meet along the under side. The interior of this proboscis is lined with delicate cilia, by whose constant vibrations a current of water is drawn into the tube and poured over the surface of the gills, for the purpose of respiration. This current may be readily perceived by any one who will take the trouble to watch, with a pocket-lens, a Cowry crawling along the side of a phial filled with sea-water. By placing the vessel between your eye and the light, and fixing your attention on the front of the proboscis, you will presently perceive the minute particles of floating matter (always held in suspension, even in clear water) drawn in various directions towards the tube, with a motion which increases in velocity as they approach, and at length rapidly sucked in and disappearing one after another within. It is an interesting sight to see, and one that cannot be looked on without delight and admiration at this beautiful contrivance of Divine Wisdom, for the incessant breathing of the respiratory organs in water charged with vivifying oxygen.

Let us look at the vivid hues of all these organs. The foot, which expands to so great a length and breadth behind the shell, is of a buff or pale orange ground-colour, delicately striated with longitudinal undulating veins of yellowish white. The mantle which embraces the shell is of a pellucid olive, thickly mottled and spotted with black, and studded with glands protruded through its substance, of light yellow; and is often edged with a narrow border of red. The proboscis is vermilion-red, varying in brilliancy in different individuals. The tentacles are of a paler tint of the same colour, speckled with yellow.

Such, then, is the beauty of the animal which inhabits this familiar and plain little shell,—a beauty of which those who know it only in cabinets can hardly form an idea; while, as the observer gazes on it placidly gliding along, he cannot avoid an emotion of surprise that such an amplitude of organs can be folded within the narrow compass of the shell, and protruded through so contracted an aperture.

You would scarcely recognise in this shell, or in the Tiger Cowry, that one so often sees on chimney-pieces, the model of an ordinary convolute spiral shell, such as the snail or the whelk. But in infancy and youth the Cowry is a shell manifestly of such a character, scarcely to be distinguished from the Olives and Volutes; a shell with a distinct spire, a long wide aperture, and a thin-edged outer lip. But when the animal has arrived at mature age, a sudden deposition of shelly matter takes place on the lip, which is greatly thickened, and which expands above so as to conceal the spire, bending inward at the same time and approaching the inner lip, so as to reduce the aperture to a very narrow line. Finally, a thick coat of enamel, or glossy porcellaneous lime, is spread over the entire surface of the shell, from the narrow aperture to the back-line, which coat takes the form of those tranverse folds which are so characteristic of the species and so elegant.

Here, clinging to the perpendicular wall of rock, sheltered snugly by an overshadowing stone, which I have just removed, is a lovely specimen of the Squin or Scallop.[9] In the ages of monkery, when men's eyes were more directed to the land where the blessed Lord Jesus once sojourned than to the place where He now is, and pilgrimage to an earthly country was more valued than that to a heavenly, this shell affixed to the hat was the accepted sign that the wearer had visited Jerusalem; and received the homage of sanctity that such a pilgrim claimed.

"He quits his cell, the pilgrim staff he bore,
And fixed the scallop in his hat before."[10]

Some mystic connexion, some secret sympathy, was assumed to exist between the scallop and St. James, the brother of the Lord, first bishop of Jerusalem. What it was appears to be irrecoverably lost in the darkness of those very dark ages, and is doubtless not worth the hunting up. We may leave such puerilities, to consider the impress of His divine hand which the All wise God has made on the shell of the mollusk that inhabits it.

These bivalves have been called the "butterflies of the sea," as well on account of the vivid and varied colours with which their broad wing-like valves are painted, as of their agile fluttering and flying movements. We frequently see them, especially for some time after having been taken and put into an unfamiliar scene, as our aquariums, shoot hither and thither through the water, with irregular zigzag flights, accompanied with fitful openings and closings of the valves. These leaps and flights seem to have no determinate object, except "the letting off the steam" of their exuberant animal vivacity; but the creatures have the power of directing their leap by a forcible ejection of water from any given part of the compressed lips of the mantle.[11]

It is a very pretty sight to see a healthy Pecten in vessel of clear sea-water. The elegant valves are opened to a considerable width, perhaps to half an inch or more, and the entire aperture all round is filled by a curtain, which drops from one to the other, perpendicularly, a little way within the margin. This is the mantle, and it is generally painted with rich colours, in irregular patterns, often of spots and marbled clouds of black on a rich green ground, or pearly-green clouds on flesh-colour—sometimes pale-yellow clouds on velvet-black; but these hues have no perceptible relation with those of the shell. Looking closely, you see that the mantle is not single, but composed of two curtains, whose edges meet in the middle. And now these are slightly separating, and giving us a peep into the interior; but the most notable thing we see is the array of long white taper tentacles which proceed from each edge, and wave to and fro in the clear water; while another row of similar organs, but larger, is affixed to each curtain along the line where it starts from the shell. And along this same line, scattered between the bases of the larger tentacles, there is a row (and a corresponding one on the other curtain) of beads, which seem to be turned out of the richest and most lustrous gems. Even the unassisted eye is arrested by the flashing brilliance, but with a powerful lens they look like rubies set in sockets of sapphire, from which the light blazes forth with incomparable brilliance. These are the Pecten's eyes, each of which possesses all the parts requisite for perfect vision.

The valves vary much in colour. Some are pure white; some white with a crimson line along the summit of each radiating ridge; some rosy, crimson, or lilac; some cream, straw-yellow, deep yellow; some dull brick-red, dark purplish-red, or sienna-brown; some are marbled with black on a red ground, making a very rich pattern.

The largest specimens, and those with greatest variety in hue, are found in deep water, and for the most part congregated in large numbers on some particular spot of the sea-bottom, which is called a scallop-bed. Such are found in Weymouth Bay, and in Torbay; and there the shell-fish can be obtained in sufficient quantity for the market. At Weymouth there is a considerable business done in these delicacies, which is, however, almost all in the hands of one dealer, from whom I have collected some details of interest.

The ordinary trawlers avoid the scallop-beds, if possible, because they are liable to have their nets torn by them; the sharp valves doubtless catching and cutting the meshes. But they often bring up many unintentionally, and a naturalist would find a trawler's refuse a most productive field: for numbers of rare and valuable zoophytes and other forms of life come up attached to the shells, which might easily be saved, but are not: the men "have no time, for they are so anxious to get their craft into a berth, and then to take out the fish as soon as the trawl is up."

Twenty bushels of scallops are sometimes taken at once; but this is rare. The average produce of the Weymouth trawlers is five bushels per week, which are readily sold at twopence per hundred; about seven hundred going to the bushel. The customers are "mostly the genteels," who eat the *morceaux* stewed with flour or scolloped. The worthy woman who commands the supply had had the trade in her hands for twenty-eight years (in 1853); she had never heard them called by any other name

Plate III

Dotted Siponcle. Sea-Cucumber.

than "Squins," though she understood they were called Scallops in some places. "Squin" is by some said to be a corruption of "Quin," after the actor and epicure of that name, who is reported to have been fond of the delicate mollusk; but I much doubt the derivation.[12]

As a proof of the tenacity of life possessed ay this species, a fisherman assured me that he once put a quantity in a bag into a cupboard and forgot them, till, after the lapse of a week, turning them out he found them alive.

But now another object of interest claims attention: for, in this cavern, closely squeezed in between the layers of stone, I see the satiny-white skin of a glorious Sea-cucumber. And now to get him out, there's the rub. So firmly imbedded is he, so deeply ensconced, that no pushing with fingers or sticks will avail; indeed, I can but just touch his body with my finger-ends poked in to the utmost. No; we must cut away the rock above and below with the strong steel chisel, by means of well-directed strokes of a heavy hammer. Slow work it is, for the rock is awfully hard: the prize, however, cannot escape, and the chief point of solicitude is not to crush it in the process. At length a fortunate blow splits off a slice of rock, which leaves the unhappy skulker defenceless. Now I get my fingers gradually behind him, and force him out, gently and tenderly; sucker after sucker he is compelled to let go, and now here he is in my hand, shrunken indeed, and squeezed flat from his very shrinking in the close crevice, but all unbroken and none the worse.

This is a much more sluggish creature than any of the mollusks that we have been capturing: no sooner are they put into water than they are active, and at once display their attractions; this animal, on the contrary, will be perhaps several days in your tank before he will feel himself sufficiently at home to unfold his splendid array of tentacles. But then it is indeed a magnificent coronet of plumes wherewith the headless king is adorned.

The Sea-cucumber soon finds himself a snug berth among the rockwork of the tank; pressing his body between the pieces just as when we saw him first, but taking care to leave space to protrude his front. Then this part evolves, and a deep collar of dark purple is seen, from which a ring of ten somewhat thick stems arises, tapering to a point and arching outwards. These are of a purplish-black hue, and are studded with short branches set on in a spiral, which again branch and branch again, each terminal point bearing a white papilla; so that the whole constitutes a series of conical aggregations of white dots clustering about the black stems, something like pointed cauliflowers, and forming, as they wave to and fro in the clear water, a very charming spectacle.[13]

The suckers, which, when the animal first came into our possession, were apparent only as little warts, arranged in five clustered rows down the angles of the body, are now seen to be long, tubes, each with an adhering disk at its extremity, by which it anchors to the surrounding stones. The mechanism of these suckers does not importantly differ from that of the same organs in the Star-fishes. Indeed, notwithstanding the very wide diversity of form and appearance between the two animals, the Cucumber and the Star are so nearly allied as to belong to the same class, that named Echinodermata; the Sea-urchins, creatures totally diverse in aspect from both, connecting the forms together.

And this Cucumber, again, is connected with the proper worms (Annellida) by some obscure animals which bear the name of Siponcles. Here is one which may illustrate the form, the Dotted Siponcle.[14] It has a cylindrical body, rounded and abruptly pointed behind, which is of a light-brown hue, with a satiny gloss but the hue resolves itself under a powerful lens into a freckling of pale dots, excessively numerous, on a brown ground, and the lustre into a multitude of close-set annular wrinkles. What is curious in the creature is the protrusion and retraction of its trunk. From the front end of the body we see rapidly protruding, by evolution of the parts, a rather slender trunk, till it attains about one-third the length of the body; then its tip expands, and is seen to be surrounded by eight rows of black points, and within these a circle of slender, white, thread-like tentacles. These latter are the representatives of the gorgeous head-plumes of the Cucumber. Immediately the long trunk is turned out to the outmost, it begins to be rolled in again; and this process goes on with equal rapidity till it is quite concealed. Then again it is unrolled, and so on alternately. Doubtless the function of respiration is performed by this action; and perhaps also food is collected and swallowed.

One species of this creature, the Hermit Siponcle,[15] common enough with us, is in the habit of appropriating old deserted shells of univalve mollusca, as the periwinkle, or the pelican's-foot, for its own residence. In this case it builds up a wall of sand-atoms, cemented by a glue of its own secreting, across the shell-aperture, leaving only a small central orifice, through which it may protrude its curious trunk.

Thus we discern the infinite and inexhaustible resources of the Divine Wisdom in contrivances which have for their object the preservation, sustentation, and comfort of worms so obscure and humble as these. Discerning, let us adore!

II.
February

What will Babbicombe Bay yield us this fine February morning? One thing at least it yields, a magnificent coast view; and this is scarcely affected by the season. Let there be only a moderately clear atmosphere, a sky chequered with blue spaces and white wind-borne clouds, and snatches of sunshine interchanging with shadows,—which last there will be, of course, with such a sky,—and such a prospect cannot fail to please.

And, indeed, this noble sweep of precipitous coast can hardly be surpassed for beauty all round the sea-girt shores of Britain. The forms of the cliffs are imposing: their broad masses of vivid colour alternating,—the white compact limestone, the bright red sandstone, becoming almost scarlet as the sun shines out full, yet prevented from being tawdry by its harmonies with the various hues of green that crown it, by its own breadth of light and shadow, by its dimming tints as it softens and mellows into the purple of the distance; the panorama of blue hills rising and fading far inland, the Tors and heights of Dartmoor and Exmoor; and the ever-changing sea, now laughing in its brightness, now frowning, and chafing in its wrath, filling so vast an area as it does from this vantage height;—these are the broader features of a scene which I will pause a moment to depict in detail, before I descend to the beach.

I take my stand on the margin of the cliff that overlooks Oddicombe, my feet upon the short soft turf, marked with fairy rings, the Doe's Head just on my left,—a remarkable projection of grey lichened limestone from the very cliff-edge, which, seen from the opposite side, bears a curious resemblance to the head of a lop-eared, cross-grained cur; but from my point of view far more forcibly presents the appearance of the face of a night-capped old man, grinning with pain;—and a fine vertical, and in some places overhanging, precipice just on my right, in whose horizontal strata scores of noisy jackdaws find resting ledges. I see them as they sit in conscious security only a few yards below the margin, their sleek grey polls wagging, and their black eyes now and then upturned, as others of the cawing tribe fly in, and seek sitting-room.

Some of the strata are strangely distorted at the western end; and here a narrow and somewhat perilous track leads down below the cliff to a grassy plateau at its foot. I scramble down, and sit on a stony shelf, overhung with sheets of ivy, and mark the bright green tufts of Sea-spleenwort springing out of the clefts, unfortunately too high to be reached.

Plate IV

Sea Lemon. Crowned Eolis. Spawn of Both.

The eye roams northward. At foot a rough broken ground slopes steeply down, shaggy with thickets of brake and bramble, and of furze which glows even now with golden blossom, varied with great tracts of broken fragments of limestone, blackened by the weather. At length this merges into a broad beach of shingle, snowy white, on which I see ladies reclining, with books and parasols, as if 'twere July instead of February. The sea bounds the beach with a line of still whiter surf, ever renewing itself as it breaks, with a sweet whispering sound. At the back is a series of most picturesque cliffs of the reddest sandstone, on the top of which I find in June the beautiful blossoms of the Purple Gromwell, one of the rarest of British flowers. The ground at the summit is very uneven; and so my eye rests on the broad opposite slopes of Woodleigh Vale, chequered with fields and hedgerows, among which the ploughmen are busy, and the teams are toiling up the steep furrows.

The formation suddenly changes again, and the limestone is seen in the fine rounded projection of Petit Tor, whose front of white marble has been laid bare by the quarriers. Beyond this is the ruddy sandstone once more rising into lofty headlands of noble shapes. At the foot of one of these an isolated rock, called, from its figure, the Bell, stands in the sea, where, even while I am writing this paper, a mournful tragedy has occurred. Two Babbicombe fishermen went out at midnight to examine their crab-pots at this rock, and did not return. The morning revealed the keel of the boat bottom-up, moored by the pot-lines, and one poor fellow entangled by his feet in the same lines, while the sea washed his hair about the surface. The other has not yet been found.

Farther on, the bluff Ness marks the harbour of Teignmouth, and as the sunlight falls on the white villas that stud the opposite side, the scene looks attractive. Then the cliff-line rapidly diminishes in height as it recedes, and the heads of Dawlish project, and we see no more till at Exmouth the land trends to the eastward, and from its white terraces faintly seen in the slanting sun now, but to stand out full and clear in the afternoon, we follow the bold, varying, beauteous coast, beauteous in its outline, but dim in its detail, for some twenty miles farther, till the straining eye finally fails to discern it somewhere between Lyme and Bridport; though Portland itself is sometimes to be seen, and I have myself made it well out, stretching far forth upon the wide eastern horizon of blue sea. Now, however, along that shining line nothing is discernible but a white speck or two, and yon ocean steamer that passes down the Channel, with a long line of black smoke on the low sky behind her.

I forsake my sheltered seat, and climb to the down, making my way towards the left, in order to see the prospect to the right. Here is a track winding down the broken slope, leading through roods of the round leaves of the fragrant Butterburr. A month ago the whole air was loaded with the delicious perfume of its lilac blossom. I make my way, slippery and tenacious enough just now, along by the hedge of a field, till I come to the edge of an abrupt perpendicular cliff. How beautiful from hence is the sweet hamlet of Babbicombe the Nether! The rugged masses of Black

Wall project from the foot of the slope into the sea, dividing Oddicombe from Babbicombe beach. Beyond it is the latter, a sweeping curve of pebbles and then of larger boulders, backed by an amphitheatre of picturesque fishing huts, and elegant villas, half hid in bowery plantations and woods, with peeps of lawns and gardens, all occupying the steep sides of the bay, up to the summit of the downs.

Beyond the beach, fine dark rock masses again project; and farther still, the prospect is abruptly shut in by a magnificent vertical cliff of great height, the northern boundary of that lovely spot of renown, Anstey's Cove.

These features, which I feebly essay to paint with many successive words, and multitudes of others which I must fain leave untouched, the eye drinks in at once, grasping the whole grand and beautiful picture at a glance, steeped as it is in loveliness. Those who have seen it may possibly find an aid to memory in recalling it in these details of mine, for I write with the scene before me; those who have not will probably find little of interest in them.

It is at the farther end of yonder beach that we must commence our marine explorings to-day; there, where the pebbles at the lowest water-line merge into larger dark stones, and a little on this side of the bounding rocks. We might get down by this path to Oddicombe beach, scramble over Black Wall, and so make our way along Babbicombe beach to the spot; but the state of the tenacious soil at this season makes such a descent unpleasant. There is a better road to the eastward, which winds among the villas, and descends direct to the spot we seek. Let us therefore pursue our walk over the downs, along the margin of the cliff, enjoying fresh aspects of the coast view as we proceed, till we reach the road.

We are among the olive-coated stones at the verge of the far-receded tide, among which the springs from the cliffs having broken out from various points in the shingle beach, are making for themselves tortuous channels on their way to the deserting sea. Their water, originally fresh of course, has, by the time it arrives here, become so brackish by washing the salt stones and sea-weeds, that the sand-hoppers and worms which inhabit the hollows under the stones are bathed in it with impunity, though, in general, immersion in fresh water is fatal to marine animals. Great tufts of bladder wrack and other *Fuci* spring from the lower stones, and now lie flaccid about, awaiting the returning tide to erect them and wave their leathery leaves to and fro. Broad fronds of *Ulva*, too, like tissue paper of the tenderest green, irregularly crumpled and waved, and nibbled and gnawed into thousands of holes, lie crisp and tempting; and tufts of a darker, duller green, and others of purple-brown, and others again of rosy crimson, stud these rough stones, and vary their ruggedness with elegance and beauty; a beauty, however, far more appreciable, and far more worthy of admiration, if we could look upon it when the flowing tide creeps up, with its calm water clear as crystal, and covers the many-hued parterre, softening and displaying the graceful outlines and the brilliant colours. Then, too, those tiny creatures would be seen agilely swimming from weed to weed, or lithely twining among the fronds, which now we have to search for in their recluse hiding-places under these rocks.

Selecting, a stone which experience teaches its is a likely one—and only experience can teach this, though in general I may say that the heaviest and flattest beneath, those which appear to have been long undisturbed, and especially those which, instead of being imbedded in the soil, rest on other stones in such a partial way that there is room for free ingress and egress to minute creatures beneath, and which have a broad surface to which they may cling in congenial darkness, are the most promising—selecting, I say, such a stone, we place both hands beneath one side, and heave with all our might to turn it bodily over. We must be careful, for many of these stones are so beset with the small shells of *Serpula triquetra*, that they cannot be handled with impunity. This is a worm which makes a tubular pipe in its defence, of hard shell, adhering to the rock throughout its length; the tube enlarges a little as it grows, and its most recent extremity, which is brilliantly white and clean, is defended by the projecting extremity of a ridge which runs along the back of the shell, the point of this ridge forming a very sharp needle-like prickle, which, as we apply our hands beneath the stone to lift, terribly cuts the fingers. On some stones we find hundreds of these treacherous shells, set as thickly as they can stand, and covering large patches; on others they are scattered, and some are quite free from them. In an aquarium the little worms protrude their breathing fans very constantly, and are pretty, though not conspicuous objects, being varied with bright blue, grey, and white. Pretty as they are, however, the collector wishes them further a hundred times during his collecting, for, in such an expedition as this, he is fortunate indeed if he come home without half of his fingers gashed with deep incisions, smarting from the sea-water, and all the slower to heal from the skin of the finger-tips being worn to thinness, in handling the stones.

But these are trifles; the fortune of war; amply compensated by the joy of victory, when we succeed in capturing some rare or lovely creature, to be displayed in triumph within the glass walls of a prison. Such an one is this beauty, which is lurking in an angle of the block we have just overturned. It needs a sharp eye to detect it; for we see no beauty yet, nothing but a little lump of whitish jelly, dappled with orange-yellow, not bigger than the half of a split pea, clinging close to the stone. It requires some care to get it up without crushing; the end of a toothpick, or a penknife, or a bit of stick cut to a point, must be inserted under it; thus we lift it, and drop it into the ready phial of clear water. It opens instantly, sprawling even before it reaches the bottom, where it at once begins to crawl, and we detect in our prize the lovely little Triope.[1]

As it swiftly glides up the glass, we see that it has an oblong body of a pellucid white hue, curiously beset with finger-like appendages. There is a row of some half-dozen or so fringing the front of the head; and down a line on each side of the body, margining the mantle, there is a row of larger ones, and all these are tipped with the richest orange colour. Just behind the frontal points there are two club-shaped organs, which start up out of holes, the sides of which form sheaths for them, into which they can be withdrawn at the will of the animal. These organs carry a number of narrow plates set parallel to each other, diagonally pointing backwards and downwards. Doubtless, this structure is intended to augment the sensitive powers of these curious organs, which are understood to be the tentacles.

Then, in the middle line of the back, but placed a little nearer the tail than the head, there is an orifice, which is the vent; remarkable because the breathing organs are arranged partly around it. There are three tiny leaves cut like the fronds of a fern, which stand up over the orifice, and are endowed with the power of absorbing for the purposes of respiration the oxygen of the air commingled in the water.

But here is an animal which possesses all these peculiarities of structure, displayed on a much larger scale. It is a fine specimen of the Sea Lemon,[2] which we oftener find clinging to the sides of perpendicular rocks, or beneath projecting ledges, than on the undersides of stones. This fellow is two and a half inches long, and an inch and a quarter or more broad; but I have met with individuals much larger than he. Its back is rounded, and its outline generally reminds one of the half of a lemon cut longitudinally. The resemblance is heightened, too, by the round warts with which the whole surface is studded, and by the colour, a yellow more or less pure, often, however, clouded, as in this instance, with purple, by which its beauty is much enhanced.

The mantle, in this Doris, reaches down to the foot on all sides, and covers the head, and is not furnished with any appendages. The tentacles, which are plated, as in the Triope, pierce through the mantle, and are sheathed; the gill plumes are large and ample featherlike organs, eight in number, forming a complete circle round the orifice, in the manner of a beautiful expanded flower.

As the Doris crawls along, it now and then lifts and puckers the edge of the mantle, and displays its under surface and that of the foot, which are of a rich orange-scarlet hue.

But we have turned a stone beneath which lurk several specimens of a much lovelier creature yet. I see by the gleams of crimson and azure which shine out from it that it must be the Crowned Eolis.[3] It looked a little heap of fibrous semi-pellucid flesh when out of water, and, like the Triope, must be immersed to display its beauties. Now in the phial of water, how elegant it is! Its body is long and slender, tapering away to an almost imperceptible point behind, of a clear translucent white. The head forms two long smooth taper tentacles, which wave hither and thither as the creature gracefully glides along; and besides these it has two other tentacles, distinguished as the dorsal pair, resembling, in their position and in their structure, those of the Doris and Triope, but not sheathed.

The chief glory of this exquisite animal, however, is in its breathing organs. These consist of clusters of finger-shaped papilla, set transversely, across the back, in about six rows, with the middle line of the back free.

Each of these papillæ is pellucid, with a central core of the richest crimson, while a very brilliant flush of steel blue is reflected from the surface, and the tip is opaque white. The combination of these hues has a most charming effect.

You would scarcely suppose such lovely creatures were fierce and carnivorous; but they are the most determined enemies of the Sea Anemones. This beautiful Eolis I have often seen assaulting an Anemone, ferociously tearing away its tentacles, or gnawing great holes in its side, and, when touched, stiffening and erecting all its brilliant papillæ, as the porcupine does its quills.

All these creatures are Mollusca very closely allied to the Cowry and the Trochus which we lately examined, but destitute of a shell. The exposure of the breathing organs is a distinguishing character (these being more commonly, in the order, concealed in a cavity), whence they are called *Nudibranchiata*, or Naked-gilled Mollusks.

At this season, wherever we find the animals themselves, we may with confidence expect to find their spawn. This is deposited in masses, which possess characteristic forms. Thus this roll, which looks as if you had made a thin ribbon of paste, half an inch wide, and rolled it into a loose scroll of two or three turns, and then affixed it by its edge to the under side of a stone, is the spawn-mass of the Sea Lemon. And here is a much more elegant scroll, of which the constituent is a slender thread, twisted into a frilled or figure-8 form, as it goes on to make the spire.[4] This has been laid by the beautiful Crowned Eolis. If you examine either of these masses with a lens, you will see that it is composed of a vast multitude of white eggs, suspended in a clear jelly, in which they are arranged in transverse rows, giving the opaque appearance to what would else be colourless and transparent.

The eggs, watched day by day under a good microscopic power, as they advance towards maturity, present a most interesting object of study. The yolk, which at first nearly fills the egg-shell, soon becomes a little elongated, with one end diagonally truncated, or, as it were, cut off obliquely; the truncated end then becomes two-lobed, "each lobe exhibiting an imperfect spiral, and having its margin ciliated. The now animated being is seen to rotate within its prison. Shortly the lobes enlarge, and a fleshy process, the rudimentary foot, is observed to develop itself a little behind them, on the medial line; a shell closely investing the inferior portion of the embryo, the lobes and rudimentary foot being uppermost. The shell rapidly increases, and assumes a nautiloid form; afterwards the foot displays, attached to its posterior surface, a circular operculum, which is opposed to the mouth of the shell. The lobes now expand into two large, flattened, ovate appendages, with very long vibratile cilia around the margins; and the larvæ are at length mature. The whole mass of spawn now presents the utmost animation. Hundreds of these busy atoms are seen, each within its transparent, membranous cell, rotating with great agility and ceaseless perseverance, the cilia all the while vigorously vibrating on the margins of the outstretched lobes. The

Plate V

Limpet. Purple. Slit-Limpet.

membranous chorion [or transparent eggshell], which by this time has become enlarged, ultimately gives way, no longer able to resist the perpetual struggle within; and the liberated larva, wending its way through the shattered shreds of the general envelope, boldly trusts itself to the open trackless water, where, doubtless, thousands and tens of thousands perish ere they find a fitting resting-place, some being swept away by resistless currents, others falling a prey to ever-watchful and innumerable enemies.

"When the larva is at rest, the oral lobes are pulled back into the shell, and the foot being drawn down, brings along with it the operculum, which closes the orifice. But when in action, the whole of these parts project beyond the opening of the shell, the foot lying back against the spire; and the oral lobes inclining forward, their cilia commence to vibrate, and the larva, with the mouth of the shell upwards, moves through the water with lively action, sinking or rising, or advancing onwards at its pleasure."[5]

The fecundity of these mollusca is immense. An *Eolis papillosa* of moderate size in one of my aquaria, deposited successively nine strings of spawn between March 20th and May 24th. The strings were exactly alike in length and arrangement; each comprised about 105 convolutions, and each convolution 200 eggs, while each egg contained on an average two embryos. Thus the astonishing number of 378,000 embryos proceeded from this one animal in about two months.

Step by step we have crept along the beach, turning stones as we went, till we are come to the great masses of sandstone rock. Here are the Purples[6] by hundreds, with their strong massive shells, some of them pure white, which, however, becomes dingy with age, some banded with brown, and some, especially the young and half-grown ones, painted with a dull but soft purplish hue. The older specimens have the inner surface of the lip tinged with a rich rosy purple. This tint on the shell we may receive as the advertisement of the colorific property that resides within, a sort of sign-board to tell us that this is the "genuine" purple-shell. And there is little doubt that it is one of those enumerated by Pliny, as used by the ancients for obtaining the renowned dye of Tyre: though the principal, and that which yielded the richest line, was probably the *Murex trunculus*, a common Mediterranean shell, which does not extend to our shores.

My readers are, I dare say, familiar with the pretty myth which professes to embody the discovery of the purple dye. The Tyrian Hercules was one day walking with his sweetheart along the shore, followed by her lap-dog, when the playful animal seized a shell that had just been washed up on the beach. Its lips were presently dyed with a gorgeous purple tint, which was traceable to a juice that was pressed out of the shellfish. The lady was charmed with the colour, and longed to have a dress of it; and, as wishes under such circumstances are laws, the enamoured hero set himself to gratify her, and soon succeeded in extracting and applying the dye, which afterwards became so famous. I have elsewhere[7] recorded my own experiments on the stain yielded by the *Purpura* before us, with the remarkable changes through which it passes before the sunlight fully brings out the colour. The use of cochineal makes us independent of molluscan dyes, and the matter is merely one of antiquarian interest, or a question of zoological chemistry.

Perhaps you may be more interested in the development of the Dog-winkle. Under the ledges of rocks we find in abundance groups of little yellow bodies, resembling ninepins in shape, set on their ends in close contact with each other, and varying in numbers from three or four to a hundred or upwards in a group. Some of them are tinged with purple at the tips; and while sometimes you find them closed, and full of a yellow creamy substance, at others they are open at the top, and empty.

These are the egg-capsules of this mollusk, and some very unusual circumstances connected with the birth of the progeny, and their development within these cases, have been discovered by Dr. Carpenter.[8] Each capsule contains 500 or 600 globules that cannot be distinguished from each other at first; but only twelve to thirty of these are developed into young animals, though their united bulk ultimately equals that of the whole mass. The greater number of these globules are not real eggs, but only "yolk-spherules," destined to afford nutriment to the true embryos, which greedily swallow them, after certain changes have taken place, and increase rapidly in bulk. It is curious, however, that they do not advance in development during this absorption of nutriment, but are, so to speak, arrested until a great augmentation of size is thus attained; then they quickly acquire the form of little free-swimming nautiloids, closely like those of the Doris and Eolis, a form which indeed is common to the early stages of all the known higher mollusca, however various may be their adult conditions.

Here are the familiar Limpets, too: let us look at *them* awhile.[9] They are not generally very attractive in appearance, the shell being coarse and rubbed, especially in the larger specimens; and in an aquarium they do not live long, and are so inert as to afford no amusement even while they survive. Yet we occasionally find examples prettily coloured; and there are facts in their economy which make them worthy of a few moments' notice.

If you look carefully over the rocks, especially when these are of a somewhat soft nature, as the slates and shales, you will find oval depressions, sometimes but just discernible, at other times sunk to the depth of an eighth of an inch, corresponding in outline to the shell of a Limpet; and in many instances you will actually see a Limpet imbedded in such a pit, which it accurately fills. Strange as it may seem, it has been ascertained that these cavities are formed by the animals, which make them their ordinary resting-places, wandering away from them nightly to feed, and returning to them to rest early in the morning.

The force with which a Limpet adheres to the rock is very great, especially when it has had warning of assault, and has had time to put out its muscular strength. Réaumur found that a weight of twenty-eight or thirty pounds was required to overcome this adhesive force. His experiments seem to prove, however, that its power is mainly owing, not to muscular energy, nor to the production of a vacuum in the manner of a sucker. If an adhering Limpet were cut quite through perpendicularly, shell and animal, the two parts maintained their hold with unabated force, although of course a vacuum, if there had been one, would have been destroyed by the incision. The power is said to reside in a very strong blue, a very viscid secretion, deposited at the will of the animal. "If, having detached a *Patella*," says Dr. Johnston, "the finger be applied to the foot of the animal, or to the spot on which it rested, the finger will be held there by a very sensible resistance, although no glue is perceptible. And it is remarkable that if the spot be now moistened with a little water, or if the base of the animal be cut, and the water contained in it allowed to flow over the spot, no further adhesion will occur on the application of the finger: the glue has been dissolved. It is nature's solvent, by which the animal loosens its own connexion with the rock. When the storm rages, or when an enemy is abroad, it glues itself firmly to its rest; but when the danger has passed, to free itself from this forced constraint, a little water is pressed from the foot, the cement is weakened, and it is at liberty to raise itself and be at large. The fluid of cementation, as well as the watery solvent, is secreted in an infinity of miliary glands with which the foot is, as it were, shagreened; and as the Limpet cannot supply the secretion as fast as this can be exhausted, you may destroy the animal's capacity of fixation by detaching it forcibly two or three times in succession."

If we remove one of these Limpets from his selected area of rock,—which we may readily do, notwithstanding the strength of his cement, if we take him at unawares, and give him a smart sudden horizontal rap with a piece of wood, or a moderated blow with a hammer,—we shall obtain a view of a structure well worth looking at. The animal is essentially like a Trochus or a Purple inhabiting a conical shell; only in this case the cone is low and simple, whereas in the others it is tall and slender, and rolled into a spire. One of the most curious peculiarities in the Limpet is its gill or breathing organ. This, we perceive, completely encircles the animal, forming a ring interrupted only at one point, it lies in the fold between the mantle and the foot, commencing on the left side of the neck, and passing quite round the body, parallel with the edge of the shell, in front of the head, till it terminates close to the point where it began. It is a long cord closely beset with tiny leaflets, and thus forming a continual plume. Each leaflet, conical in outline, is permeated with blood-vessels, and clothed with minute *cilia*, whose constant vibrations cause the circumambient water ever to play over the surface of these organs in ceaseless currents, bringing fresh supplies of oxygen to be respired; and this is absorbed by the blood through the thin membrane by which they are protected.

There is a very pretty little shell, not uncommon in deep water off these coasts, but rarely found by the shore collector, though it does occasionally venture to peep at daylight at the verge of extreme low-tide. It is the Slit Limpet,[10] which by the older naturalists was placed in close alliance with the Limpets proper, as if a member of the same family. They were, however, deceived by paying too exclusive attention to the form of the shell, which is a cone, somewhat rounded, and nearly simple, the summit being slightly turned over in a backward direction. The margin of the shell is delicately notched, the points being the extremities of the radiating ridges; for the entire surface is covered with reticulations, one series of alternate furrows and ridges proceeding from the summit to the margin, and another series crossing these at right angles, running round the shell parallel with the margin. The animal has its sides ornamented with short fleshy processes, and possesses two symmetrical gill-plumes, one on each side. It is rather attractive in appearance, but I cannot tell you anything of its manners; for though I have kept specimens in the aquarium, they are so habitually sluggish, and so reluctant to allow one a peep beneath the edge of the jealous shell, that I could learn nothing about their ways;—if indeed they have any.

Another curious form closely related to this is the Keyhole Limpet,[11] whose shell is of a long oval outline, of a lower cone, reticulated, like the Slit Limpet, but pierced at the summit with a double hole, or rather a perforation apparently made of two holes broken into one, something like a keyhole. This orifice, like the slit in the former case, is for the discharge of the effete water taken in in breathing.

See! here is the soft red sandstone lying in great beds, pierced through and through with smooth round holes, just as if bored with a carpenter's auger, big enough to admit a man's thumb. What agency has been in operation to effect these perforations? Let us try to discover.

A few good blows with the stout hammer on the chisel-head serve to split off a great slice of the coarse red sandstone. The holes run through its substance, but they are all empty, or filled only with the black fœtid mud which the sea has deposited in their cavities. Yes; these are too superficial; they are all deserted; the stone lies too high above low-water mark: we must seek a lower level. Try here; where the lowest spring-tide only just leaves the rock bare. Ha! now we have uncovered the operators. Here lie, snugly ensconced within the tubular perforations, great mollusca, with ample ivory-like shells, which yet cannot half contain the whiter flesh of their ampler bodies, and the long stout yellow siphons that project from one extremity, reaching far up the hole towards the surface of the rock.[12]

We lift one from its cavity, all helpless and unresisting, yet manifesting its indignation at the untimely disturbance by successive spasmodic contractions of these rough yellow siphons, each accompanied with a forcible *jet d'eau*, a polite squirt of sea-water into our face; while, at each contraction in length, the base swells out, till the compressed valves of the sharp shell threaten to pierce through its substance.

Strange as it seems, these animals have bored these holes in the stone; and they are capable of boring in far harder rock than this; even in compact limestone. The actual mode in which this operation is performed long puzzled philosophers. Some maintained that the animal secreted an acid which had the power of dissolving not only various kinds of stone, but also wood, amber, wax, and other substances, in which the excavations are occasionally made. But it was hard to imagine a solvent of substances so various, and to know how the animals' own shells were preserved from its action; while, confessedly, no such acid had ever been detected by the most careful tests.

Others maintained that the rough points which stud the shell enable it to serve as a rasp, which the animal, by rotating on its axis, uses to wear away the stone or other material; but it was difficult to understand how it was that the shell itself was not worn away in the abrasion.

Another zoologist, rejecting this hypothesis, maintained that the edges of the mantle and the short thick foot are the instruments employed; and that, though these fleshy organs seem little fitted for such work, they are really endowed with the requisite power in the shape of crystals of flint which are deposited thickly in their substance. Strange to say, however, other accurate observers fail to detect these siliceous crystals, and therefore reject the hypothesis.

Another suggested that the stone was removed in invisible particles by the constant action of currents in the water, produced by vibratile cilia seated on the soft parts of the animal; but this supposition was found untenable on examination.

Actual observation in the aquarium has proved that the second hypothesis is the true one. M. Cailliaud in France and Mr. Robertson in England have demonstrated that the Pholas uses its shell as a rasp, wearing away the stone with the asperities with which the anterior parts of the valves are furnished. Between these gentlemen a somewhat hot contention was maintained for the honour of priority in this valuable discovery. M. Cailliaud himself used the valves of the dead shell, and imitating the natural conditions as well as he could, actually bored an imitative hole, by making them rotate. Mr. Robertson, at Brighton, exhibited to the public living Pholades in the act of boring in masses of chalk. He described it as "a living combination of three instruments, viz., a hydraulic apparatus, a rasp, and a syringe." But the first and last of these powers can be considered only as accessory to the removing of the detritus out of the way, when once the hole was bored, the *rasp* being the real power. If you examine these living shells, you will see that the fore part, where the foot protrudes, is set with stony points arranged in transverse and longitudinal rows, the former being the result of elevated ridges radiating from the hinge, the latter that of the edges of successive growths of the shell. These points have the most accurate resemblance to those set on a steel rasp in a blacksmith's shop. It is interesting to know that the shell is preserved from being itself prematurely worn away by the fact, that it is composed of arragonite, a substance much harder than those in which the Pholas burrows. Yet we see by the specimens before us that such a destructive action does in time take place, for some of these

Plate VI

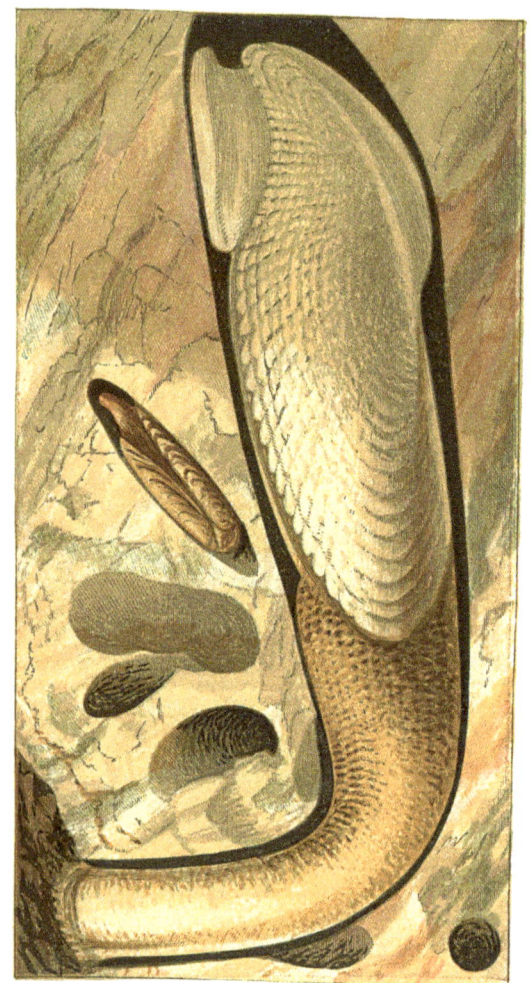

Red-Nose. Finger-Pholas.

have the rasping points much more worn than others, many of the older ones being nearly smooth.

The animal turns in its burrow from side to side when at work, adhering to the interior by the foot, and therefore only partially rotating to and fro. The substance is abraded in the form of fine powder, which is periodically ejected from the mouth of the hole by the contraction of the branchial siphon; a good deal of the more impalpable portions being deposited by the current as it proceeds, and lodging as a soft mud between the valves and the stone. Mr. Hudson,[13] who watched some Pholades at work in a tide-pool in the chalk, observed the periodic ejection of the cloud of chalk-powder, and noticed the heaps of the same material deposited around the mouth of each burrow. The discharges were made with no regularity as to time. Mrs. Merrifield[14] records a curious fact. "A lady, watching the operations of some Pholades which were at work in a basin of sea-water, perceived that two of them were boring at such an angle that their tunnels would meet. Curious to ascertain what they would do in this case, she continued her observations, and found that *the larger and stronger Pholas bored straight through the weaker one*, as if it had been merely a piece of chalk rock."

Mr. Ross, of Rhyl, having a Pholas in his aquarium, prepared a piece of wood, by excavating a shallow cavity, about a quarter of an inch deep, in which he set the animal, whose shell was two inches long. "After a short time the animal attached its foot to the bottom of the hole and commenced swaying itself from side to side, until the hole was of sufficient depth to allow it to proceed in the following manner:—It inflated itself with water, apparently to its fullest extent, raising its shell upwards from the hole; then holding by its muscular foot, it drew its shell gradually down. This would have produced a perpendicular and very inefficient action, but for a wise provision of nature. The edges of the valves are not joined close together, but are connected by a membrane (extension of the mantle), and instead of being joined at the hinge (umbo) like ordinary bivalves, they possess an extra plate, attached to each valve of the shell, which is necessary for the following operation:—In boring, this mollusk, having dilated itself with water, draws down its shell within the hole, gradually closing the lower anterior edges until they almost touch. It then raises its shell upwards, gradually opening the lower anterior edges, and closing the upper, thus boring both upwards and downwards. The spines are placed in rows, like the teeth of a saw; those towards the lower part of the shell being sharp and pointed, while those above, being now useless, are not renewed."[15]

In this limestone cliff we shall find other borers, for you may see even at a considerable distance how holed and honeycombed its surface is; the cavities being so numerous, so close, and so irregular in their direction, that the whole face of the rock is fashioned into small sharp-edged shapeless points. Nor need we be long in finding the industrious masons who thus rough-point acres upon acres, nay miles upon miles, of limestone rock. Here in ten thousand orifices you discern little double-tipped knobs of crimson flesh, which, as soon as you disturb them, shoot at you a column of water and then disappear within their fortress, having exhausted their artillery. The fishermen know them well, and use them for bait, applying to them the familiar but expressive soubriquet of Red-noses.[16]

It is not so easy to get at these as at the Pholades, because of the superior hardness of the stone which they excavate. With the chisel, however, we need not fail of uncovering a few, especially as their burrows are but shallow. Here they are, half-a-dozen in a block as big as your fist. Ugly, uncouth, bemired, the valves not nearly containing the shapeless flesh, they are not particularly attractive creatures, maugre the brilliant hue of their blushing siphons. Like Mrs. Merrifield's Pholas, these Saxicavæ habitually break into one another's houses, as we see here, and even cut one another's shells and bodies through and through most ruthlessly. They will live very well out of the rock, and may be kept a considerable time in the aquarium.

There is no doubt that the burrowing Mollusca are slowly but surely effecting changes in the configuration of rocky coasts, by destroying the rock. It is true their excavations extend but a few inches in depth; but then, as the force of the elements readily breaks down the thin partitions left standing, and discovers a new face, so the borers are continually renewing their attacks on this; and so in time the cliffs are worn away, while the debris of impalpable mud is deposited upon the shallows, entering into new combinations, and filling up estuaries and harbours.

III.
March

Perhaps the most effective aid to the investigation of natural history which the present age has produced is the invention of the aquarium, and particularly its application to marine forms of life. Depending on that grand principle of organic chemistry, of world-wide prevalence, that the emanations from animals and vegetables are respectively essential to the continued life each of the other, it was discovered that the relative proportions of number and bulk in which organic beings of the two kinds could healthfully live together was easily determined; and since the fact that the creatures were inhabitants of water, whether fresh or salt, presented no exception to the universality of the law, they had but to be placed together in a suitable ratio, enclosed in a vessel containing water, and an aquarium was established. Improvements in the form of the vessel, in the mode of exposing the contents to observation, in the impact of the rays of light, in the arrangement of the interior, and other points of value, have indeed been progressively made; whereby the practical availability of the invention for the purposes of experimental natural history has been augmented; but some of us have found little difficulty, even from the very first announcement of the discovery, in maintaining the collections of sea-water, with their living plants and animals, unchanged from year's end to year's end. I may be perhaps excused for observing, that I have at present in use a large tank, full of marine creatures, in which the water has been unchanged for four years, and on which I look with peculiar interest, because it was the first tank ever made for private use. This very aquarium has afforded, and still affords the opportunity for the observation of many interesting details of the structure and habits of the lower forms of animal life, details which constitute the basis not only of my works on marine natural history already published, but of the present series of papers also. We collect the creatures, indeed, abroad, and there gather up some broad facts of interest concerning their modes of life; but it is at home, in the quiet of the study, with conveniences and aids to examination, experiment, and record at command, that they must be studied. The aquarium becomes in fact an apparatus, whereby we bring a portion of the sea, with its rocks, and weeds, and creatures, to the side of our study-table, and maintain it there.

Thus an opportunity of close and valuable familiarity with sea-productions is open to multitudes who have never seen the broad expanse of ocean, nor searched its prolific shores; and facilities for extending the

Plate VII

Snowy Anemone. Dead-Man's Finger. Rosy Anemone. Lucernaria. Smooth Beadlet.

bounds of zoological science are everywhere enjoyed, which till lately were restricted to a very few naturalists, whose residences were situated on certain favourable spots upon the coast. Yet both modes of investigation are necessary. He who has never seen marine animals except in the confinement of an aquarium, cannot but be conscious of many chasms in his knowledge, which are filled up by him who is in the habit of collecting his own specimens in their proper haunts; and who, by finding them *in ferâ naturâ*, can, when he studies them at leisure in his tanks, make such allowances as are necessary for the variations in habit which may be dependent on the difference between their present artificial, and their original natural, conditions of existence.

While we rejoice then in tanks and vases of crystal water, filled with the lovely forms and brilliant hues of sea-weeds and sea-anemones, I invite my readers to accompany me on a few hours' visit to the charming creatures at their own homes. The season is propitious; the sun has just passed the vernal equinox, and the genial warmth of spring is diffusing new life into the cold blood of the animals that dwell beneath the waters; the equinoctial storms that lately raged have blown themselves out, and are succeeded by a quietude whose effect is delightfully seen in yonder mirror-like ocean: it is the time of spring-tide; and the near approach of the hour of lowest water will afford us unusual facilities for finding species only to be invaded under such conditions.

Let us then scramble down to the beautiful Anstey's Cove, along the steep path tangled with briers and ferns; where the swelling buds of the hawthorn and honeysuckle are already bursting, while the blackbird mellowly whistles in the fast-greening thicket, and the lark joyously greets the mounting sun above us. Yonder on the shingle lies a boat, newly painted in white and green, for the attraction of young ladies of maritime aspirations; she is hauled up high and dry; but the sinewy arms of honest Harry Bate, who hearing footsteps has come out of his little grotto under the rock to reconnoitre, will soon drag her down to the rippling waves, and, "for the small sum of a shilling an hour," will pull us over the smooth and pond-like sea, whithersoever we may choose to direct him.

"Jump aboard, please, Sir! Jump in, ladies! jump in, little master!" And now, as we take our seats on the clean canvas cushions astern, the boat's bottom scrapes along with a harsh grating noise over the white shingle-pebbles, and we are afloat.

First to the caverns just outside yonder lofty point. The lowness of the tide will enable us to take the boat into then, and the calmness of the sea will preclude much danger of her striking the rocks; especially as watchful Bate will be on the alert, boat-hook in hand, to keep her clear. Now we lie in the gloom of the lofty arch, gently heaving and sinking and swaying on the slight swell, which, however smooth the surface, is always perceptible when you are in a boat among rocks, and which invests such an approach with a danger that a landsman does not at all appreciate. Yet the water, despite the swell, is glassy, and invites the gaze down into its crystalline depths, where the little fishes are playing and hovering over the dark weeds. The sides of the cavern rise around us in curved planes, washed smooth and slippery by the dashing of the waves of ages, and gradually merge into the massive angles and projections and groins of the broken roof, whence a tuft or two of what looks like samphire depends. But notice the colonies of the Smooth Anemone or Beadlet[1] clustered about the sides; many of them are adhering to the stone walls, several feet above the water. These have been left uncovered for hours, and are none the worse for it. They are closed, the many tentacles being concealed by the involution of the upper part of the body, so that they look like balls, or hemispheres, or semi-ovals of flesh; or like ripe fruits, so plump and succulent and glossy and high-coloured, that we are tempted to stretch forth the willing hand, to pluck and eat. Some are greengages, some Orleans plums, some magnum-bonums,—so various are their rich hues; but look beneath the water, and you see them not less numerous, but of quite another guise. These are all widely expanded; the tentacles are thrown out in an arch over the circumference, leaving a broad flat disk; just like a many-petalled flower of gorgeous hues: indeed, we may fancy that here we see the blossoms, and there the ripened fruit. Do not omit, however, to notice the beads of pearly blue that stud the margin all round, at the base of the over-arching tentacles. These have been supposed by some to be eyes; the suggestion, however, rests on no anatomical ground, and is, I am afraid, worthless; though I cannot tell you what purpose they do serve.

Away! for I wish to explore another scene not less romantic than this, and which I know by experience to be much more prolific in strange and beautiful forms of life. Harry shall pull us round yonder low point, which bears the appellation of Hope's Nose, calling on the way to look at some one of the inlets that lie between the long projecting points at the foot of Black Rock. Here the boat floats over dense forests of great brown sea-weeds, the *Laminariæ*, which lift their dark: masses, and wave to and fro, with a majestic dignity. Here is the narrow crumpled blade of the Oarweed, of a rich yellow brown; and the wavy stem of the Furbelows springing from its hedgehog-like bladder; but chiefly is the forest composed of vast plants of the Tangle, whose broad deep-brown fronds of a substance like stout leather, French-polished, divide into many long straps, slide over each other, and flap to and fro in the heave of the sea. Yonder we see on the broadest part of a frond, just before it divides, what seems a flower, as large as a chrysanthemum, but of the liveliest peagreen hue, every long petal tipped with rosy pink. Hand over the boat-hook, and carefully lift the tangle to the surface. Now we have it fully in view. It is the green variety of the Opelet;[2] so called because it is scarcely capable of in-folding the walls of the body over the disk and tentacles; these therefore remain habitually *open*, though the animal is at times much less expanded than at others. We now see it in its most charming condition; the short fawn-coloured column inflated, the mouth elevated on a strong cone in the centre of the wide saucer-shaped disk, and the numerous tentacles arranged in groups, as if several stems sprang from the same root, long, slender, very flexible, twisting about like the snaky locks of Medusa's head, all of the most delicate light green, with a rich satin lustre, and all tipped with the richest crimson-lilac or light rose,—a most beautiful harmony of colours. The animal adheres by a broad base firmly to the disk of the tangle, and awaits, as it waves hither and thither, the approach of one of the little fishes that play heedlessly at bo-peep among the fronds. No sooner does one of them touch the far-stretching tentacles, than a virulent and penetrating poison shoots through its frame; its vigour is benumbed in an instant; it ceases to struggle; its powerful fins strike the water no more; others of the fatal tentacles enwrap themselves around it, and drag it towards the mouth, already protruding and expanding in expectation of the morsel; where it is in a few minutes engulfed, and soon digested in that capacious maw.

It is not very uncommon for a single specimen of this species to become two by a perpendicular division. The whole process has been observed. A little notch first appears in the margin of the disk, which extends, cutting through the tentacles of that side, splitting the disk across, proceeding through the tentacles on the opposite side till it divides the margin there also. Meanwhile, it has advanced downward in an equal ratio, till it has reached the base; and at length there are two half-opelets still adhering in the closest proximity. Now, however, the two raw and open surfaces close up, and the bases glide gradually apart. A thick wall of flesh forms between the stomach and the wound, and new tentacles develop themselves on this. The two Opelets are complete.

Half-an-hour's vigorous pulling has doubled the long promontory of Hope's Nose, a wilderness of stones, like what I suppose, from published descriptions, the foot of Mount Sinai to be, and brought us, between two raised beaches, into the pretty cove of Meadfoot, capped by elegant villas. These beaches, evidences of the lifting of the land, for they surely once stood, as beaches stand now, at the sea-level, are situate, the one on the main, the other on the Thatcher, a rocky islet some two hundred yards off shore. A few minutes more, and we are in a wild scene indeed. Isolated rocks stand up, in angular masses, upright columns, and sharp peaks, out of the sea, which is quite deep, even at lowest spring-tide. The coast itself too is rugged, precipitous, and in many spots quite perpendicular; one bold promontory, which runs out with a narrow knife-edge summit, is perforated by a natural archway of lofty elevation, of very striking aspect. It is distinctly visible for miles along the shores of Torbay, and is dignified with the name of London Bridge.

Here, then, is our fishing-ground to-day. Threading the slender passages between the perpendicular rocks, or creeping-in close under their overhanging landward sides, where no ray of the sun has ever penetrated, we hang on by the points and groins, and eagerly peer below. Into one lane our boatman hesitates to venture. It is but just wide enough to allow the boat to pass; indeed here and there she cannot without rubbing her gunwales; and if a stronger swell than usual were to roll-in from seaward while entangled, her side might be stove-in before she could be extricated. However, its gloom looks so tempting, and the water among the islets is so very smooth, that we succeed in persuading him, and we push and drag into the very midst of the watery alley. The rocks rise close on either hand like lofty walls, and descend as perpendicularly, deep and far down beneath our keel; as we can well see, for the water is of lustrous transparency.

And what a sight is here! Hundreds of Anemones of many species are studding the walls almost as thick as they can be packed. Every tiny crevice, every hollow, every hole left by *Pholas* or *Saxicava* (and the rock is riddled and honeycombed by these burrowing mollusks), holds its little knob of plump flesh; some lolling out with a dewdrop hanging from the end; some just filling the cavity, and allowing the tips of the crowded tentacles to peep out as a speck of white, or of orange, or of rosy lilac, according to the species; and some retreated to the bottom of their stony fortress, to be detected only by the probing touch. Other forms too there are;—dead men's fingers, white and yellow; worms, green and brown and grey, twining in and out, and grasping the sharp edges of the rock; tunicate mollusks, simple and compound; univalves and bivalves; sponges of all bright colours by hundreds:—what a maze, what a teeming world of life it is!

All this is at and above the level of the eye. Now let us bend over the boat's gunwale, and gaze below, with our faces brought nearly to the surface of the sea. Here the sight is far more wonderful, and far more attractive; for here the life is seen in all its fullest activity, every creature performing its functions, and pursuing its instincts with the most single earnestness, self-contained, and altogether regardless of the myriad fellow-beings that surround it and press upon it, in this eager contest and struggle for maintained existence.

A yard or two below the surface the eye is caught by a great oyster projecting from the vertical wall. It is a strange situation for an oyster to be in, but it shows how the infant young, in their free-swimming form, so different from their ultimate condition, may be carried by the aid of their own cilia, and the sea-currents, into the most improbable situations, and may there find circumstances congenial for permanent settlement.[3] Perhaps, however, its brown and rough shell would scarcely have attracted our notice, but for the rider that sits upon it. A specimen of the Deadman's finger,[4] of noble dimensions, has selected this shell as the seat of its dominion; and we can discern the three or four great lobes of which it consists all surrounded by the gauzy cloud that tells of the thousands of translucent polyps projected from every part of its periphery. Fine as is that specimen, however, there are scores of others, many of which are of equal dimensions, and more easily accessible. By the aid of the hammer and cold-chisel, we may easily secure a specimen without harming it, after searching a while to select one which is seated on some projection of the rock that can be struck off. Thus removed, and at once transferred to one of our collecting jars, the curious compound animal will in captivity display its beauties, though, it must be confessed, it is often rather bashful before company. The lobes into which the mass is divided are sufficiently like stumpy fingers to have given it a popular designation, while their dull white hue has suggested that the fingers are those of a corpse. The animal is sometimes, however, called Cows' paps, and sometimes Mermaids' gloves; but I think this latter is a book name.

When we examine it in the aquarium, after it has recovered its equanimity disturbed by the rude shocks of the hammer battering about its castle, we see that the lobes are greatly swollen and sub-pellucid, from the imbibition of water into the canals with which its whole substance is penetrated. When out of water the surface was studded with shallow pits, as if the poor thing had at some period of its history been afflicted with the small-pox. Now, however, these pittings reveal their true character; for each has protruded itself in the form of a long but slender polyp, of exquisite translucency and perfect symmetry. It resembles a tubular flower with eight narrow pointed petals, which arch outward like those of a campanula or tulip. Each petal carries on its edges a row of very slender transparent filaments, arranged like the teeth of a comb, which also arch downward, and greatly augment the beauty of the flower-like polyp.

Structurally, this polyp is closely allied to the common forms of the Sea Anemones; the most obvious peculiarity being, that a multitude are combined into one mass, with a common life animating the whole. The fleshy mass is of a spongy texture, full of branching water-canals, and containing a multitude of calcareous spicula of characteristic forms. They resemble gnarled branches of oak, with the branchlets broken off, leaving ragged ends. The skin of the polyps contains, at certain fixed spots, groups of similar spicula, but much more minute. The microscope is necessary to discern these, as well as some other details of the organization of this very interesting creature.

The technical character by which this animal with its allies is distinguished from the proper Anemones, is that its plan of organization is fashioned on the number *eight*, whereas the true Anemones have *six*, as their characteristic number. Thus, however numerous the tentacles of an anemone may be, and in the case of the Daisy or the Plumose, they often amount to several hundreds,—the young animal began with six, and the increase is normally a multiplication of six, though accidental irregularities do occur. On the other hand, the tentacles of the Alcyonium are permanently eight, as are the vertical partitions of the interior of the body; and by consequence, the chambers into which those membranous partitions divide it.

But we must not allow the interest attaching to these forms to divert our attention from the Anemones themselves. All the species which we saw on the rock above the water, are here below it, and all displaying their beauties in an incomparably more charming fashion. We can compare the whole submerged wall to nothing else than a parterre of most brilliant flowers, taken bodily and set on end. The eye is bewildered with their number and variety, and knows not which to look at first. Here are the Rosy Anemones,[5] with a firm fleshy column of rich sienna-brown,

Plate VIII

Dahlia Wartlet.

paler towards the base, and with the upper part studded with indistinct spots, marking the situation of certain organs which have an adhesive power. The disk is of a pale neutral tint, with a crimson mouth in the centre, and a circumference of crowded tentacles of the most lovely rose-purple, the rich hue of that lovely flower that bears the name of General Jacqueminot. In those specimens that are most widely opened, this tentacular fringe forms a blossom whose petals overhang the concealed column, expanding to the width of an inch or more; but there are others in which the expansion is less complete in different degrees, and these all give distinct phases of loveliness. We find a few among the rest, which, with the characteristically-coloured tentacles, have the column and the disk of a creamy white; and one in which the disk is of a brilliant orange, inclining to scarlet. Most lovely little creatures are they all.

Commingled with these charming Roses, there are others which attain a larger size, occurring in even greater abundance. They are frequently an inch and a half in diameter when expanded, and some are even larger than this. You may know them at once by observing that the outer row of tentacles, and occasionally also some of the others, are of a scarlet hue, which, when examined minutely, is seen to be produced by a sort of core of that rich hue pervading the pellucid tentacle. The species is commonly known as the Scarlet-fringed Anemone.[6] The inner rows of tentacles, which individually are larger than those of the outer rows, are pale, marked at the base with strong bars of black. The disk is very variable in hue, but the column is for the most part of the same rich brown as we saw in the Rosy. Yet, though these are characteristic colours, there are specimens which diverge exceedingly from them, and some approach so near the Roses, as to be scarcely distinguishable from them. Generally, however, the scarlet-cored outer tentacles, and a peculiar habit of throwing the tentacular margin of the disk into crumpled folds, will be found sufficient to determine this very handsome kind of Anemone from its nearest allies.

There are multitudes too of a charming, little kind, which, on account of the pure whiteness of the crown of tentacles, is known as the Snowy.[7] The disk is of the same spotless hue; and the column of a light drab deepening into pale olive towards the summit. With the exception of its colours, this species has a very close resemblance to the Rosy, with which it is generally associated, even as we see it here. And here is the Orange-disk,[8] one of exceeding loveliness, which you might fancy a cross-breed between the Rosy and the Snowy, having the rich brown column of the former, and the white tentacles of the latter; but that it has a character of its own in the disk being of the most brilliant orange-red. All these are scattered in the most abundant profusion, looking like gems sown on the rough rock; or, as I compared them before, like gorgeous composite flowers, of which you might easily fancy the little tufts of green and purple *Algæ* to be the proper leaves. There are also others, less conspicuous, the Daisy, the Sandalled, the Cave-dweller, the Translucent,[9] more or less numerously mingled with the rest, of which I have not space here to speak, but whose history I have elsewhere written in detail.[10] And we see here and there, for the most part crowded into groups, another interesting kind, the Plumose,[11] which differs much in appearance from its associates, having a taller column much more pellucid, and a crown of tentacles so short, so numerous and so dense, as to form a large confused tuft of frills, which cannot be separated into rows. This kind is always of self-colours, which, however, may be light olive, fawn-brown, orange, flesh-colour, or pure white. Those which the tide has left exposed, loll out of their holes and droop; but under the water they stand erect, with a noble boldness. Each group generally contains individuals of all sizes, and may be considered as a single family of several generations, or, to speak more correctly, of several series of offsets, of different ages. For it is highly characteristic of this species to increase by spontaneous division. When a large individual has been a good while adherent to one spot, and at length chooses to change its quarters, it does so by causing its base to glide slowly along the surface on which it rests;—the glass side of the tank, for instance. But it frequently happens that small irregular fragments of the edge of the base are left behind, as if their adhesion had been so strong, that the animal found it easier to tear its own tissues apart than to overcome it. The fragments so left soon contract, become smooth, and spherical or oval in outline; and in the course of a week or fortnight each may be seen furnished with a margin of tentacles and a disk; transformed, in fact, into perfect though minute Anemones. Occasionally a separated piece, more irregularly jagged than usual, will, in contracting, constringe itself, and form two smaller fragments, united by an isthmus, which goes on attenuating until a fine thread-like line only is stretched from one to the other; this at length yields, the substance of the broken thread is rapidly absorbed into the respective pieces, which soon become two young Anemones.

All the kinds which we have seen in this locality belong to one great family, the *Sagartiadæ*, a group which includes nearly one-third of the seventy species of Anemones and Corals which we have on the British coast; and certainly the most beautiful and the most known, taking them one with another. They are distinguished by a remarkable peculiarity; the skin of the body is pierced with minute holes, capable of being opened and closed at will, out of which can be forced curious slender threads, which ordinarily lie coiled up in great profusion in the interior of the animal. These threads are almost entirely composed of those extraordinary capsules, called *cnidæ*, or nettling-cells, found indeed in most of the tissues, but nowhere in such abundance as here, which eject with amazing force a poisonous filament having the strength and elasticity of a wire, and furnished with reversed barbs, but of almost inconceivable tenuity. The filaments, projected by myriads at the pleasure of the animal, penetrate deeply into the flesh of other soft-bodied creatures, and cause immediate paralysis and speedy death.[12]

The waning day and the turning tide warn us homeward; but we shall have time to visit a fine dark overarched pool in the rocks which I know on our route. Here it is; noticeable because of its being the chosen residence of a colony of that magnificent species, the Dahlia Wartlet.[13] All round the curving sides of the sea-washed basin, crowding one upon the other beneath the projecting angles, or seated in single majesty on some prominence, we see them flaunting the most gorgeous colours, and attaining a diameter of expanse that no other, at least of our common forms, can rival or approach. The wide but low column, rough with coarse warts, may be olive, or deep green, or purple-crimson, or light green splashed and streaked with scarlet like an apple; the disk is equally varied, but generally displays diverging bands of rich red which fork and embrace the tentacles; while the tentacles, short, stout, and conical, may be white with pellucid rings, deep crimson, or of the highest flush of rose, with a broad ring of lilac. Widely expanded, the Crassicornis is as good a mimicry of the great dahlias of our gardens, as the Sagartiæ are of the daisies and pompone chrysanthemums. Even bees are occasionally deceived. Mr. Couch, when once looking at a fine specimen which was expanded so close to the surface that only a thin film of water covered the disk and tentacles, saw a roving bee alight on the tempting surface, evidently mistaking the anemone for a veritable blossom; the tenacious tentacles instantly seized it, and though it struggled a good deal for its liberty, retained the disappointed bee till it was drowned, when it was soon consigned to the insatiable stomach. The story reminds us of the well-known fact that the flesh-flies, deceived by the carrion smell of some of the Stapeliæ, sometimes lay their eggs on the flowers; both cases showing that animal instinct is not quite so unerring as it is frequently represented.

Attached to the thin crumpled leaf of an Ulva in this pool is an animal, having much of the texture, and somewhat of the form, of an Anemone. Formerly, indeed, it was associated in the same group, but it is now ascertained to have more affinities with the translucent and often colourless free-swimming jelly-fishes. From its resemblance to an elegant lamp, it is called *Lucernaria*.[14] We must suppose a *Medusa* to be turned hollow upwards, and an adhesive foot to be produced from what was before the summit of its "umbrella;" and little more is necessary to constitute a *Lucernaria*. The most observable peculiarity is that the tentacles, which are very minute, and have the form of a globose head seated on a short stem, are disposed in compact groups of as many as seventy, which groups, eight in number, like so many round balls, are seated on projecting angles of the margin; while from the centre of the hollow rises a mouth, with four protrusile lips in form of a square. The colour is a dull dark red or liver brown. The animal preys on other creatures, which it captures by means of poison-capsules, and swallows, much as the anemones do.

And thus we wend our way homeward; meditating much as we glide across the smooth bay, on the wondrous elegance of form, the exquisite brilliance of colours, the great variety, the instincts, the powers, the most elaborate apparatus, bestowed on these humble creatures,

Plate IX

Green Opelet. Orange-Disk Anemone.

of no apparent use whatever to man; indeed, until quite recently, utterly neglected by him and unknown, though exhibiting their loveliness under his very eyes, and close to his doors. We meditate on these things, and ask, For what purpose is all this profuse expenditure of power, wisdom, taste, skill? We hear the answer in the choral praise of those who know more of these matters than we can yet attain to,— "Thou hast created all things, and *for thy pleasure* they are, and were created."

Plate X

Spinous Cockle. Banded Venus.

IV.
April

Shall we explore the sands to-day? A bright sandy beach well exposed to the sea is no bad hunting-ground for the naturalist, bare as it looks, and proverbial as is its character for sterility,— "barren as the sand on the sea-shore." And specially is it likely to be productive, when, as is often the case, the wide reach of yellow sand is interrupted by one or more isolated areas of rough rocks. Goodrington Sands, lying in the hollow of Torbay, afford just these conditions; and thither will we bend our steps this April morning.

So we make our way along the dusty highroad, that leads from Torquay southward, skirting the shore, now and then getting peeps of the rocks and the retiring tide, over the massive sea-walls, as the successive coves open and again shut-in by bounding hedgerows as we cross the bases of the intervening headlands. Wild hyacinths are peeping among the rank foliage of the arums and nettles; and harts-tongue ferns, and primroses are everywhere, clustering in treat masses, or studding the green banks in single stars; the bright rose-campion smiles, and the ever lovely germander speedwell, brightest, sweetest of spring flowers, gladdens us here and there, like "angels' eyes," as our rustics poetically call these pretty azure flowers.

As we proceed, we pause to wipe our foreheads, and turning round, see Torquay behind us, covering and crowning its amphitheatre of hills, like a queenly city, surely the most beauteous of all our watering-places;—and beyond it on the left, we see the old church tower of Marychurch, on its elevated plateau, standing out massive and dark against the sky.

We pass through the outskirts of the long straggling village of Paignton, and mark how picturesquely it is embosomed in the midst of its apple orchards; the old-fashioned cottages buried in the trees, so that only the time-stained roofs of brown thatch rise here and there, like islets in a wide sea of blushing blossom. And now extensive osier grounds lie on either side; the young tender-green shoots, the hope of the harvest, rising thickly from the uncouth pollard stumps; while the still water glimmers everywhere around their roots.

A narrow lane leads off abruptly on our left, into which we turn, and in a moment are in a mossy, flowery, ferny region. The open gate of a villa reveals a little girl "perambulating" a baby amid the bowers and blossoms of a sweet garden, whose numerous old tamarisk trees, rough and bristling, guard the wall, just breaking into their plumy foliage. And then we open the expanse of shore and sea, and the wheels of the carriage are suddenly six inches deep in the soft sand. How brightly the wide silver sea is glancing and sparkling under the climbing sun! Scarcely a breeze breaks its mirrory face, though far out in the offing lines and bands of deep blue show that there are intermitting puffs ruffling the water; and the craft that creep along the horizon have evidently got a working breeze, though the yachts in the half-distance sit like white swans, their motionless prows pointing every way, and "floating double," on the molten looking-glass.

These are the Goodrington Sands; for there on the left is the projecting bluff of red sandstone, horizontally stratified, known as Roundham Head, and beyond it in the distance we see Hope's Nose, and its two guardian islets, the Orestone and the Thatcher. On the other side, the long wall of land terminating in Berry Head projects to an equal distance, and we are in the bottom of the deep bight, nearly equidistant from both.

Immediately in front of the debouchure of the little green lane, beginning some way down the beach, and stretching away into the sea, there is a mass of low black rock, leprous with barnacles, and draped with ragged tufts of oar-weed and tangle and bladder-wrack, sweltering and blackening in the sun. It is much broken up, and narrow winding lanes paved with sand pierce it in all directions; and shallow pools of quiet water sleep everywhere in the hollows. Sweet little sea-gardens are these pools: bright green leaves of ulva float like tinted cambric in the water; tufts of chondrus are glittering with steely reflections of gemmeous blue; large broad leaves of dulse, richly, darkly red, afford fine contrasts with the green sea-lettuce; and one and all give ample shelter to thousands of vigilant, busy, happy, living creatures. It is treacherous walking; for the footing is very uneven, and the glare of the sun on the water renders it difficult to see where to tread; while the advance and recess of the wavelets on the sand between, give to the bewildered brain the impression that everything is sliding from under the foot.

What is that object that lies on yonder stretch of sand, over which the shallow water ripples, washing the sand around it and presently leaving it dry? It looks like a stone; but there is a fine scarlet knob on it; which all of a sudden has disappeared. Let us watch the moment of the receding wave, and run out to it.

It is a fine example of the great spinous cockle,[1] for which all these sandy beaches that form the bottom of the great sea-bend of Torbay are celebrated. Indeed the species is scarcely known elsewhere; so that it is often designated in books as the Paignton cockle. A right savoury *bonne bouche* it is, when artistically dressed. Old Dr. Turton, a great authority in his day for Devonshire natural history, especially in matters relating to shells and shell-fish, says that the cottagers about Paignton well know the "red noses," as they call the great cockles, and search for them at the low spring-tides, when they may be seen lying in the sand with the fringed siphons appearing just above the surface. They gather them in baskets and panniers, and after cleansing them a few hours in cold spring-water, fry the animals in a batter made of crumbs of bread. The creatures have not changed their habits nor their habitats; for they are still to be seen in the old spots just as they were a century ago: nor have they lost their reputation; they are indeed promoted to the gratification of more refined palates now, for the cottagers, knowing on which side their bread is buttered, collect the sapid cockles for the fashionables of Torquay, and content themselves with the humbler and smaller species,[2] which rather affects the muddy flats of estuaries than sand beaches, though not uncommon here. This latter, though much inferior in sapidity to the great spinous sort, forms a far more important item in the category of human food, from its very general distribution, its extreme abundance, and the ease with which it is collected. Wherever the receding tide leaves an area of exposed mud, the common cockle is sure to be found; and hundreds of men, women, and children, may be seen plodding and groping over the stinking surface, with naked feet and bent backs, picking up the shell-fish by thousands, to be boiled and eaten for home consumption, or to be cried through the lanes and alleys of the neighbouring towns by stentorian boys, who vociferate all day long,— "Here's your fine cockles, here! Here they are! Here they are! Twopence a quart!"

It is on the north-western coasts of Scotland, however, that the greatest abundance of these mollusca occurs, and there they form not a luxury, but even a necessary of life to the poor semi-barbarous population. The inhabitants of those rocky regions enjoy an unenviable notoriety for being habitually dependent on this mean diet. "Where the river meets the sea at Tongue," says Macculloch, "there is a considerable ebb, and the long sand-banks are productive of cockles in an abundance which is almost unexampled. At that time (a year of scarcity) they presented every day at low water a singular spectacle, being crowded with men, women, and children, who were busily employed in digging for these shell-fish as long as the tide permitted. It was not unusual also to see thirty or forty horses from the surrounding country, which had been brought down for the purpose of carrying away loads of them to distances of many miles. This was a well-known season of scarcity, and, without this resource, I believe it is not too much to say, that many individuals must have died for want."[3]

The isles of Barra and North Uist, in the Hebrides, possess also enormous resources of the same character. "It is not easy to calculate," says Mr. Wilson, "the amount of such beds of shell-fish, but we may mention that, during a period of great distress which prevailed a good many years ago, all the families in the island (then about two hundred in number) resorted, for the sake of this food, to the great sands at the northern end of Barra. It was computed that, for a couple of summers at the time alluded to, no less than from one hundred to two hundred horse-loads were taken at low water every day of the spring-tides during the months of May, June, July, and August. We were pleased to hear it observed that the shell-fish are always most abundant in years of scarcity."[4]

These Barra beds are of great antiquity. A very old writer, Dean Monro, thus notices them:— "This ile is full of grate cokills, and alledgit be the aunceint countremen that the same cokills comes down out of the fore-said hill throw the said strype in the first smalle forme that wee have spokyn of, and aftir theyr comying down to the sandes growis grate cokills allways. Ther is no fayrer and more profytable sandes for cokills in all the worlde."

But all this time our fair "cokill" has been lying at our feet, snapping, and gaping, and thrusting forth and back his great coral foot, waiting our leisure to take him up. No longer shall he be neglected. The bivalve shell is a fine solid house of stone, massive, strong, and heavy, elegantly fluted with prominent ribs that radiate regularly on both valves from the curved beaks, which ribs are beset with polished spiny points. The hues of the shell are attractive, though not at all showy; they consist of tints of yellowish and reddish browns, rich and warm, arranged in concentric bands, and gradually fading to a creamy white at the beaks. Unlike the scallops, the cockles have the two valves alike in shape, and from the bent beaks meeting each other, and the curvature of the outline, they present, when viewed endwise, a very regular and beautiful heart-shape, whence the scientific name of the genus is derived, *Cardium*, from êáñäßá, the heart.

The animal which inhabits this strong fortress is handsomer than bivalves usually are. The leaves of the mantle are thick and convex, corresponding to the shell-valves; the edges are strongly fringed in the neighbourhood of the siphons, which are short tubes of considerable diameter, soldered, as it were, together. The mantle has a soft spongy character towards its edges, but towards the back, where it lines the valves, it is very thin and almost membranous. The hue of the former parts is very rich, a fine brilliant orange, with the shaggy fringe of tentacles paler; the siphons are also orange, with the inner surface of the tubes white, having a pearly gleam.

But what was that scarlet knob that we saw protruded and retracted but now? Ha! as it lies, slightly gaping, the lips of the mantle recede, and we catch a peep within of the gorgeous colour. Suddenly the valves open to their full extent, like the folding-doors of a drawing-room, allowing exit to a richly dressed lady. Here comes the vermilion tenant! Place for my lady! But what is she? And what is she about to do in her gorgeous raiment? Nay; 'tis but the cockle's foot; a monopod he is: this is all the foot he has. It is clad in neither shoe nor stocking; and truly it needs it not. Never was the silken-hosed foot of cardinal arrayed like this. But see to what an extent the organ protrudes! four inches from the valves' edges does its tip reach; smooth, lubricous, taper, with a knee at the upper part, and the toe bent in the form of a hook. As to its general appearance when thus extended, I have compared it to a finger of polished carnelian; but Mr. Pingsley thinks that this resemblance will not hold, the foot being too opaque for that gem: he likens it to a long capsicum, which is, however, too dull and too dark; and he tells a story of a certain (mythic, I fear) countess who, seeing it for the first time, exclaimed, "Oh, dear! I always heard that my pretty red coral came out of a fish, and here it is, all alive!"

Nay; after all, it is what it is; and those comparisons just help one who has never seen it, to form some conception of its appearance; but by one who has, all will be rejected as inadequate.

And as to what the brilliant organ is going to do, that we see. For the long taper foot being thrust to its utmost, feels about for some resisting surface,—that stone, half buried in the sand, for instance; which no sooner does it feel than the hooked point is pressed stiffly against it, the whole foot by muscular contraction is made suddenly rigid, and the entire creature,—mantle, siphons, foot, shell and all,—is jerked away in an uncouth manner, "quite permiscous," as the fisherman hard-by says, to a distance of some foot or more. But the cockle can leap on occasion much more vigorously; one has been seen to throw itself clear over the gunwale of a boat when laid on the bottom-boards.

Thus we see one use of the hooked tip is to afford a stronger spring; but it has a more direct bearing on the burrowing habits of the animal. Like all the rest of its beautiful tribe, this species is a dweller in the deep sand, into which it can penetrate with considerable power and rapidity. In order to do this, the foot is straightened, and the sharp point is thrust perpendicularly down into the wet sand. The muscular force exerted is sufficient to penetrate the soft sand to the whole length, when the point is suddenly bent sidewise, thus obtaining a strong holdfast. The whole organ is now strongly contracted in length, and the animal and shell are dragged forcibly to the mouth of the burrow, the edges of the valves downward and piercing the sand a little way. The straightened point is then pushed an inch or two farther down; again hooked, and another pull is made. The shell descends a little farther into the yielding sand, and the same interchange of processes goes on till the animal is sufficiently buried. To read this description you would suppose it a most clumsy, and ineffective, and slow business; but indeed this is very far from its character. The elongations and contractions are made with great rapidity; and almost with the quickness of thought the unwieldy cockle, when in full vigour and thoroughly alarmed, disappears into his sandy fortress; so fast, indeed, that you must be very alert to overtake him and prevent his descent, if you have no appliances but your two hands.

Cuvier, in his elaborate and beautiful dissections of the Mollusca, has demonstrated that this important organ is mainly composed of an immense multitude of muscles, circular, longitudinal, and transverse, wonderful in their complexity and arrangement, but most perfectly adapted to impart variety, force, and precision to its movements. In these respects the human tongue perhaps presents the closest parallel to its organization. It is remarkable that at its upper or basal part it is hollow, and encloses some of the viscera of the body.

Here, under this low-lying ledge of rock, is another shell, which in beauty perhaps excels even the gorgeous cockle. It belongs to a genus pre-eminent for loveliness, to which the name of the Goddess of Love has

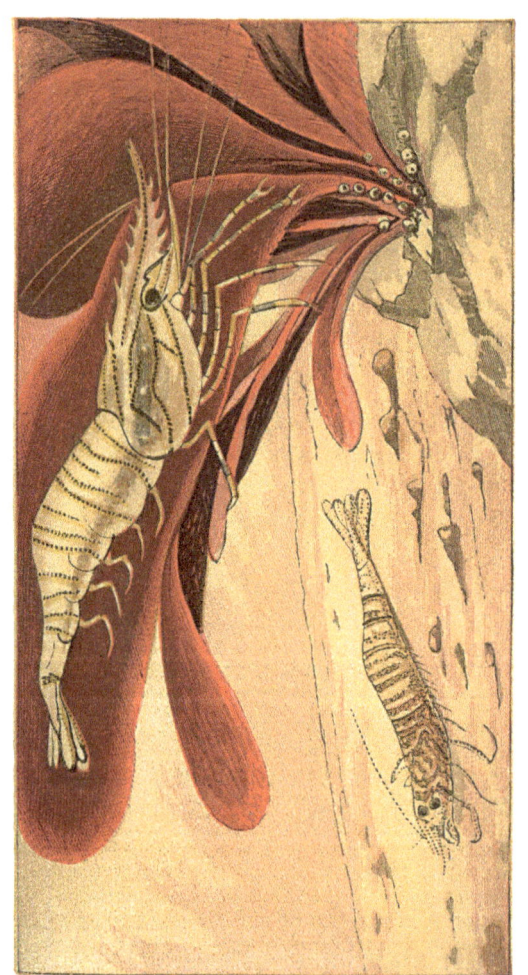

Plate XI

Common Shrimp. Great Prawn.

been assigned. This is the Banded Venus.⁵ The most prominent and obvious character is that the shell-valves are covered with ribs, more or less strongly marked, which, instead of running fan-like from the beaks to the edges, as in the cockles, are concentric, being parallel with the edges. In this species these ribs are well marked, about a dozen in number, broad, flat, sharply defined, and nearly equally distant. They impart to the shell, which is very convex, and nearly round, an aspect of great strength combined with elegance. The colours, too, are very ornamental: broad bands of brownish lilac, varied with warmer tints, widening as they go, radiate from the beaks to the margins, relieved by a whitish ground. The hues vary in different individuals; the bands being sometimes rusty brown, or purple; and the ground yellow, or pale orange; and the contrasts are in some better marked than in others; but when fresh and unrubbed the shell is always a beautiful one.

    The specimen before us is alive. I will drop it into this shallow pool in the rock. See, the valves are opening, and a large foot of a waxy whiteness, almost semi-pellucid, protrudes, thicker and more ovate than that of the cockle, but not capable of such elongation. The siphons, however, are proportionally longer; they are separate at their extremities, and project considerably from the shell.

    But while we are gazing at the beauty of our little Venus, we become cognizant of the presence of another spectator. He has slowly come out from beneath the shadow of that long dark-brown leaf of *Laminaria*, that floats like a crumpled ribbon across the pool, and now rests on the tuft of *Iridæa*, that fine scarlet weed of leathery texture, that grows in the shaded corner. It is a Prawn;⁶ and a fellow of noble dimensions. Is he too attracted by the fair shell? or rather is not his attention occupied by us? Yes; the latter is the true case; as you may discern by his long-stalked eyes, steadily staring upwards. He wonders what our two faces can mean; and, as we remain still, he ventures forth to take a fuller view.

    An elegant creature is the common prawn, or rock-shrimp, as the fishermen designate him, by way of distinction from another sapid crustacean that inhabits these shores. His armour of proof, composed of plates that slide so smoothly one under another, sustains the most lustrous polish, and is ever subject to the animal's efforts to keep it so; for, whenever he has a moment's leisure from more pressing avocations, he is constantly engaged in cleaning it with the brushes which those slender fore-limbs of his carry. Like a true soldier, like a knight of chivalry, the Prawn lives, eats, sleeps in armour. How completely is his body encased in defensive mail; and he carries his tempered weapon too. Look at the serrate sword which he always points at the foe whom he faces? Who would rashly provoke such a weapon as this? Stiff and firm in substance, long, pointed, two-edged, keen on both edges, curved sabre-like, and cut into acute teeth; it does seem a most formidable affair: and yet, truth to tell, I do not know what use the owner makes of it. Though I have been for many years in the practice of keeping these elegant animals in my aquaria, I have never seen one smite a foe with his two-edged sword.

Perhaps like the cane over the looking-glass in a nursery, its mere presence is sufficient to keep in awe encroaching enemies, whose hearts sink when they behold the sharp-toothed weapon.

Exquisitely painted is the Prawn. His ground colour is semi-pellucid olive-grey, on which transverse lines of black are drawn; and specks and dashes of sparkling white, symmetrically arranged and well defined, are scattered here and there, especially upon the broad swimming plates that serve as his principal instruments of locomotion. His limbs, too, are ringed with blue and orange, a felicitous combination!

I have just alluded to the tail as a motive power. It is a very curious organ, consisting of five plates, so hinged that they can play over each other, or be spread out in shape of a fan, and each plate beset on its edges with a most delicate fringe of stiff bristles. To see its use, you have only to approach the animal. He instantly darts away with force; all the while, however, keeping his face to the foe, as becomes a soldier so armed. Now this retrocessive power is his great *cheval de bataille*. When gently exploring he crawls among the weeds on the tips of his long feet; when swimming at ease, he glides gracefully along by the rapid paddling of the false feet, of which he carries five pairs beneath his abdomen. But when alarmed, he forcibly throws forward this plated tail, expanded to the utmost, bending the last joints of the body from the hump on his back, and thus strikes a powerful forward blow on the water, by the impact of which the whole prawn is jerked backward to a distance of several inches.

But he is gone; and it were useless to look for him any more in this wilderness of sea-weeds, and amid the cavernous recesses of those rocky ledges, where he enjoys ample means of retreat and concealment. For, even if you did catch a momentary glimpse of him again, it would be only as he darts from one shelter to another, and he would presently be far out of your reach in the obscurity of some inexplorable hole.

Let us turn to the beach and follow the water's edge. Let us see what this fisherman is so busy about, and what that horse is doing as he paces backward and forward belly-deep in the sea, from one end of the beach to the other, then retracing his steps, as if he were ploughing the shallows. And why does the fisherman watch the horse so attentively? Hark! what says he? He shouts to the diminutive urchin that rides the horse to come in; and now he eagerly goes down to the edge of the sea, as the beast and his little rider come ashore. We will go and see.

The man is civil and communicative, and lets us into the whole secret; though now indeed that we are on the spot, it is sufficiently patent. The horse draws behind him an implement called a keer-drag; a net, which is stretched upon an oblong iron frame, that forms its mouth. Behind, the net tapers to a point, but is left open there in the making, and only tied with a string. The iron frame keeps the net-mouth open, and being attached by a bridle to a rope, which is fastened to the horse's harness, scrapes the sea-bottom as he proceeds; whatever is collected passing into the net, and accumulating at the narrow point.

Now the shallows just here are alive with swarms of another edible species of crustacea, the Shrimp,[7] *par excellence*; or, as the people here say, the sand shrimp, to distinguish it from the prawn, which, as I have observed, they call the rock shrimp. And this sand shrimp finds a ready sale in the Torquay market; the fisherman getting, as he tells us, a shilling a quart from the fishmongers.

The horse, doubtless nothing loath, for his toil must be great, wading on soft sand in three feet of water, and dragging that heavy apparatus behind him, walks to dry land, where, as soon as the keer-drag is ashore, the man seizes it, cries "whow!" to the obedient animal, and, having spread a cloth on the sand, proceeds to untie the string, and pour out on the cloth the struggling contents. "It is a very good haul," says the fellow; "there's more nor two quart there!" So, being in a good humour, and naturally civil besides, we venture to propound a bargain; that, for a small coin of the realm, we may be allowed to pick out all the "rubbish;" *i.e.*, everything that is not a shrimp, and convey it to our own private reservoirs; a pleasant agreement for both parties; for the net gathers many curious creatures of great interest to the naturalist, though of no value whatever to the fisherman. Shrimps, however, are the staple; there are probably a hundred of these to one of all other kinds, lumping these latter all together. And very fine these shrimps are. Mr. Bell gives two inches and a half as the total length of the species,[8] and I do not remember that I ever before saw one that exceeded that size: but here, the great majority are upwards of three inches; and a very considerable number are full three and a half. They are mostly females loaded with spawn, which they carry entangled among the false feet beneath the body.

In general figure the shrimp resembles the prawn: it, however, carries no sword-like rostrum; and the front pair of feet, instead of terminating each in a pair of claws, have a strong hook which bends down upon a short spine. The limbs too are very much shorter, and the animal is less elegant. The colour is a pale warm brown; but when examined closely this is seen to resolve itself into a freckling of black, grey, brown, and orange specks, arranged so as to make a kaleidoscopic sort of pattern. When highly magnified many of the dots take star-like forms.

It is amusing to see how rapidly and cleverly the shrimp takes its place in the sand. If there be an inch or two's depth of water, the animal quietly sinks on the bottom; then, in a moment, you see a little cloud of dust (so it seems) rise up along each side, and the body sinks till the surrounding surface is nearly level with its back. Then you perceive the value of the peculiar style of colouring: the freckling of specks of various tints of brown, grey, and red, so exactly resembles the hues of the sand, that you might look close at a shrimp so sunken, and yet not discern it. The eyes, however, which are set on the top of the head, like a Dutchman's garret windows, are keeping a bright watch upward, and here it lies, quiet and, against most enemies, safe. The iron lip of the drag, however, scrapes up with its edge the upper inch of sand-bottom, routs out the poor shrimps, which dart upwards, to find themselves within the mouth of the ever-advancing net. The agency in the burrowing is the false feet, which, waved rapidly to and fro, brush up the fine sand with the currents that they make in the water, and throw it up in those clouds on each side, presently to fall again on the body, and help to conceal it.

But there are more things than shrimps in the gleaming, working, struggling mass of life before us. Not to mind the uncouth soldier-crabs, dragging about their despoiled shells, which, numerous and conspicuous as they are, we shall neglect for another occasion,—we have other fish to fry. Here are sundry examples of that remarkable race, the proper Flatfishes. These thin, brown, long-oval ones are specimens of Soles, of which there are two kinds here, the Common Sole, uniform dull brown, and the Lemon Sole, of a more freckled tint, pale orange brown, with darker spots.[9] The fisherman considers them marketable if they are not less than four or five inches long, and bundles them into his common depository, under the title of tea-dabs, a name which sufficiently indicates their destiny.

Now every one has looked at hundreds of pairs of soles raw and ready, but perhaps not all have ever adequately remarked the singular anomaly presented by their structure, or are aware how unique their tribe is among animals. That one surface is positively coloured, while the other is fleshy white, is no great matter; for many creatures, and fishes in particular, are darker above and paler below. The flat Rays are equally abject, and show a like contrast of hues; but, *structurally*, the colours in the Sole are not respectively on the back and belly, though they are certainly above and below. These fishes, in fact, swim and lie *on one side*; and so they have one side dark and one side light.

This habit, however, imposed upon them, involves other very important aberrations from ordinary forms. Let us suppose that the eyes had been placed, like those of the Chætodons (very thin, wide, and flat fishes of the tropical seas), one on each side of the head. That eye which belonged to the white or inferior side, would be rendered useless, since it would be almost perpetually buried in the mud of the bottom. Hence, by an unprecedented exception to the symmetry which marks the organs of sense in all other vertebrate animals, both of the eyes are placed on the same side of the head, one above the other. They are, however, frequently not in the same line, and one is often smaller and less developed than the other.

In addition to these peculiarities, we may remark, that the spine makes a sudden twist near the head to one side; that the bones of the head are not symmetrical; that the two sides of the mouth are unequal; that the pectoral and ventral fins of the under side are generally smaller than those of the upper; and that the dorsal and anal fins generally correspond to each other, the one fringing the whole length of the dorsal, the other that of the ventral edge of the body.

We must not suppose that these peculiarities are defects and mistakes; nor, like Buffon, when he found some structure or habit which was at variance with his preconceived notions of fitness, accuse the all-wise God of bungling in His work. They are merely examples of that inscrutable wisdom, those inexhaustible resources of power and skill, which can and often do delight to attain the most worthy ends by the most unexpected roads, in which we can only follow, as the way is opened up to us, and wonderingly adore. Let us hear what Yarrell says on these strange modifications. "The Flat-fishes ... are, by this depressed form of body, admirably adapted to inhabit the lowest position, and where they occupy the least space, among their kindred fishes. Preferring sandy or muddy shores, and unprovided with swimming-bladders, their place is close to the ground, where, hiding their bodies horizontally in the loose soil at the bottom, with the head only slightly elevated, an eye on the under side of the head would be useless; but both eyes placed on the upper surface afford them an extensive range of view in those various directions in which they may either endeavour to find suitable food, or avoid dangerous enemies. Light, one great cause of colour, strikes on the upper surface only; the under surface, like that of most other fishes, remains perfectly colourless. Having little or no means of defence, had their colour been placed only above the lateral line on each side, in whatever position they moved, their piebald appearance would have rendered them conspicuous objects to all their enemies. When near the ground they swim slowly, maintaining their horizontal position; and the smaller pectoral and ventral fins on the under side are advantageous where there is so much less room for their action, than with the larger fins that are above. When suddenly disturbed, they sometimes make a rapid shoot, changing their position from horizontal to vertical; if the observer happens to be opposite the white side, they may be seen to pass with the rapidity and flash of a meteor; but they soon sink down, resuming their previous motionless, horizontal position, and are then distinguished with difficulty, owing to their great similarity in colour to the surface on which they rest."[10]

On several occasions I have, when examining the contents of the shrimpers' nets, found a pretty little species of flat-fish, which, though we find it not at this moment, is a pretty constant inhabitant of these sandy beaches. It is too small and too worthless for the fisherman to have a distinctive name for it, but our systematic books call it a Topknot,[11] and assign to it near consanguinity with the majestic and delicious turbot. It is marked as very rare; but I have seen three or four come up at a haul of the drag, and have found it among the rocks. Not long ago, I took a specimen by turning over a flat stone in a sandy pool in this ledge. It was indeed small, not exceeding an inch and a half in length; the ordinary size of those that occur as the shrimps' companions in captivity; but their utmost growth scarcely attains five inches.

The specimen I allude to I took home, and observed at leisure. In a white saucer it was a charming little object, though rather difficult to examine, because, the instant the eye with the lens was brought near, it flounced in alarm, and often leaped out upon the table. When its fit of terror was over, however, it became still, and would allow me to push it hither and thither, merely waving the edges of its dorsal and ventral fins

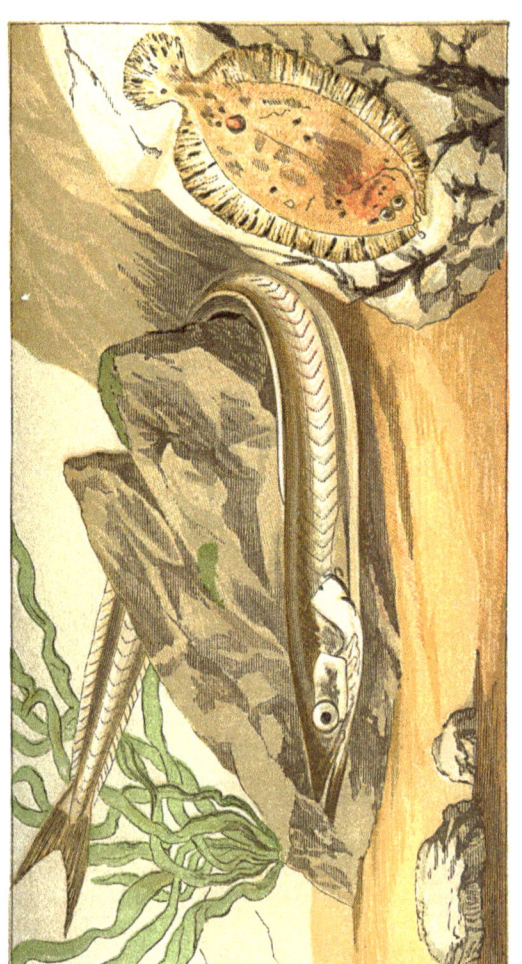

Plate XII

Sand-Launce. Topknot.

rapidly as it yielded to the impulse. The shape of these fins gives to the outline of the fish a form resembling an oblong parallelogram with the corners rounded, and the fan-like tail projecting; but the outline of the body is much more oval. The first ray of the dorsal is a little lengthened; whence the name of Topknot. We have two little species of Turbot with this peculiarity, called Muller's Topknot, and Bloch's Topknot. This was the former. Yarrell, indeed, distinguishes the two by saying that this one has "the first ray of the dorsal not longer than the succeeding rays;" or, in other words, that it has no topknot at all. It may be that it is obliterated in age, but in this half-grown specimen, it was quite conspicuous, projecting like a little horn from the forehead, about one-fourth longer than the second and following rays. In Bloch's Topknot it is, indeed, more marked, for it there runs off into a slender filament, of more than twice the length of the rays. The fins were exquisitely delicate, and were very pretty in their markings, every tenth or twelfth ray being black interrupted with white; the middle ray between these was black at the tip, and the central one of these subordinate divisions was again more slightly specked. This had a very pretty effect. The body was pellucid yellowish brown, studded with irregular faint clouds and stronger specks of dark brown, and bearing one conspicuous ring-like mark near the tail. The flesh was so translucent, that the stomach and principal viscera could be distinctly seen, and the accumulation of the chief blood-vessels here, gave a crimson flush to these parts.

Alarm had a curious effect, probably dependent on the quickening of the circulation. When I tried to catch the little fish, all the spots and markings became instantly deepened and vivified, and particularly those of the fins, so that the change seemed magical. I have observed the same thing in the Gobies, and some other fishes.

The eyes were very beautiful and interesting. As in all this family of Flat-fishes, they are set close together on the same side of the head, the upper one inclined slightly upward, the lower downward. Viewed with a lens, the iris was seen to be pale green, with radiating dark bands, and the pupil surrounded by an edge-line of ruddy gold. The iris projects into the pupil with an angle, making it crescent-shaped. The eyes move quite independently of each other, and very curious it was to look down with a lens upon the quaint little face, and see one eye quickly turned up towards the beholder, while the other remained still, or presently turned in the opposite direction.

Now and then it curved the head and tail downwards, and leaped out of water, clearing the side of the saucer in which it was confined; then, when put back, it lay some seconds on its back (or rather on its wrong side), with the dorsal and ventrals incurved, and thus the whole body concave, as if in tetanus; but when turned over it soon recovered.

What is this writhing, wriggling thing, that looks like a narrow tape of burnished silver? It is a Sandlaunce,[12] and very slyly is it endeavouring to make its way down to the rippling edge of the wave, to liberty and life. But not so fast, pretty Launce! we want to have a look at you, and to introduce you to a very jolly set in our aquarium at home. Now don't flounce and dart round the jar so angrily: you can't get out, and may as well be philosophic.

Do you see the remarkable projection of the lower jaws? With that sort of spade the little silvery fish manages to scoop out a bed for itself very quickly in the wet sand, and so lie hid. It is numerous enough in these bays, and it is in request among fishermen, who use it largely as bait, and who, to obtain it, cast a seine, and enclose vast multitudes, which are thus dragged up on the beach high and dry.

A short time ago I saw a paragraph in the *Times*, from some Jersey correspondent, who complained of the recent scarcity of fish, and accounted for it by the following curious catenation of links. A number of sharks had recently appeared in the offing, which frightened away the shoals of porpesses, which ordinarily came to feed on the fishes, which fed on the Sand-launce. Now when the porpesses were there the fishes were driven with the Launce into the shallows, and were readily taken; but, on being relieved of these persecutors by the intruding sharks, were free to retire to the deeper water, where the fishers could less easily entrap them. The writer stated, however, that at length the sharks had departed, the porpesses had returned, the fishes were consequently driven in shore, and were again devouring the Launce. The whole account has something of the "House that Jack built" twang, and I do not quite pin my faith on the philosophy of the explanation.

Be that as it may, I can vouch for the Launce making a very attractive tenant of an aquarium, where it will live a considerable time. The pearly gleams of lustre from its sides are very beautiful, and such as no pictorial art can reproduce.

V.
May

We are far from having exhausted the treasures of the teeming sands. Another visit to their broad expanse may yield other objects of interest not inferior to those we lately discovered there. Let us, then, seek the shore, where our humble friend the shrimper, with his wading horse, under the guidance of his shrill-voiced little son, still pursues his indefatigable calling.

Again the keer-drag is drawn up the tawny beach, the bag is untied, and the sparkling, crawling, jumping heap spreads itself over the sand, beyond the limits of the insufficient cloth.

A little silvery fish wriggles from the mass, and, by a few lateral vibrations, in an instant buries himself in the soft wet sand, all but the upper surface of his head and back. Our attention is drawn towards this object; but our friend the shrimper shouts rather abruptly a note of warning. "Mind what ye be 'bout! that 'ere's pison! He's a sting-bull, he is." Thus armed, we use caution in our approaches, and look well before we touch. As we see it now, it certainly presents a noteworthy appearance. A large head, with a wide mouth opening at very upward angles; two staring eyes, set in the crown so as to look upward instead of sideways, and intently watching our intentions; a short fin on the back, of which the membrane is of the deepest velvet black, and the rays, which are stout sharp spines, are white; these rays are now stretched to the utmost, like a fan widely expanded, so as to offer the threatening points in all directions to a foe;—these are all the features we can discern, except a narrow line of olive presently lost in the sand, which marks the buried body.

In spite of the good man's earnest warnings to have nothing to do with so venomous a creature, we must contrive to take possession of it for study at home and by the aid of our hand-net we find no difficulty in lifting it and transferring it, an unwilling guest, to a glass jar of sea-water. We now discern it more fully and distinctly; though it manifests its indignation at this tyrannical suspension of the *Habeas Corpus* Act, by flouncing around the glass, and scattering the water hither and thither. This wrath, however, gradually subsides, and our captive philosophically makes up his mind to his fate.

It is the Lesser Weever;[1] a name corrupted from the French, who call it Vive, from the length of time which the fish will *live* out of its native element. It also bears the names of sting-fish, sting-bull, and sea-cat, among English fishermen; on the shores of the Mediterranean it bears

Plate XIII. Fifteen-Spined Stickleback. Lesser Weever.

the title of spider, and the ancient Romans called it sea-dragon. The specific names,—*vipera* and *draco*, viper and dragon—which are appropriated to this species and another which is nearly allied to it, make up an extensive list of aliases, all combining to give this pretty little fish a thoroughly bad reputation. All these titles point to a habit and a power possessed by it of inflicting severe wounds, which without doubt are of a highly inflammatory character, and are slow and difficult to cure. These are effected by the rays of the first dorsal fin, which, as we have just seen, are erected and spread in a way which indicates a perfect consciousness of their power, and by certain spines, long and acute, set on the gill-covers, one on each, pointing backward. These all are of needle-like sharpness, and are wielded most effectively. Yarrell tells us that if trod upon, or only touched, while on the watch, nearly buried in the sand at the bottom of the water, it strikes with force either upwards or sideways; and Pennant says that he had seen it direct its blows with as much judgment as a fighting cock. Fishermen hold it in great dread; and the name of sting-bull is said to be due to its power of piercing even the proverbial thickness of a bull's hide.

Cuvier considers the imputation of venom to the wounds made by the Weever as a popular error. He says, "They cannot inject into the wounds they inflict with their spines any poisonous substance, properly so called; but, as these spines are very strong and sharp-pointed, and can no doubt pierce the flesh to a considerable depth, these wounds, like all others of the same description, may produce dangerous consequences if care is not taken to enlarge them, and to allow the blood to flow; this perhaps, is the most certain, as the simplest remedy, and much preferable to the boasted applications of the ancients."

This is oracular; but it does not appear that the decision of the great French anatomist was grounded on any definite experiments. Mr. Couch, on the other hand, has known three men wounded successively in the hand by the same fish (the Greater Weever), and the consequences have been felt in a few minutes as high as the shoulder. It is certain that the spinous bristles of certain caterpillars have the power of inflicting envenomed wounds, which in some cases even prove fatal, notwithstanding the minuteness of the organs, and evidence appears very strong for the injection of some highly irritant poison by means of these prickles of the Weevers.

The flesh of these fishes is esteemed for the table; but such is the general apprehension of danger attendant upon touching them, heightened also by their great tenacity of life, that the fishermen usually cut off the first dorsal and the gill-spines as soon as they capture them; while in Spain and France these precautions are enforced by legal penalties, on such fishes being exposed in the market without having been disarmed.[2]

According to Mr. Couch smart friction of the wounded part with olive-oil is the most effectual remedy; and this fact again suggests analogy of the evil with the effects produced by the bites of venomous snakes and the stings of insects.[3]

Our little fish is not uncomely in its form or the distribution of its sober colours. The upper parts are light olive, with lines of ill-defined reddish spots running lengthwise; the sides are silver-grey, tenderly washed with blue; the under parts pearly white: the cheeks and operculum are richly adorned with pearly reflections; these parts are destitute of scales, which is the chief distinction between this species and the Greater Weever, after the size; this species rarely exceeding five or six inches in length, whereas its congener attains double those dimensions, and even more.

In the tank, it is not particularly interesting; it grovels on the bottom among the pebbles, and will cover its body with the sediment so far as it is able; where it lies for hours, watching upward. Doubtless this is its habitual mode of obtaining its food; lying motionless in wait, nearly concealed, the eyes and the mouth both opening upwards, so that the former can observe, and the latter seize, any vagrant crustacean, or annelid, or young fish-fry that unsuspectingly swims within reach. Its motions when its energies are aroused are rapid, sudden, and forcible; and it probably rarely misses its victim when it makes its snap; while the multitude of minute creatures that roam continually over every part of the sea-bottom give no lack of opportunities for the exercise of its instincts. He fares sumptuously, no doubt.

Here is in the drag a specimen of an interesting tribe of fishes. It is the young of the common Thornback, a little thing about five inches in width, and in its infantile grace and beauty much more attractive than the older ones we are accustomed to see on the fishmonger's table. It flaps and flutters in impatience at being dragged out of its element, and exposed to ungenial air: we will quiet its anxiety by lifting it into yonder shallow rock-pool. Now watch it. How easily and gracefully it glides around its new abode, moving along by an undulation of the edges of the broad pectoral fins, a movement which Yarrell describes as something between flying and swimming. Now it lies still on the sand-floor of the pool, motionless, save that the two oval orifices just behind the eyes are constantly opening and closing, by the drawing across each or back, of a film which exactly resembles an eyelid, and which on examination with a lens we see to be edged with a delicate fringe. The action is so closely like the winking of an eye, that an observer seeing the fish for the first time might readily suppose the orifices to be the organs of vision. They are, however, outlets of the gills, called spiracles; the ordinary gill-apertures are five on each side, placed semi-circularly on the inferior surface of the body, as you see when I turn the fish on its back,—a demonstration which it resents and resists with all its might: these upper orifices communicate with the gill-chambers by canals, and you may see the water now and then strongly driven out of them.

The eyes are these knobs just in front of the spiracles; or rather these are the orbits, the pupil looking sideways and somewhat downward. If you use the lens again, you perceive that there is a singular protection to the pupil in the form of a fan-like array of about a dozen stiff points arching over it.

The general form of the fish is beautifully symmetrical; it is nearly a rhomboid, with the two front sides slightly excavated, and the two posterior sides convex. At the point where these latter unite, there are two smaller fins (the ventrals), and the body is continued very slender to a considerable length, tapering to a point, near which two upright dorsals are placed. The pectorals, as in all this tribe, are of enormous size, forming the lateral angles of the rhomboid, and extending in front of the head to the tip of the snout.

The colours are beautiful, but not at all gaudy. A warm olive brown is the ground hue, on which numerous roundish black spots, with softly blending outlines, are set in symmetrical patterns, and there are also rows of pale spots. This combination of hues is elegant. The slender prolongation of the body is edged with a narrow stripe of pure white. The colour of the whole under surface is richly iridescent, like mother-of pearl.

At present we see only a few of the curved spines appearing, chiefly in the vicinity of the eyes, which in the adult become so conspicuous and remarkable; being something like strong rose-spines, each set on an oval button of bone, imbedded in the skin.

Another draught presents us with the Fifteen-spined Stickleback,[4] a little fish, remarkable for its form, but much more so for its habits. It is ordinarily about five or six inches in length, very slender and lithe, from which circumstance, combined with a protrusion of the jaws, which gives it a sinister expression, it is on some parts of the coast called the Sea-Adder. The lower jaw projects considerably beyond the upper, which indicates that the fish habitually takes its food front a point above the level of its own body. The dorsal and anal fins are high and short, so as to form, when erected, nearly equal-sided triangles; but the former is preceded by fifteen minute sharp erectile spines, each of which has its own little membrane, and all together represent the spinous portion of the dorsal fin in such fishes as have but one, as the Blennies, or the first dorsal in such as have two, as the Weevers. The caudal is narrowly lozenge-formed, as ordinarily carried, but becomes fan-like when expanded. The colours are deep sepia, or olive-brown, cast into streaks and irregular clouds, on the sides, where they are interrupted by white, and by a rich golden yellow, that extends over the inferior surface: the dorsal and anal fins are white, each crossed by a broad conspicuous band of brown; the eyes have golden irides.

We frequently see this attractive little fish hovering about the long tufts of wrack and tangle that hang from perpendicular rocks, and from the quays and wharves of our harbours. It diligently hunts about for its minute crustacean prey, in picking off which it assumes all varieties of position "between the horizontal and perpendicular, with the head downward or upward," thrusting its projecting snout into the tufted weed, and snatching its morsel with a sudden jerk.

It is, however, in its domestic relations that this little fish presents itself in the most interesting aspect. It was known ages ago to Aristotle, that some fishes are in the habit of forming nests, in which they deposit their eggs, and bring up their young with a parental care not inferior to that of birds. Until lately, however, this fact was supposed to be fabulous; and fishes were believed by the greatest masters of modern zoology to be utterly destitute of the parental instinct. Recent research has in this, as in so many instances, proved the exactitude of the old Stagyrite's knowledge, and we now know that several fishes of different families nidificate. The Sticklebacks, most of which inhabit in common our marine and fresh waters, are remarkable for the manifestation of this faculty, as was first shown by Mr. Crookenden, of Lewisham, in 1834, and as has since been proved, with many interesting details, by Mr. A. Hancock and Mr. Warington. Our Sea-Adder, which is exclusively marine, was first ascertained to be a nest-builder by the late Dr. George Johnston, who mentioned the fact in the "Transactions of the Berwickshire Naturalists' Club" in 1839. But the most interesting account is that of Mr. R. Q. Couch, who noticed the facts on the coast of Cornwall, and thus records them in a paper read before the Royal Institution of that county:—

"During the summers of 1842 and 1843, while searching for the naked mollusks of the county, I occasionally discovered portions of seaweed and the common coralline (*Corallina officinalis*) hanging from the rocks in pear-shaped masses, variously intermingled with each other. On one occasion, having observed that the mass was very curiously bound together by a slender, silken-looking thread, it was torn open, and the centre was found to be occupied by a mass of transparent, amber-coloured ova, each being about the tenth of an inch in diameter. Though examined on the spot with a lens, nothing could be discovered to indicate their character. They were, however, kept in a basin, and daily supplied with sea-water, and eventually proved to be the young of some fish. The nest varies a great deal in size, but rarely exceeds six inches in length, or four inches in breadth. It is pear-shaped, and composed of sea-weed or the common coralline as they hang suspended from the rock. They are brought together, without being detached from their places of growth, by a delicate opaque white thread. This thread is highly elastic, and very much resembles silk, both in appearance and texture: this is brought round the plants, and tightly binds them together, plant after plant, till the ova, which are deposited early, are completely hidden from view. This silk-like thread is passed in all directions through and around the mass, in a very complicated manner. At first the thread is semi-fluid, but by exposure it solidifies; and hence contracts and binds the substance forming the nest so closely together that it is able to withstand the violence of the sea, and may be thrown carelessly about without derangement. In the centre are deposited the ova, very similar to the masses of frog-spawn in ditches.

"Some of these nests are formed in pools, and are consequently always in water: others are frequently to be found between tide-marks, in situations where they hang dry for several hours in the day; but whether in the water or liable to hang dry, they are always carefully watched by the adult animal. On one occasion I repeatedly visited one every day for three weeks, and invariably found it guarded. The old fish would examine it on all sides, and then retire for a short time, but soon returned to renew the examination. On several occasions I laid the eggs bare, by removing a portion of the nest; but when this was discovered, great exertions were made to recover them. By the mouth of the fish the edges of the opening were again drawn together, and other portions torn from their attachments and brought over the orifice, till the ova were again hid from view. And as great force was sometimes necessary to effect this, the fish would thrust its snout into the nest as far as the eyes, and then jerk backwards till the object was effected. While thus engaged it would suffer itself to be taken by the hand, but repelled any attack made on the nest, and quitted not its post so long as I remained; and to those nests that were left dry between tidemarks, the guardian fish always returned with the returning tide, nor did they quit the post to any great distance till again carried away by the receding tide."

It is worthy of note that the newly-hatched young from these nests were so unlike the full-grown Stickleback, and so like the common smooth Blenny, that Mr. Couch concluded that there had been some error in his observation, and that the nest truly belonged to the latter fish. Further research, however, proved that the Stickleback was indeed the parent; and the transition from the infantile Blenny-like outline of the face, high, bluff, and almost perpendicular, to the true Stickleback outline, lone, slender, pointed, with the far-projecting lower jaw, is something remarkable.

But now the tide has reached its lowest mark; and as we wander over the wet sand at its very verge, our attention is attracted by every tiny object that breaks the uniform level, even at a considerable distance. Some of these are worm-casts thrown up by busy Annelids, working away in the sand to reach a lower and therefore a wetter level, as the upper stratum dries in the sun. But others are Crabs, of two or three species. One of them is the somewhat uncommon and very beautiful *Portumnus variegatus*, of which a great number are left by the sea, but all of them dead; some of them, however, from their freshness, only recently defunct. The shape of the carapace, or body-shell, is very elegant, and the colours, though sober—a light drab, mottled and pencilled with pale lilac—are pleasing: the hindmost pair of feet terminate in thin swimming-plates, but they are narrow, and exhibit the natatory character in only a subordinate degree.

Other Crabs are alive and active, though, to be sure, in a somewhat sluggish way. Here we catch sight of a slight movement in the wet sand, and, stooping, we perceive a pair of antennæ, much beset with short bristles, projecting from the surface. They wag to and fro, and presently up pushes a shelly head, with its pair of stalked and jointed eyes, and two tremendously long angular arms, furnished with awkward-looking nippers at their extremities. Another effort, and the whole Crab emerges from his sandy burrow, and displays his pale buff-coloured shell, wrinkled across, and armed with sharp spiny points at its front and edges. We easily take him up, for his means of escape are feeble, as he uncouthly

Plate XIV

Masked Crab.

shuffles on his short legs over the sand; and his bellicose instincts are not strongly developed, nor, if they were, have those long levers of arms any formidable powers of offence. Latreille gave to the genus the title of *Corystes*; which signifies a warrior armed for battle, from κορυς, a helmet, but its inoffensiveness belies the appellation.[5] Pennant had already conferred on the species the name of *Cassivelaunus*, the ancient British chief immortalized by Caesar. If you were to ask me why this obscure crab should bear a name so renowned, I can answer only by conjecture. The carapace is marked by wrinkles, which, while in some specimens they suggest nothing, in others, especially old males, bear the strongest and most ludicrous resemblance to the face of an ancient man. I have taken specimens in which the *vraisemblance* was so perfect as to strike me, and others to whom I showed it, with amazement. Now Pennant, as is well known, had strong sympathies with his British ancestry; and perhaps, by a not extravagant stretch of imagination, his playful fancy saw the features of the grand old Celtic warrior perpetuated on this Crab, which he first met with, too, be it remembered, on the Welsh coast.

Mr. Couch, in his Cornish Fauna, notices the unusual length of the antennæ. "These organs," he says, "are of some use beyond their common office of feelers; perhaps, as in some other crustaceans, they assist in the process of excavation; and, when soiled by labour, I have seen the Crab effect their cleaning by alternately bending the joints of their stalks, which stand conveniently angular for this purpose. Each of the long antennæ is thus drawn along the brush that fringes the internal face of the other, until both are cleared of every particle that adhered to them." This suggested use of the antennæ does not seem to me to be a very felicitous guess of the excellent Cornish naturalist: I should fancy them to be somewhat inefficient instruments in excavation: perhaps I can help him to a better. I have observed that, when these Crabs are kept in an aquarium, they are fond of sitting bolt upright, the antennæ placed close together, and also pointing straight upward from the head. This is, doubtless, the attitude in which the animal sits in its burrow, for the tips of the antennæ may often be seen just projecting from the sand. When the chosen seat has happened to be so close to the glass side of the tank as to bring the antennæ within the range of a pocket lens, I have minutely investigated these organs, without disturbing the old warrior in his meditation. I immediately saw, on each occasion, that a strong current of water was continuously pouring up from the points of the approximate antennæ. Tracing this to its origin, it became evident that it was produced by the rapid vibration of the foot-jaws, drawing in the surrounding water, and pouring it off upwards *between the united antennæ*, as through a long tube. Then, on examining these organs, I perceived that the form and arrangement of their bristles did indeed constitute each antenna a semi-tube, so that when the pair were brought face to face the tube was complete. It is difficult to make this arrangement intelligible by mere words; but I may say that if either of the antennæ were broken off in the middle and viewed vertically, the bristles would be seen to project from each side of the inner face, in a curved form, each making about a fourth of a circle, so that the two corresponding bristles enclose, with the body of the antenna, a semicircle. Of course, those of the opposite antenna make another semicircle, and, when placed face to face, the points of the bristles just cross each other, and a circle is enclosed. Now, the whole length of the antennæ (about an inch and a half) is closely beset with these bristles, and thus a long row of rings is formed with very narrow interspaces between them; and these rings do in effect constitute a tube quite sufficient to retain the stream of water that is poured through it.

I think then that we may, with an approach to certainty, conclude that the long antennæ are intended to keep a passage open through the sand, from the bottom of the burrow to the superincumbent water, for the purpose of pouring off the waste water, rendered effete by having bathed the gills; and it is one of those exquisite contrivances and appropriations of structure to habit which are so constantly exciting our admiration in the handiwork of the ever blessed God, which cannot be predicated by the *à priori* reasoner, however astute, but are ever rewarding the research of the patient observer.

Our walk along the sands with steady downcast poring gaze suddenly ends, and we find ourselves among low ledges of black rock (ruddy, however, in its recent fractures, for it is the old red sandstone), clad with sweltering weed, and intersected by little sparkling pools and basins, in which the tiny fishes and entangled prawns shoot hither and thither at our approach. It is the low-lying ridge in the midst of the broad sandy bight that I have already spoken of. Well, *n'importe*; there is plenty of game to be obtained here, and all is fish that comes to our net. What have we here, creeping over the broad brown leathery leaf of this *Laminaria*? Is it a little scrap torn from an old newspaper? It looks like it at the first glance, only that it moves steadily onward with a smooth gliding motion, which shows that it possesses a life of its own. Examine it closely: it is exactly like a bit of white paper, about as large as a rose leaf, and cut into that shape, only with an even edge, its clear white surface marked all over with black parallel lines, some thinner, some thicker, running lengthwise, and as clear as if drawn with a pen. What answers to the base of the leaf is the head of the creature, the pointed end being the tail, where the two most strongly marked black lines meet; from the head end arise two curious ear-like leaflets, which are studded with crowded black dots, and are thrown back upon the general surface. With a lens we may discern on the surface of the body, just between these ear-like tentacles, a group of black specks. These are ascertained to be veritable eyes, notwithstanding; their number, for they have a cornea, a light-refracting body surrounded with pigment, and a nerve-bulb.

As the animal glides over the surface of the smooth weed, or over the inequalities of the rough rock, we see that its thin papery margin is frequently thrown up into waves, or folds, more or less distinctly revealing the inferior surface. The movement is very even and uniform, but the mode by which it is effected has not been satisfactorily explained. It has been asserted that certain staff-like bristles which project from the skin are used as oars, but this seems doubtful. It is certain that the whole body of the animal, as of the entire class to which it belongs, is densely clothed with minute vibratory cilia; and these, while they probably serve as organs of locomotion in freely swimming, do also without doubt make the whole skin a highly delicate and sensitive organ of touch.

It is asserted of the near allies of this species, and. probably is equally true in this case, that if an individual be cut to pieces, every portion continues to live and feel, from whatever part of the body it may be taken; and what is not a little remarkable, each piece, even if it be the end of the tail, as soon as the first moment of pain and irritation has passed, begins to move in the same direction as that in which the entire animal was advancing, as if the body were actuated throughout by the same impulse; and, moreover, every division, even if it is not more than the eighth or tenth part of the creature, will become complete and perfect in all its organs.[6]

You would naturally expect to find the creature's mouth at the front end, where the two tentacles are placed, and the group of eyes, but you would search for it there in vain. It is, in fact, situated most strangely in the very midst of the belly; that is, at the very centre of the inferior surface. And its structure is not less peculiar than its locality. It consists of an orifice, in the midst of which lies a sort of trumpet of enormous extent when opened, but when not in active use thrown into many folds, which, when the animal wishes to seize prey, are thrust forth, and being partly opened, take the appearance of many irregular tentacles radiating in all directions, at the centre of which is the œsophagus, leading immediately into a much ramified intestine. The name which is given to this elegant and interesting creature is *Eurylepta vittata*.[7]

But here is another member of the same class of strange creatures. On turning up a large flat stone, we expose to the light of day what might readily be mistaken for a very long thong of black leather, or rather a narrow strip of Indian-rubber, twisted and tied together, and coiled in all possible contortions. If you take hold of it, you find it not so easy to secure it as you expected, for it is excessively lubricous and soft, and withal so extensile and so tough, that you may pull one of the coils to almost any length without lifting the rest of the creature. However, you at last contrive to raise the slippery subject, and commit it safe to your tank at home, in which it will live an indefinite while; often invisible for weeks at a time, lying concealed under some of the stones, then seen perhaps in every corner of your aquarium at once, stretching from one stone to another, and coiling around every groin and projection, folded back upon itself, until in the multitude of convolutions you despair of finding head, tail, or any end at all to the uncouth vermin. You may soon discover the signs of its presence, however, in another way, for its voracity is great, and it is a ferocious foe to the tube-dwelling worms; such as the lovely *Sabellæ* and *Serpulæ*, thrusting its serpent-like head into their tubes, and dragging out the hapless tenant to be quickly swallowed.

Plate XV

Banded Flat-Worm. Long-Worm.

The animal is named *Nemertes Borlasii*, or sometimes *Borlasia longissima*, in allusion to Dr. Borlase, the historian of Cornwall. It is also occasionally termed the Long-worm, *par excellence*, a name whose appropriateness will appear from the fact that it sometimes reaches a length of thirty feet, with a breadth of an eighth of an inch.

Mr. Kingsley has drawn the portrait of this ciliated worm; and if he has painted it in somewhat dark colours, and manifested more than a common measure of antipathy to it, we must confess that the physical and moral lineaments of the subject do in some degree justify the description. I will quote his vivid words.

"There are animals in which results so strange, fantastic, even seemingly horrible, are produced, that fallen man may be pardoned if he shrinks from them in disgust. That, at least, must be a consequence of our own wrong state; for everything is beautiful and perfect in its place. It may be answered, 'Yes, in its place; but its place is not yours. You had no business to look at it, and must pay the penalty for intermeddling.' I doubt that answer: for surely, if man have liberty to do anything, he has liberty to search out freely his Heavenly Father's works; and yet every one seems to have his antipathic animal, and I know one bred from his childhood to zoology by land and sea, and bold in asserting, and honest in feeling, that all without exception is beautiful, who yet cannot, after handling, and petting, and admiring all day long every uncouth and venomous beast, avoid a paroxysm of horror at the sight of the common house-spider. At all events, whether we were intruding or not, in turning this stone, we must pay a fine for having done so; for there lies an animal, as foul and monstrous to the eye as 'hydra, gorgon, or chimera dire,' and yet so wondrously fitted for its work, that we must needs endure for our own instruction to handle and look at it. Its name I know not (though it lurks here under every stone), and should be glad to know. It seems some very 'low' Ascarid or Planarian worm. You see it? That black, slimy, knotted lump among the gravel, small enough to be taken up in a dessert-spoon. Look now, as it is raised and its coils drawn out. Three feet! Six—nine at least, with a capability of seemingly endless expansion; a slimy tape of living caoutchouc, some eighth of an inch in diameter, a dark chocolate-black, with paler longitudinal lines. Is it alive? It hangs helpless and motionless, a mere velvet string across the hand. Ask the neighbouring Annelids and the fry of the rock fishes, or put it into a vase at home, and see. It lies motionless, trailing itself among the gravel; you cannot tell where it begins or ends; it may be a strip of dead sea-weed, *Himanthalia lorea*, perhaps, or *Chorda filum*; or even a tarred string. So thinks the little fish who plays over and over it, till he touches at last what is too surely a head. In an instant a bell-shaped sucker mouth has fastened to its side. In another instant, from one lip, a concave double proboscis, just like a tapir's (another instance of the repetition of forms), has clasped him like a finger, and now begins the struggle; but in vain. He is being 'played,' with such a fishing-rod as the skill of a Wilson or a Stoddart never could invent; a living line, with elasticity beyond that of the most delicate fly-rod, which follows every lunge, shortening and lengthening, slipping and twining round every piece of gravel and stem of sea-weed, with a tiring drag such as no Highland wrist or step could ever bring to bear on salmon or trout. The victim is tired now; and slowly, yet dexterously, his blind assailant is feeling and shifting along his side, till he reaches one end of him; and then the black lips expand, and slowly and surely the curved finger begins packing him end foremost down into the gullet, where he sinks, inch by inch, till the swelling which marks his place is lost among the coils, and he is probably macerated into a pulp long before he has reached the opposite extremity of his cave of doom. Once safe down, the black murderer contracts again into a knotted heap, and lies like a boa with a stag inside him, motionless and blest."[8]

VI.
June

We are on the narrow shingle-beach of Maidencombe, or, sometimes, more familiarly, Minnicombe; one of the slight indentations of this line of coast, which, from the mouth of the Exe to Start Point, runs nearly north and south, and so looks right up-channel, and receives the full violence of the keen and blustering east winds.

Away down the gentle slope till we come to the line where the wavelets are kissing the rock, where the next step would put us into King Canute's circumstances, where the sea is washing to and fro the shaggy weed, and just preventing it from assuming the shrivelled and blackened condition, into which the tufts a little above are fast falling under the baking powers of this June sun; and here, on these very weeds, now submerged, now dry, are crawling some uncouth beings of a dark liver colour or purple-brown hue. The creature passes by the name of Sea-hare;[1] a not inappropriate designation, for I have often seen it in postures when the resemblance to a couching hare was spontaneously suggested. Around Weymouth, where it is common, the fishermen and shore-boys call it the Sea-cow; which is not a bad hit, though not so happy as that of hare. In each case, the feature which strikes the imagination and suggests the comparison with the quadruped, is the pair of tentacles which stand erect, but a little diverging, from the back of the head, and which consist of an expanded lamina infolded at the base, and, as it were, cut off slantingly, so as to look like a hare's ears. There are, indeed, two pairs of tentacles of similar structure; but the front pair are more commonly stretched forward horizontally, and held near the ground, so as to be much less conspicuous.

The animal is one of the Sea-slugs, allied, not remotely, to the *Doris* and the lovely *Eolis*, which occupied our attention some time ago. The order to which it belongs is, however, distinguished from them by having the breathing organs covered. In our Sea-hare these take the form of complicated leaflets, which are placed upon the middle of the back, and are protected by a broad plate of shell, somewhat like a watch-glass of irregular outline, very thin and transparent, and very brittle when dry. During life, this shelly plate is imbedded in the substance of the skin of the back, a thin layer of which clothes it; so thin that it can be very readily seen and felt notwithstanding. The mantle is much developed, forming two great irregular wing-like lobes, which stand up on each side of the body, and at pleasure either arch over the gill-shield, or are depressed,

Plate XVI — Sea-Hare.

and widely expose it. It is reported that these mantle-lobes are capable of being used as swimming-fins, by their undulations; but I doubt the correctness of the observation.

When full-grown, our Sea-hare is three inches in length, and upwards of an inch high. Its body is of a slimy, fleshy, slug-like texture, varying much in colour; sometimes being dark olive-green, sometimes red-brown, sometimes deep purple, occasionally clouded with blue: sometimes the hue is uniform; at others, it is varied by light dots, or handsomely marked with dark rings enclosing white areas. Its figure is extremely versatile; so that, when crawling, it scarcely exhibits the same outline for two minutes together.

See what has happened. On dropping one of the slimy beasts into this phial of clear sea-water, it immediately resented the incarceration by beginning to pour out from beneath the lobes of the mantle a thin stream of fluid of the most royal purple hue, which freely diffused itself through the water. And see! it is still copiously exuding; and the whole contents of the bottle are now fast becoming of so fine and rich a tinge, as already to veil the form of the animal. Attempts have been made to employ this secretion in the arts; but the hue is fleeting. According to Cuvier, it assumes in drying the beautiful deep hue of the flower known as the sweet scabious, and remains long unaltered by exposure to the air. The purple tint is readily transferred to spirit, when the animal is immersed in it; the tincture retains the colour for a while, but ultimately becomes of a deep clear port-wine tint. Linen, dyed with the fluid, soon fades to a dingy brown.

It is a curious coincidence that this mollusk possesses a more recondite analogy with herbivorous mammalia, than a fleeting resemblance of form. Professor Grant has shown that it has three stomachs, like the ruminants. First, a short narrow gullet dilates into a large membranous crop; a curved bag, which is generally filled with pieces of coarse sea-weed. This large crop or paunch occupies the right side of the body, and opens laterally into the middle stomach, which is the smallest of all, and performs the part of the gizzard. Its coats are thickened; and the interior callous lining is besat with firm horny processes, in the form of rhomboidal plates or molar teeth, which serve to compress the, softened vegetable matter transmitted in small portions from the first stomach. The third cavity of this complex apparatus is placed on the left side of the body; its interior surface is studded with sharp, horny spines, resembling canine teeth, to pierce and subdivide the coarse food, and thus prepare it for the action of the gastric juice and other fluids accessory to digestion, which enter the stomach from adjacent organs.[2]

The complexity of this structure has reference to the coarseness of the materials on which the animal subsists; the leathery fronds of the olive sea-weeds, which slowly and with difficulty yield their nutritive elements to the digestive functions.

This great, flabby Sea-Slug has a mythic history full of wild romance. Our species has been often called *depilans*, because the fluid which exudes from it was said to have the power of causing the hair to fall from the human head which it touched; and the common species of Southern Europe retains the appellation in the records of science. The Mediterranean fishermen have so great a horror of it that no bribes will induce them to handle it willingly; and they tell strange stories of wounds being produced, limbs being mortified, and even death itself being caused, by accidental or foolhardy contact with the potent creature.

Bohadsch has given, on the authority of personal observation, a minutely circumstantial account, which it seems a hyper-scepticism to doubt. When removed from the sea, and placed in a vessel, there exuded a large quantity of a limpid and somewhat mucilaginous fluid, exhaling a sweetish, sickening, peculiar smell: but besides this, and distinct from its purple secretion, the *Aplysia* excreted also a milky liquor, formed in an internal conglobate gland, which seems to be analogous to the kidney of vertebrate animals. As often as he took the *Aplysia* from the vase of seawater and placed it on a plate with the view of more narrowly examining its structure, the room was filled with a nauseous odour, compelling his wife and brother to leave the room, lest sickness and vomiting should follow. He himself could scarcely endure it, and during the examination had repeatedly to go out and breathe a purer air. His hands and cheeks swelled after handling the creature for any length of time, and as often as it ejaculated its milky secretion; but he is uncertain whether the swelling of the face proceeded from the halitus merely, or from his having accidentally touched it with the hand besmeared with the liquid: probably the latter was the real cause, for when he purposely applied some of it to his chin, some hairs fell from the part.[3]

We may add to this account, as being in a measure confirmatory of its probability, the statement of a perfectly dependable naturalist, Mr. Charles Darwin, that he found a species of *Aplysia* at St. Jago, one of the Cape Verd Isles, from which "an acrid secretion, which is spread over its body, causes a sharp stinging sensation, similar to that produced by the *Physalia*,[4] or Portuguese man-of-war."[5] And yet I have myself freely handled *Aplysiæ* in health and vigour, both here and on the coast of Jamaica, without perceiving the slightest unpleasant sensation.

But in the days of ancient Rome the poor Sea-hare had a far more terrific reputation. In those dark days of the Empire when no one's life was secure against insidious assassination, and when professed poisoners were at the command of such as could afford to pay their hire, this mollusk was an essential element of the fatal draught. "Locusta used it to destroy such as were inimical to Nero; it entered into the potion which she prepared for the tyrant himself; and Domitian was accused of having given it to his brother Titus. To search after the Sea-hare was to render one's-self suspected; and when Apuleius was accused of magic, because, forsooth, he had induced a rich widow to marry him, the principal proof against him was that he had hired the fishermen to procure him this fearful animal."[6] He succeeded, however, in showing, to the satisfaction of his judges, that his object was merely the gratification of laudable scientific curiosity.

Peering into the deep and narrow fissures with which the rocky ledge is cleft, we observe some shells which properly belong to the deep sea bottom, but have been doubtless washed into the shallow, by some heavy ground-swell, and left where we now see them. Here are several fragments, and one or two nearly perfect specimens, of what looks like an elephant's tusk in miniature, but is really the shell of a small Gastropod mollusk commonly known as the Tusk-shell.[7] In colour, form, and curvature, the resemblance is complete, but the length of a perfect shell rarely exceeds an inch and a half, with a diameter of one-eighth of an inch at the larger end. The animal is remarkable for having long been a subject of dispute with learned zoologists as to its true affinities; by some being considered as a true mollusk allied to the Limpets, by others as a worm allied to the *Serpulæ*. Anatomy determines it to be rightly located by the former opinion, and yet the possession of red blood, and some other peculiarities belonging to the *Annelida*, indicate a curious relationship with this class, so that we may consider it as one of those interesting forms which link together two great divisions of the animal kingdom.

When the Tusk-shell is found alive, we rarely can see more of the soft parts than a sort of white cushion occupying the mouth of the shell, and occasionally protruding or receding, with a little conical point projecting from the centre of it. You might keep it for weeks, as I have done, and see no more, by the most assiduous watching, than this; but at some fortunate moment you might perchance see the whole foot, of which this little cone is the extremity, thrust far out of the cushion-like collar, when you would discern a wide lobed membrane, fringing the base of the foot, trumpet-like in shape, or resembling the blossom of a convolvulus, with the thick and pointed foot projecting from its centre like a pistil.

These sluggish white mollusks ordinarily live on the muddy sea-floor, or burrow in it, where they devour minuter animals, such as *Foraminifera*, and the spawn and larval forms of their fellow Mollusca. They are rarely taken alive at a less depth than ten fathoms.

But we have also an example of a much rarer shell, the Torbay Bonnet, or Cap of Liberty.[8] The shape, which is exactly that of the ancient Phrygian bonnet, or the modern emblem of liberty, is sufficiently commemorated in all the appellations by which it is known, both scientific and popular. This specimen is but an empty shell, but the freshness of the colours, and the beautiful polish of the interior show that the animal cannot have been long dead, for the porcellaneous smoothness and gloss of shells very soon become defaced after their exposure by the death and decay of the soft parts. The interior of this shell is of a most lovely rose-pink, very glossy, and the exterior is nearly of the same hue, though this is concealed by a horny skin which closely invests it, and is covered with a shaggy pile that projects even beyond the edge, in the form of a ragged yellow fringe. This rough epidermis is of a hue varying from a bright yellow-olive to a dull wood-brown; it is frequently rubbed off in the upper parts, when the natural hue of the shell is there seen.

This species is rare enough, and large enough, and handsome enough to be a prize worth finding, when picked up in so fresh a condition as this; but, of course, it is more valuable when it occurs in a living state. But this scarcely ever happens except by dredging, or by trawling. I have frequently had it brought to me by trawlers both at Weymouth and Tenby, oftenest by the former, who get it in deep water, from thirty to fifty fathoms, on the western side of Portland.

The living animal is not unworthy of its elegantly painted house. Its colour is usually pale yellow, with a rose-pink mantle, bordered by a fine orange-coloured fringe. The head is large and swollen, furnished with tentacles, which carry the eyes at their bases. The tongue-ribbon carries seven rows of teeth, of which the central one differs in shape from the rest.

I have kept a specimen in the aquarium for a considerable time, with very little addition to my knowledge as the result. It remained adhering to the scallop shell on which it was found almost all the time I had it, occasionally shifting a hair's-breadth to the one side or the other. Almost always the fringed edge of the shell was so closely applied to the support as absolutely to forbid intrusion; but now and then a very slight lifting of the edge all round gave me the narrowest possible peep at the broad cream-coloured foot adhering to its rest. Thus it went on tantalizing me, till after some months I lost it, I forget how.

A close ally of this form is a pretty shell which we often obtain by dredging, called the Cup-and-Saucer Limpet. It is a pretty little white porcellaneous cone, with a curved plate of thin shell projecting from the side of the interior, like a semi-cup within the cup. It is named *Calyptræa*. Both this and the Torbay Bonnet have been ascertained to manifest domestic instincts, in sitting on their eggs till they are hatched. According to MM. Audouin and Milne Edwards, the parent *Calyptræa* "disposes them under her belly, and preserves them, as it were imprisoned, between the foot and the foreign body to which she adheres, her patelloid shell thus serving not only to cover and protect herself, but as a shield to her offspring. These eggs are oval bodies of a yellow colour, enclosed in membranous capsules, which are elliptical, flattened, translucid, and filled with an albuminous matter. The number of these little capsules varies from six to ten; they are connected among themselves by a footstalk, so as to represent a sort of rosette; each of them contains from eight to ten eggs. It appears that the young *Calyptræa* are developed under this sort of maternal roof, and do not quit it until they are in a condition to affix themselves, and are provided with a shell sufficiently hard to protect their own bodies."[9]

Along the margins of these shallow rock-pools with sandy bottoms, we see many little grey shrimp-like creatures, with thick-set arching bodies, which swim rapidly, and with much vibration of the abdominal feet, from weed to weed. If we catch one and lay it on the rock or on the wet sand, it appears very helpless, for its vertically thin shape and arched attitude preclude the possibility of its crawling: it falls upon its side, and vainly struggles round and round as on a pivot, or makes aimless jerks by throwing out the tail. It is of a greenish blue, or glaucous colour, marked with red dots. This is the common Locust Screw,[10] which is so confined to sea-water, that it has been affirmed that if put into fresh water it presently dies. But the experiments of Mr. Robertson negative this statement:[11] he has found that five out of seven, after being eighteen hours in rain-water, continued to live upon being returned to salt water.

I delight to trace the manifestations of parental love in these tiny, forms of animal life. It had long been known that the females of this species display a solicitude for their infant offspring, which they carry for some time about with them; but the following very pleasing details of maternal manners have recently been observed by my relative, Dr. James Salter, and by him communicated to the learned zoologists who are now engaged upon the history of this order:—

"On catching a female with live larvæ, nothing is seen of the progeny till the parent has become at home in the aquarium, when the little creatures leave her, and swim about in her immediate neighbourhood. The plan I have adopted to watch this curious habit of maternal protection has been to place a single individual in a bottle of sea-water. After a time, and that soon, the little crustacean seems at ease, and swims slowly about, when the young fry leave, and swarm around her in a perfect cloud; they never leave for more than half or three-quarters of an inch, and as she slowly moves about they accompany her. If, now, one taps the sides of the bottle with one's finger-nail, the swarm of larvæ rush under their parent, and in a second are out of sight. The parent now becomes excited, and swims about quickly, as if trying to escape; but on letting the bottle containing her rest quite still on a table, she soon gets composed, when out come the young larvæ again, and swim about as before. This may be repeated as often as the observer wishes, and always with the same result. I have only seen this in one species, but it is quite a common species in Poole Harbour, and I have watched the interesting habit many times."[12]

Every little stream and ditch of running water in our lanes and fields abounds with a species, which, except for the fresh-water habit, and a little difference in the shade of colour,—the latter being of a yellowish, instead of a bluish grey,—is so absolutely identical with the Locust Screw, that, notwithstanding it is registered under a name of its own, *Gammarus pulex*, it is difficult to believe that the two are not of common parentage. Certain facts observed in Sweden give colour to such a suspicion. The large inland seas of fresh water, Lakes Wetter and Wener, in the south of that country, are situated on high ground, and have the surface of their water 300 feet above the level of the Baltic, whereas the bottom is 120 feet below such level. In these lakes (which appear to have been lifted up with the gradual uprising of the country) have been found several genera and species of Crustacea, three of which are Amphipoda, which are affirmed to be identical with marine ones, viz., *Gammaracanthus loricatus* (Sabine, Ross, Kröyer), *Pontoporeia affinis* (Lindström), and *Gammarus cancelloides* (Gerstfeldt).

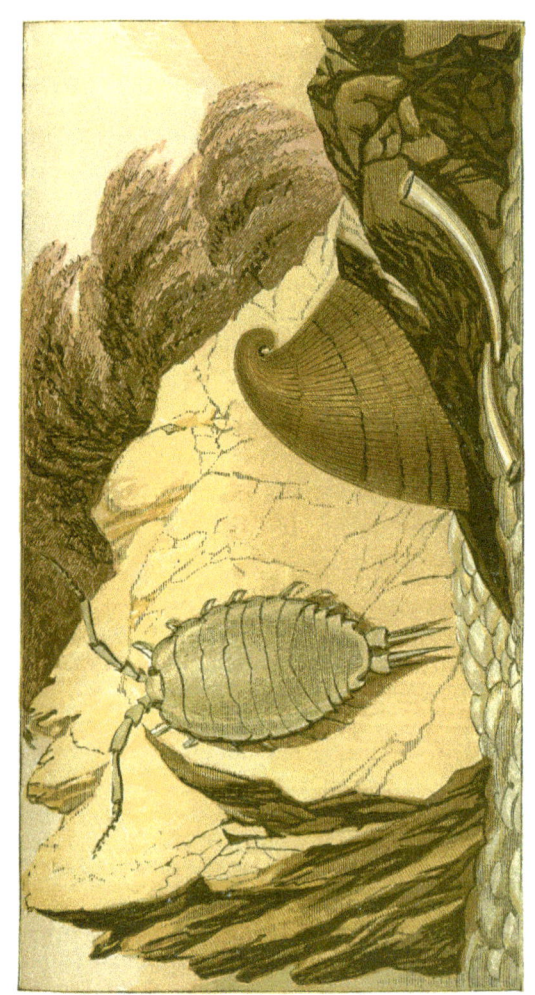

Plate XVII

Ligia. Torbay Bonnet. Tusk-Shell.

The first is now only known to exist in the Arctic seas, the second in the Baltic, and the last was found in Lake Baikal, in Central Asia. It is therefore suggested by Lovèn, that the land was raised so as to convert these waters from marine bays into inland lakes. These marine species were retained within the basins, the waters of which have since been changed, through the agency of springs, into fresh water; and with the gradual transfer of the water, the habits of the animals have also changed gradually, and that without any outward alteration of form. Professor Lovèn thinks that there is sufficient evidence to show that this change in the condition of these lakes must have taken place during the great glacier period, at a time when the animals now found in it (and which are known at this day only to inhabit the extreme north) could have lived in the same latitude as the south of Sweden. The evidence of these fresh-water lakes suggests that similar changes in the relative position of sea and land may have been the cause of our having fresh-water Crustacea nearly allied to marine species in our rivers and inland streams.[13]

Crawling about perpendicular faces of rocks, generally at a considerable distance above high-water mark, we may find a crustacean, not very remotely allied to these, of rather large size.[14] It is broad and flat, a form which marks it as belonging to another order, though in many peculiarities of structure agreeing with its near neighbours the high-backed Screws. The present species crawls readily with its fourteen short strongly-hooked feet, with which it clings to every little roughness of the stone. It swims much less effectively: indeed, I have never seen it spontaneously in the water; and those which I have captured on the rocks, and transferred to an aquarium, have died after a very brief interval. They have little agility under any circumstances, and trust rather to craft than to power for their safety. When alarmed, they instantly gather in their feet, and drop from their hold; and, as I have said that the positions in which they are found are for the most part perpendicular surfaces, such as cliffs and sea-walls, their one trick is often successful.

Thus the *Ligia* makes a decided approach to an aërial or terrestrial mode of life; which, indeed, is strictly the habit of some species with which every cultivator of flowers is only too familiar. I refer to the little Wood-lice, or Buttons, or Sows, as they are variously called, so abundant in gardens, especially in pits and frames, and so annoying for their depredations on our cherished plants. These garden pests are scarcely to be distinguished as to their structure from the semi-marine *Ligia*, particularly those flatter and softer species (*Porcellio*), which do not roll their body into a complete ball.

In all these creatures we find maternal care. The females carry their eggs in a sort of pouch or sac, placed beneath the breast, which opens when these are hatched to afford exit for the infant progeny. These have from the first the same form and appearance as the adult, except that they have at first six pairs of feet instead of seven. They cling about the body of the mother, and are carried by her in her rovings with affecting solicitude.

About the sloping ledges of low-lying rock, especially those which are covered with young mussels, so closely that between their blue-black shells, packed and tied together with byssus-threads, you can scarcely thrust a penknife, we very commonly see slender Worms of a vivid grass-green hue gliding in and out. Their movements are very graceful, and if we examine them closely, we discern the presence of a multitude of minute points along each side of the body, which in turn are thrust out and as quickly retracted. If we put the little creature into a vase of water, we see fresh powers and organs of locomotion; for the back bears a double series of leaf-shaped fins, overlying one another, which act as broadoars rowing the lithe and graceful worm through the sea.

This species[15] is not more than three inches in length; but there is another[16] much less common, which is larger, richer in colours, and altogether a finer species. A specimen which I lately found was about a foot in length when crawling, and nearly a quarter of an inch in width. The whole body was divided into distinct segments, which in this individual were about two hundred and ten in number; though, according to MM. Audouin and Milne Edwards,[17] they sometimes amount to nearly five hundred, and the worm has been found two feet in length. The head is small, terminated by two pairs of very minute antennæ, but surrounded at what we may call the neck by four pairs of rather long feelers (tentacular cirri), with a fifth pair which are minute and rudimentary.

The colours are very beautiful. The leaf-like fins of the sides, which are somewhat heart-shaped, are of a yellowish green hue, occasionally clouded with blackish; the middle portion of the back, which is exposed, is of a rich brown, but flushed with the most glowing iridescence of blue and purple; while the whole under parts are of a pearly flesh-colour. As it crawls over the stones, it throws its body into the most elegant lateral curves, while its suppleness and great length cause it to cling close to the rock; and thus its outline takes the form of every projection and depression over which it is wandering.

When disturbed, and often without any apparent provocation, we see the under side of the tiny head rise from the ground, swell out, and turn itself inside out, as you turn a stocking, until a great pear-shaped bag is protruded, fully eight times as long, and thrice as broad as the entire head. Its whole surface is rough and papillose, and around its extremity, which is the largest part, there is a row of small knobs or warts. This curious organ is found under similar conditions in very many Annelids; it is commonly called the proboscis, or evertile œsophagus; but in truth it is a special and peculiar apparatus, with little analogy with anything found in higher animals: it is in some species furnished with strong horny teeth, and is doubtless employed for the capture of living prey, and the conveyance of it to the stomach.

The tail of the specimen I refer to was evidently being renewed after having been accidentally lost. For the body-segments ended abruptly, and were followed by a portion, not more than an eighth of an inch long, white, and excessively delicate; but which, when examined with a powerful magnifier, displayed a division into segments, each segment carrying its proper cirri; I could count twenty segments within that minute space, the last of which carried the usual pair of stylets.

I find among my notes a record of a specimen of *Phyllodoce*, which, if not identical with this, was closely allied to it, in which I observed the continuance of vitality after the severance of the creature into parts. It was sent to me from Torquay, when I lived near London. When it arrived I found that about an inch and a quarter of the anterior extremity was detached from the remainder, which measured about four inches. The former was motionless, contracted, and seemed lifeless; the latter moved freely. I put both into an old aquarium. The long posterior portion glided about among the stones for two days, exactly like a living healthy animal; the anterior part remained motionless and contracted until the third day, when I saw it also gliding over the stones in a most lively manner, rearing its head, and feeling about in the manner of a caterpillar. Eight days after its arrival, the head portion was still active and apparently healthy, but the hinder part had become motionless and was evidently dead. I find no further record of the case, and probably the anterior part ultimately died without reproduction; but the length of the period of its survival in apparent vigour, renders it not improbable that in the open sea, under the influence of abundant oxygen, and suitable food, the wanting parts might have been renewed to the fore-part, if not to both.

To return to my more recent captive, however. I killed it for cabinet preservation by putting it into fresh water, where it presently died, with the noticeable circumstance that it threw out mucus in such profusion that the whole body was enveloped in a mass, much thicker than itself, of clear jelly, excessively tough and tenacious.

The most common members of the class *Annelida*, that we meet with in these situations, are different species of the genus *Nereis*, which are for the most part worms of considerable size, usually brown or green, with a changeable metallic lustre above, and brilliantly pearly beneath. They have a distinct head, of a squarish form, terminating in two swollen fleshy knob-like antennæ, and furnished with four pairs of thread-like tentacular cirri, which project on each side like a cat's whiskers. The body is plump, though somewhat flattened, and bears on each side a row of fleshy foot-warts, which are pierced for the extrusion of the curious bristles that are so characteristic of these marine worms.

We can scarcely turn one of these flat stones which lie half-buried in sandy mud at the water's edge without finding one or more of this tribe. Let us try. Here at once is a specimen, one of the finest as well as one of the commonest of all.[18] The upper surface is of a warm fawn-brown; but the beautiful flashes of iridescent blue that play on it in the changing light, and the exquisite pearly opalescence of the delicate pink beneath, are so conspicuous as to have secured it the title of "Pearly," *par éminence*. As you gaze upon it you see the great dorsal blood-vessel or heart, as a dark red line running along the middle of the back. This, at irregular intervals of five to fifteen seconds, contracts almost to invisibility, and

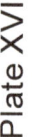

Plate XVIII

Pearly Nereis. Rainbow Leaf-Worm.

then expands again, taking the form of a string of beads in each process.

This, however, is only a part of the great circulating system in this fine worm. In it the red blood flows from the tail towards the head; at the under side of the body, there is a similar vessel (the ventral), through which the blood flows from the head towards the tail. Besides these, there are four other longitudinal vessels in the interior of the body, one above and one below the intestine, and one on each side, all of which are connected by transverse branches. Thus there is a double circulation. "The great dorsal," says Dr. Williams, "the reservoir of the centripetal streams of the body, may be likened to a right ventricle (the lungs cut off), and the great ventral to a left ventricle. The duty of the former is to collect the refluent blood of the system; of the latter to circulate it again."

Our *Nereis* is furnished with two pairs of dark blue eyes, and with an evertile proboscis, which consists of two segments. The one first protruded is beset on its upper side with some largish horny points, arranged in two groups, which are continued round to the under side in a band of irregular lines of points. The second segment has four groups of points, the groups of oblong outline, radiating from the strong black jaws, which are protruded last, and can be widely opened and closed.

Here, too, we have an Annelid of very different form and appearance.[19] It is a mean-looking worm, about an inch and a half long, of flattened shape, blunt at each end, apparently covered with a smooth skin of a dull brown colour; but on being touched it presently throws itself into elegant serpentine curves, and then what appears to be the upper skin is seen to be composed of a great number of round flat membranous plates or shields, arranged in two rows overlapping each other. These, though of large size, are attached to the body only by a small point in the centre of their under side, so that when the animal moves, the edges of these shields are lifted, and reveal their true structure, sliding upon one another in a singular manner.

In captivity I have found the animal inert, prone to seek concealment in the corners of the glass vessel beneath other animals or stones, and remaining still for a long time together; but, if disturbed, manifesting impatience and much agility, swimming through the water with strong lateral undulation, as already described. I have been struck with the deciduous character of the broad leaf-like shields. As soon as the animal was in my possession, one and another of these appendages was cast off at almost every time that I roused it to action; and even when allowed to remain quiet, the denuding process went on, so that in a few days it was nearly half naked. This process of self-mutilation will sometimes go on till scarcely a single shield remains out of the double series.

This dull-coloured Scale-worm presents peculiarities of structure which are eminently worthy of careful examination. The body, like that of the other species we have just been considering, is composed of many rings or segments, each of which bears on its upper surface a little wart or tubercle on each side, to the summit of which is slightly attached the circular leaf-like shield just described. Beneath the shadow of this broad shield the segment projects laterally into another tubercle, whence issue the organs of motion, which in these Annelids are of highly curious structure. In this species they consist of a bundle of straight bristles of exquisite tenuity, and having a silky lustre; they are of unequal length, the upper ones being the longest, and the pencil diminishing pretty regularly downwards. The microscope shows them to be about one hundred in number in each bundle; and each bristle to be a delicate oar consisting of a slender stem, apparently tubular, dilated at the tip into a narrow blade terminating in a minute hook. A fibrous structure is seen to run diagonally across the blade, the edge of which is set with minute barbs pointing outwards, resembling very fine and very short bristles. The whole bundle is connected with a long slender rod of cartilage, which, doubtless acted upon by proper muscles, moves to and fro through the muscular sheath, protruding the bundle of bristles, or entirely retracting them within the body. The bristles, when protruded, slightly diverge, so that the dilated blades of these hundred oars strike with full force upon the water in rowing, if such indeed is the nature of their action, as some have supposed. In the act of withdrawal, however, into the narrow compass of the muscular sheath, the blades slide one upon another, so as to present a surface considerably diminished. But why is each bristle hooked and barbed? The obvious supposition is that these organs act like the pole of a ferry-boat in the shallows; the barbs, pointing outwards, serving to catch any roughness of the surface, and thus to *push* the animal by their resistance, while the terminal hook may serve to *pull* in an analogous manner. But then the barbed and hooked edge is the *upper* one of each oar, a circumstance which renders such an explanation at first sight unsatisfactory. Perhaps, however, the habit of the animal of living under stones, may in some measure account for it; the edge and point of each bristle being intended to act upon the surface of the object above it, beneath which it is forcing its way.

A secondary pencil of bristles also issues from the upper side of each of these tubercular sheaths, so as to project diagonally upwards and outwards beneath the edge of the shield-leaf. This pencil consists of between thirty and forty bristles, which are connected with a cartilaginous rod exactly similar to that of the primary bundle. These bristles run off to a very fine point, and each one is marked on both sides with serratures so delicate as to be only just discernible with a magnifying power of 300 diameters. There are thus about 270 movable bristles of exquisite structure in each segment, which multiplied by 36, the number of segments in the body, gives a total of 9720 distinct organs of motion possessed by this animal, besides the broad leaf-like shields, which perhaps may act as fins, and the short tentacular feet, one of which is placed beneath the primary bristle-sheath, on each side of the segment.

By dissection after death, I have found the proboscis in the form of a long oval sac, very muscular and firm, of a blackish hue, lying in the anterior part of the body, which, on being cut open, showed four horny teeth placed in its neck so as to meet each other in the centre. I have never seen the protrusion of this organ during life, but if it is capable of being wholly everted, as in many species, these teeth must be turned on the outside, where they would seem to be of little use. Possibly, however, the eversion may be only just sufficient to bring these teeth to the margin, when their action might be made very efficient by the slightest alteration in the contraction of the sac.

Some species of this genus construct for themselves enveloping tubular cases, out of mucus given off from their bodies, and fragments of shells. In these they ordinarily live concealed, but are sufficiently active when they leave their houses. Some shine with a phosphorescent radiance in the dark.

In the great class of Worms, special organs for locomotion are often altogether lacking; and, where found, are only rudimentary. Alternate swellings and contractions of certain portions of the body are a great source of progression; and these are effected by the fluids of the interior, which are driven to a given part of the cavity, and momentarily imprisoned there by the contraction of the circular tegumentary muscles before and behind it; the body swelling at that place. "The muscles of the integument are then excited to action, and the fluid is forcibly compressed forwards or backwards, according to the direction of the muscular agency. Nearly all Annelids are struck with paralysis when this fluid is made to escape from its cavity by a puncture through its external walls. The power of voluntary motion is suspended; the body of the worm becomes passive and flaccid."[20]

These details convey but a feeble and imperfect notion of the numerous and elaborate contrivances which are so profusely bestowed upon these mean and grovelling worms; but they show how careful is the Creator of their well-being; how lavish of His mercies towards His meanest creatures. How unreasonable, then, is it for those to doubt His ever-watchful and unerring tenderness towards themselves, who have been made the objects of His *redeeming* love, and who, on the ground of redemption, "are of more value" in His sight, than all these His lower creatures put together!

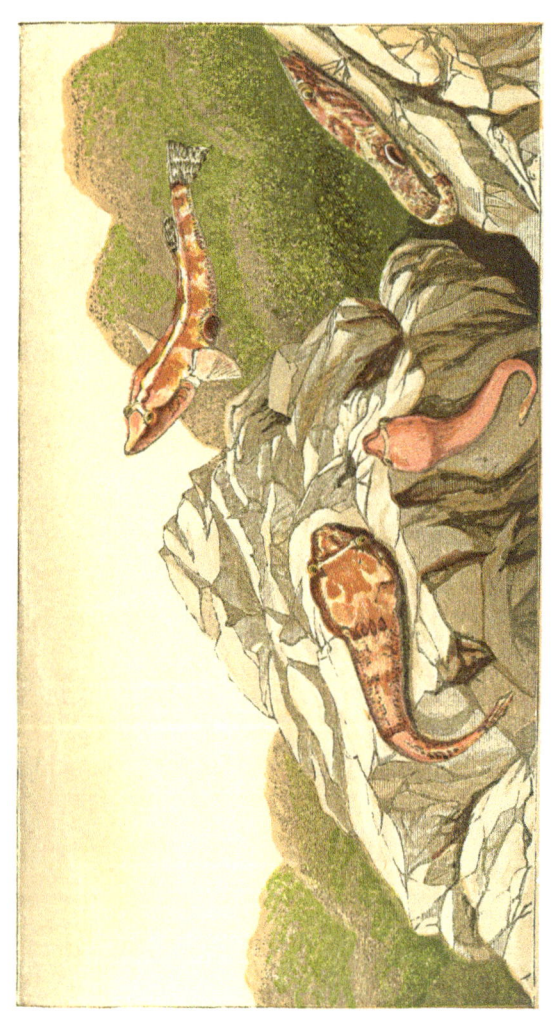

Plate XIX

Two-Spotted Sucker.

VII.
July

A mile or two eastward of Babbicombe and Petit Tor, in from ten to fifteen fathoms water, there lies a stretch of flat stony bottom, reaching away from the island known as the Ore Stone, towards the mouth of the river Exe. This is a bit of ground to which a boatman whom I occasionally employ often resorts with the dredge, and rarely or never without a fair harvest of curious and interesting creatures. Among other things he brings me from time to time numerous specimens of what Yarrell calls the Bimaculated Sucker;[1] the propriety of which name will be evident the moment you examine one of these little fishes alive. Cuvier named the group in which they are found (a group comprising very few species) *Discoboles*, because the ventral pair of fins are united so as to form a circular disk or saucer, by means of which the fishes have the power of adhering firmly to any solid object larger than the circumference of the disk. Yarrell substitutes the term *Cyclopteridæ* for the family group; the name *Cyclopterus*, used for the principal genus, expressing the same thing, that the fins are united in a circular fashion. The word *bimaculatus*, signifying two-spotted, alludes to two remarkable and conspicuous oval spots of dark purplish brown or red, situated one on each side of the body, just behind the pectoral fin. These spots, being comparatively large, and separated from the general colour of the body by a well-defined white ring, constitute a very striking and beautiful feature in these little fishes.

Their form is flattened; they have a broad shovel-shaped muzzle, prominent eyes, looking rather upwards, and the head much widened behind; the head, indeed, constitutes more than one-fourth of the entire length; and at its hinder part, or where the gills open, is far wider than any other part of the fish. They rarely exceed an inch and a half in length. The general hue above is pale red; but in some specimens they become a nearly uniform lake-purple, in others the hue is a clear orange; while yet in others it is almost white. A hand of white, bounded by darker lines, almost invariably connects the two eyes. Frequently the hue of the body is varied by clouds and patches of dark reddish brown, which patches have a tendency to assume a constant pattern, quite recognisable when you look at a good many specimens together. In the hinder half and on the sides the ground colour is apt to be minutely divided or mottled, the interspaces being of a delicate azure or lilac; and when examined with a lens, the whole surface seems sown with gold dust. The dorsal fin is set very far back, and, as well as the caudal, is prettily pencilled with dark brown: the under parts are pearly white.

The eyes are exquisitely beautiful, and as they are prominent, very movable, and especially as they are moved quite independently of each other, they at once attract and fix the admiration of the beholder. The large pupil is of a deep lustrous green, the iris of the most brilliant orange gold, and the whole set as it were in the midst of a globe of the purest glass. On the whole I scarcely know of a more attractive little fish than this.

This little Sucker is easily reconciled to captivity. I have in my aquariums some individuals which were captured nearly a year and a half ago; and they are still in the full enjoyment of health and activity. They are pleasing little things: they scuttle from spot to spot with a spasmodic sort of bustle, wagging their tails much from time to time, so that in movement as well as in form they remind one of tadpoles. They are generally seen, however, anchored to the sides of the vessel, or to the prominent knobs of the stones by their sucker, and here they remain for an indefinite time, sometimes for hours, at others only a few seconds, throwing their beautiful eyes about in insatiable curiosity, fanning the water with their transparent pectorals, or whisking the painted tail about. Now and then they make a sudden snap, doubtless at some passing animalcule, with an audible sound, and the emergence of a bubble of air from the top of the water, whence the muzzle is frequently projected. They have an awkward habit of throwing themselves out of a shallow vessel; and if you are not on your guard you may find your little pets dead and dry on the carpet. They are inquisitive little things; if a new stone or shell or tuft of serpulæ is put into their vessel they soon discover it, and may be seen exploring it in every part; and it is amusing, when *you* are examining *them* with a lens, to note how thoroughly mutual is the investigation; for you can see by the direction and motion of the eyes that the little fish is watching you as interestedly as you are observing him.

I do not think that the adhesion of the ventral sucker is effected exactly as has been supposed, by a vacuum produced in the area of the united ventral fins; but by the combined action of some minute fleshy sucking disks, which are arranged in two groups, in front of and behind the united fins. The conjoined fins do not appear to me to make a vacuum. The fish has a curious habit of coming to the surface of the water, and there floating perfectly still, back downward, the entire belly-surface dry. The ventral disk is then seen as a shallow cup, quite dry and shining. If touched, the little fish hurries along the surface, with some splashing, till it acquires impetus enough to go under at an oblique angle, when it presently turns over, and adheres to the bottom, or side of some stone. I have seen this practice frequently, but only, I think, at night.[2]

This principle of a vacuum produced by the retraction of the centre of a fleshy disk, while the margins remain in close contact with a solid body, is of extensive application in the lower forms of animal life, and especially in the class Echinodermata, comprising what are popularly known as Star-fishes, Sea-urchins, and Sea-cucumbers.

I have on other occasions noticed the elaborate and wonderful mechanism of the sucker-feet as they appear in the commoner species of the class. I need not therefore repeat those details, but look at a few other particulars in the economy of the animals whose locomotion is dependent on this curious contrivance.

There is a pretty little species abundant enough hereabout, chiefly affecting shores on which numerous angular masses of stone lie irregularly scattered and heaped one on another. Yet they seem to have a predilection, for they do not occur in all our localities even though these conditions be not lacking. Livermead Point, and the south side of Anstey's Cove, beneath the cliffs, are favourite spots for them, the former especially, where we can find the little Gibbous Starlet,[3] for such is its name,— at all times of the year, when the tide is sufficiently out. The retiring tide here leaves a shallow pool of considerable area, which then continues to run out by a narrow channel among the rock boulders, a winding rivulet of salt water; along whose borders, by turning over the loose blocks, scores of this pretty Star are exposed, clinging to the wet sides and roofs of the dark passages by means of their sucker-feet. Forbes has given two figures of the species, but manifestly taken from dead specimens, and from very small ones too. He says, "large specimens measure only an inch across;" from which I infer that on the shores of the Isle of Man, where he was familiar with it, the Starlet does not attain the dimensions it reaches on our mild southern coast. He indeed alludes to one in Mr. Ball's collection, which measured one inch and five lines in diameter. Specimens, however, of this size are quite common with us, nor would one of an inch and a half be looked upon as at all exceeding the modest and proper range of the species.

It is of a pentagonal figure, with the margin a little receding between the angles, but not so as to cause the latter to form distinct arms. The body is flat below, and plump and cushion-like above, of a yellowish olive hue, with the very edge of a golden orange tint, while a spot of the latter colour, a little out of the centre, marks the situation of a remarkable organ called the madreporiform tubercle, the proper use of which has not as yet been satisfactorily determined. Just at the extremity of each angle, but a little below, is situated a wart of rich crimson hue, which is supposed to be an eye, being seated on a small ganglionic swelling of a nerve that passes along the ray. It is true no crystalline lens has as yet been detected on the pigment dot, either in this species or any other (for the specks are found in the same position in all the proper Star-fishes), but they are manifestly of the same character as similar specks in *Rotifera*, and other humble animal forms, which in some examples are connected with an indubitable lens. It might seem at first as if the situation of these eyes were not very favourable to vision; but, in truth, they command the ground just before and around the ray-tip, and also the water in a horizontal direction; and as there is one at each of the five angles, the entire circumferent space is viewed at each moment. Add to this, that the animal is in the habit of very frequently turning up the tip of one or other of

Plate XX

Purple-Tipped Urchin. Rosy Feather-Star. Starlet.

its rays, when the range of vision would take in the zenith; and we shall perceive that no position in any other part of the body could be so suitable for the location of eyes as these selected. It is not to be supposed that distinct definition of objects is attained by these rudimentary organs; but the animal is probably conscious of the difference between light and darkness, and may also discern the sudden approach of any object, either by its interception of light, or by its colours, though its features and form may be indistinct. Such a degree of visual perception, though very imperfect in our esteem, may be of great use to this sluggish creature, and amply sufficient for its need.

The whole upper surface of this Starlet is covered with six-sided convex plates, each of which is crowned by a group of short blunt spines; the number in each group varying from one to nine; four to six, however, most commonly; arranged in a diverging tuft. Over the madreporiform tubercle, the tufts are stouter, and bend towards each other, as if to protect this delicate organ, which, whatever its function, is grooved with sinuous furrows, visible only with a considerable magnifying power, like the rounded masses of coral from the tropical seas, called brain-stones.

On the under surface similar stout short spines are arranged in transverse bands across each ray, interrupted, however, by the central furrow, which is perforated with two ranges of orifices to give issue to the sucker-feet, which thus form a double row. These organs do not differ importantly either in structure, function, or appearance, from those in the Cross-fishes, in the Sea-cucumbers, or in the Urchins.

In health and activity the whole upper surface is covered with a forest of short pellucid tubes, closed at the tips, which protrude from pores in the plates, and stand erect, moving, however, to and fro at the will of the animal; they are evidently filled with fluid. I cannot find any notice of these organs: they are probably connected with respiration.

What a wonderful piece of mechanism is a Sea-Urchin! Accustomed as I am to the multitudinous contrivances and compensations that present themselves at every turn to the philosophic naturalist, often as surprising and unexpected as they are beautifully effective, I am yet struck with admiration at the structure of an *Echinus* whenever I examine it anew. A globular hollow box has to be made, of some three inches in diameter, the walls of which shall be scarcely thicker than a wafer, formed of unyielding limestone, yet fitted to hold the soft tender parts of an animal, which quite fill the concavity at all ages. But in infancy the animal (and, of course, its box, as this must be full) is not so big as a pea; and it has to grow till it attain its adult dimensions. The box is never to be cast off, and replaced by a new one; the same box must hold the infant and the veteran Urchin. The limestone, not being a living tissue, but an inert earth, can grow only by being deposited. Now the vascular tissues are within, and the particles they deposit must be on the interior walls. This would indeed augment the amount of limestone in the box, but it would be at the expense of the contained space. The thicker the walls, if thickened from within, the less room in the cavity; but what is wanted is *more* room, ever more, and more. The growing animal feels its tissues swelling day by day, by the assimilation of food, and its cry is, "Give me space! a larger house, or else I die."

How is this problem solved? Ah? there is no difficulty. The inexhaustible wisdom of Jehovah the Creator has invented a beautiful contrivance for the emergency. The box is not made in one piece, nor in ten, nor in a hundred; six hundred distinct pieces go to make up the hollow case; all so accurately fitted together, that the perfect symmetry of the outline is not broken; and yet, thin as their substance is, they retain their relative position with unchanging exactness, and the slight brittle box possesses all requisite strength and firmness.

Each of these symmetrical pieces of shell is enveloped by a layer of living flesh, a vascular tissue of exceeding thinness, which passes up between the joints where one meets another, on every side, and not only so, but actually spreads itself over the whole exterior surface. So that when you take up an Urchin into your hand, and having rubbed a small space clear of spines, look on it; you have not, as you may suppose you have, exposed the surface of the shelly box, but only the flesh that covers it; yet this is so transparent and colourless, so inconceivably thin, so absolutely adherent at every point, that its presence will not be discernible to feeling or sight, without the aid of high microscopic powers.

This being so, the glands of the investing fleshy tissue secrete lime from the sea-water, which holds it in solution, and constantly deposits it, after a determinate and orderly pattern, on every part of the surface of each shelly piece; the inner face, the outer face, and each of the sides and angles of the polyhedron grow together, and all so evenly, that while the dimensions increase, both of thickness and superficies, the form characteristic of that individual piece is maintained with immutable mathematical precision. Thus the volume and capacity of the box grow with the growth of the individual segments, and it ever keeps the globose shape at first imposed upon it.

But this is but a small part of the mechanism of this interesting tribe. If you put into a basin of sea-water one of the pretty kind[4] which we find so abundantly under stones at low water,—whose green spines are tipped with rosy purple, like the tentacles of an *Anthea*,—you will presently observe it marching majestically along by means of the hundreds of sucker-feet, which it possesses in common with the Star-fish. Now, if you have in your cabinet the empty box of an Urchin of this same kind, and taking it in your hand, hold it up to the light, and look into the cavity from the under or mouth side, you will have a very interesting spectacle. The light streams in through a multitude of minute holes, as smooth and regular as if drilled with a fairy's wimble; and these holes are arranged in a pattern of elegant symmetry. They run in lines, like meridians, from pole to pole of the flattened globe; but instead of being set at uniform intervals, they constitute five principal sets or bands, with blank intervals between, about twice as wide as the drilled bands. Then each band comprises two series, each of which contains a double row of orifices.

These last, again, do not constitute a single unbroken line, but an interrupted or zig-zag line, which is, in fact, made up of a number of short diagonal rows; three holes in each diagonal, set one after another.

Put the living and the dead together. These tiny orifices, as minute as the point of the finest cambric-needle could make in a bit of paper, afford exit to the suckers, which are, of course, equally numerous. Through these pass the slender pellucid tubes, filled with elastic fluid, which carry at their tips a flat ring of calcareous shell, affording to each the form and firmness to make each one an adhesive sucking disk, in the centre of which a tiny vacuum is created at will by muscular retraction.

But this is not all. Again, look at the living Sea-Urchin. It bristles with the rosy-tipped spines, which have a satiny lustre, owing to the reflection of the light from the delicate ridges and furrows with which the whole is fluted, like an Ionic column in miniature. How they are all moving, and swaying, to and fro on their bases, quite independently of each other, however, making circles and traverses in the water with their points, as the mast-heads of a ship do among the clouds in a gentle swell, when seen from the deck. Professor Agassiz fell into the egregious blunder of supposing that the spines were the organs of locomotion in the Urchins, denying, with much contempt, the theory which attributed this office to the suckers. One can only wonder whether he ever saw a living Urchin in motion, as one moment's glance at the phenomenon is sufficient to prove how utterly his theory was false, as Forbes has well shown.

However, let us once more observe the empty denuded box from the cabinet; and now on the exterior. Between the principal bands of pores (called *ambulacra*, from their fancied resemblance to walks in a garden), as also between the two series which constitute each band, the space is studded with hemispherical warts, of very diverse size, which look as if turned in ivory, unpolished; and each wart is crowned with a smaller wart of like material, but bearing the most perfect polish.

At the bottom of each spine there is a cavity exactly fitting this second wart, and equally highly-polished in its interior. During life the spine was seated on the wart, not united to it, but moving upon it in all directions, with perfect smoothness and freedom; a ball and socket joint, in fact. It was held in its place by an investment of muscle, which completely enclosed both the wart and the base of the spine, having one insertion in the unpolished wart, and the other in a remarkable ring or shoulder of the spine, visible just above the socket.

These are but two or three salient points of interest in the structure of this little unvalued, disregarded creature. I could relate much more; indeed, I think it would not be difficult to write a bulky volume of the history and biography of a single Sea-Urchin, of which every page would display the glory of God. But I have not space for that here.

We sometimes, but very rarely, find on this coast a very lovely form of this class of animals, the Rosy Feather-star.[5] It consists of ten long attenuated arms, radiating from a common centre, composed each of about forty slender joints of stone, and each joint carrying a pair of diverging beards, also many-jointed, all of which together, by their number and arrangement, give to the arm the aspect of a beautiful feather. Around the central point of radiation, a small cup-like body gives origin to the arms, which are double, a pair springing from a single basal joint. Within the cup the soft parts of the animal are chiefly located, the organs of the vital functions; and from the convex surface spring a number of jointed stony threads, like necklaces, much shorter and slenderer than the arms, which serve as claspers, gripping and holding firmly the projections of the rock, by means of strong curved claws with which they are terminated, in shape like those of an eagle.

The whole elegant creature is of a lively rose tint, interrupted by patches of bright yellow, disposed with no regularity or apparent order; the whole, both the yellow and the rosy portions, studded with crimson clots. Edward Forbes, if I rightly understand him, considers these dots to be ovaries, which he estimates at upwards of 57,000 in number.

In infancy the Feather-star is seated at the extremity of a long slender jointed stalk, attached at its lower end, whence it rises erect, like a plant. Indeed the whole animal, in this condition, with its cup-like base and elegantly incurving arms, seated on its tall stem, has so close a resemblance of outline to a flower, that the fossil specimens, which are very numerous, and of large size, are known as Lily-stones, and technically as *Encrinites*, which word has the same allusion. After a while, the radiating portion, or flower, separates from the stalk, and swims freely, contracting its arms to give the impulse, in the manner of a *Medusa*.

Who, on looking at these two creatures side by side,—the Sea-Urchin and the Encrinite,—would imagine that they possessed any close natural relationship, or would suspect that they could have been framed on the same model? Yet it is really so; there is a common plan of structure in both; pervading, too, many intermediate forms, which at first sight would seem to manifest as little resemblance to the one as to the other. It would, in fact, be easy to select from any well-furnished museum a continuous chain of specimens, whose links approach each other so closely as to form an unbroken series from the Urchin to the Feather-star.

Among the Urchins proper there are some species, such as the Sphere Sea-egg, and the one known as Fleming's, which have a figure not far from that of a globe. Others are much more depressed, of which the little Purple-tipped is a notable example. Still the spherical shape is conspicuous. From this rounded form other species, more and more flattened, gradually lead to the *Scutella*, which takes the form of a thin round plate, quite flat beneath, but slightly convex on the upper surface. The structure is the same as before, but the spines appear to the naked eye only as very minute hairs; but, when magnified, are found to be of the most elaborate workmanship, each having a movable socket-joint. In the genus *Clypeaster*, the round outline is changed for a five-sided figure, the angles of which in succeeding species project more and more, and the spaces between become more and more indented, till we arrive at the Starlets, and at length to the Cross-fishes (*Asteriadæ*). The rays gradually becoming longer and more slender, we are brought to those in which they are so lengthened as to resemble the tails of so many serpents, whence they are named *Ophiura*. In succeeding genera, such as that called Medusa's head (*Gorgonocephalus*), the central part is still further diminished, and the rays are divided into branches of great length and number. Each ray, soon after its commencement, separates into two more; these again into two others, and so on to an astonishing extent. Upwards of 2500 ramifications have been counted on a single specimen, presenting a living net, by the contraction of which any small animal once touched would inevitably be detained. The sucker-feet are no longer found, these animals changing their position by dragging themselves along by their flexible arms. Finally, we have the Feather-stars, which, as we have seen, in their infant condition, and the Lily-stars, which throughout life (as the abundant fossil species in our own land, and that noble one which still exists in the West Indian seas), consist of slender-jointed arms, with feather-like filaments, seated at the free extremity of a tall jointed stalk, also furnished with whorls of filaments, which is fixed by its base to the solid rock.

Altogether, the series presents us with one of the most instructive and most marvellous examples of the vast variety of external form and internal structure which may be assumed by almost insensible modifications of one plan of organization; and so of the unfathomable resources of wisdom in the ever-blessed God. For every one of these links,—and there are multitudes which I have not named, found either in remote seas or in a fossil condition, that fill up the gaps with close gradations—displays an essentially common model; and the least fragment of the stony skeleton of any one would be sufficient to enable a competent naturalist to decide authoritatively, the instant he looked at it beneath his microscope, that it belonged to the great class Echinodermata. The calcareous shell of which the framework is composed,—a glass made of lime,—is deposited in a fashion which, while common to all, is found nowhere else throughout the whole animal kingdom.

Let us turn from these investigations, fascinating as they are, to examine the ways and means of two or three other creatures, familiar enough to us who habitually explore the sea-margin. I allude to certain members of the great class Crustacea, not Crabs nor Lobsters exactly, but called so by courtesy, something in fact between both. My dredger's hauls are always sure to contain, creeping in the tangled thickets of *Laomedea*, *Antennularia*, and other of the flexible Polyps, or playing at bo-peep from the interstices of the *Serpula* masses,—numerous specimens of a tiny Crab,[6] with a circular flat shell, no bigger than a split-pea, large wide claws, and very long antennæ, like two hairs. They are of various colours, sometimes pure white, sometimes chocolate-brown, and often clouded with different hues. Minute as they are, they are not despised by great fishes; for the heavy-sided, clumsy-headed cods, that occupy so large an area on the fishmonger's slab, are often found to have their stomachs packed full with these little Crabs; which doubtless the glutton picks off

Plate XXI

Olive Squat-Lobster. Shaggy Flat-Crab. Scarlet Squat-Lobster.

one by one, enjoying the taste of the savoury atom as it rolls over his fat fleshy tongue.

But we may much more easily procure specimens of his bigger brother, the Shaggy Flat-crab,[7] which abounds under nearly every flat stone at low-water on Babbicombe beach, and indeed almost everywhere else, under the like conditions. He is a curious subject, though far from attractive as to his *personnel*, for he is, I regret to say, of irreclaimably dirty habits. You never find him but he is begrimed and saturated, so to speak, with the impalpable red mud of which our soil consists,—the *débris* of the red sandstone. Yet blame him not. He is more hirsute than a modern swell; his hands and his face are as hairy as Esau's; a dense short pile of stiff bristles stands out from all his prominences, and catches and entangles the sediment in the midst of which he loves to riot. I say again, blame him not; we must not infer that he likes dirt for its own sake, because he gets his living in it, any more than the sweep or the dustman chose his trade because he had a *penchant* for the grime. Nay, dirty as our little flat friend is, he is endowed with organs expressly for the purpose of cleaning himself, and fails not to use them too. On first looking at him you would suppose, comparing him with other Crabs, that he was short of one pair of feet; yet presently, from a narrow, almost invisible crevice behind, he jerks out two jointed limbs, as slender as bristles, which, however, are each terminated by a tiny two-fingered claw, and are beset throughout their length by stiff short hairs standing out at right angles, like a brush. These feeble limbs are indeed cleansing brushes, with which he keeps certain portions of his person clean, applying them with the greatest ease to the whole surface of the abdomen, and under-side of the carapace or body-shell, while the delicate fingers of the little hand are used to pick off adhering matters that cannot be removed by brushing. Then having done his washing, he cleans his brushes with his mouth, and snugly folds them up, and packs them away in their groove till he wants them again. Yet with all this, he remains, as I said at first, a dirty subject notwithstanding.

A curious chapter in the history of this little creature, which I have put on record elsewhere,[8] is, I think, so very instructive, that I may venture to repeat some parts of it here. Let me premise that the Crab habitually lives under stones, a habit for which the remarkable flatness and thinness of all its parts adapts it; he has somewhat of the appearance of having been crushed flat by the pressure of the stone under which he lives. He does not wander much to seek his food, but expects it to be brought to him, he making provision for its conveyance.

The organs which he employs for this end are the outer foot-jaws or pedipalps, which are of unusual length, and are fringed with incurving hairs. Watching a Flat-crab beneath a stone close to the side of my tank, I noticed that his long antennæ were continually flirted about; these are doubtless sensitive organs of touch, or some analogous sense, which inform the animal of the presence, and perhaps of the nature, of objects within reach. At the same time I remarked that the outer foot-jaws were employed alternately in making casts; being thrown out deliberately, but without intermission, and drawn in, exactly in the manner of the fringed hand of a barnacle, of which both the organ and the action strongly reminded me. I looked at this more closely with the aid of a lens; each foot-jaw formed a perfect spoon of hairs, which at every cast expanded, and partly closed. That this may be better understood, I may say that the foot-jaw resembles a sickle in form, being composed of five joints, of which the last four are curved like the blade of that implement. Each of these joints is set along its inner edge with a row of parallel bristles, of which those of the last joint arch out in a semicircle, continuing the curve of the limb; the rest of the bristles are curved parallel or concentrical with these, but diminish in length as they recede downwards. It will be seen, therefore, that when the joints of the foot-jaw are thrown out, approaching to a straight line, the curved hairs are made to diverge; but as the cast is made, they resume their parallelism, and sweep-in, as with a net, the atoms of the embraced water. The microscope revealed to me a still higher perfection in this admirable contrivance. I then saw that every individual bristle is set on each side with a row of short stiff hairs, projecting nearly at right angles to its length; these hairs meeting point to point those of the next bristle, and so on in succession, there is formed a most complete net of regular meshes, which must enclose and capture every tiny insect or animalcule that floats within its range; while, at each out-cast, it opens at every mesh, and allows all refuse to be washed away or fall to the around. For we are not to suppose that the captures thus promiscuously made are as indiscriminately swallowed. A multitude of atoms are gathered, which world be quite unfit for food; and a power of selection resides in the mouth, whether it be the sense of taste or touch, or any other analogous but recondite perception, by which the useful only is admitted, the worthless, or at least the injurious, being rejected.

Companions of the Flat-crabs, closely allied to them in all essentials of form and structure, yet widely separated by general figure and appearance, and to some extent by habits too, are the Squat-lobsters. They, too, are somewhat flat, but they are more decidedly lobster-like, with a distinctly jointed abdomen as broad as the body, terminating in wide and strong swimming-plates. This portion is, during rest, thrown-in under the body, much more completely than a true lobster or prawn can do it, and yet is by no means so permanently set in that position as in the true crabs. The Flat-crabs and the Squat-lobsters constitute an intermediate group between the short-tailed and the long-tailed Crustacea, the Flat-crabs inclining to the one, the Squats to the other alliance. When the abdomen is wrapped-in, the outline of the Squat is nearly oval, particularly in the commonest species, the Olive or Scaly Squat.[9] That of the Scarlet or Embleton's species[10] is a longer ellipse. The front runs out into several sharp spines, as do also the edges of the carapace; and the inner edges of the front limbs, which carry long and stout claws, are very spiny. More formidably armed in this respect, however, than either, is another species, found occasionally at low-water, the Painted or Spinous Squat,[11] all the limbs being set, on both edges, with stout sharp prickles. The last named is the largest kind, being sometimes four inches long; then the Olive, which is commonly from two to two and a half; while the Scarlet rarely exceeds an inch and a half. They differ very much in colour, the Olive being of a dull blackish green, with narrow transverse lines of pale yellowish; the Painted somewhat of the same general line, but with the eyes and the tips of the claws of the most vivid scarlet, while the body is varied with lines and spots of an equally brilliant azure. Embleton's is of a more or less bright red, varying from a light orange or warm cream colour to a full orange, clouded with patches of deep scarlet. The last is an inhabitant of deep water, obtained only by the dredge; by this means, however, I obtain it in considerable numbers. The other two are found, the first abundantly, the second rather rarely, under stones in our coves. I have found, in autumn, in such situations, several specimens of small size, rather smaller than full-grown Embletons, which I conclude to be the young of the Painted. The whole body is pale blue, tessellated all over with black and reddish brown; the legs are banded with red, and the hands are of the same colour. They have a very pretty appearance.

The whole race are very cautious and timid. With the long claws, and the longer antennæ, stretched out to their utmost in front, the suspicious Squat feels the unknown ground with delicate touches; should he touch any object that moves, he gives on the instant a vigorous flap with the broad incurved tail, and shoots backward through the water to the distance of several inches. At the same moment all the legs are thrown forward in the line of the body, to diminish the resistance. Mr. Couch says: "It is very remarkable to witness the accuracy with which they" [he is speaking of the Painted species specially] "will dart backward *for several feet* into a hole very little larger than themselves: this I have often seen them do, and always with precision." This would surely be a remarkable feat for an animal in the air; how much more through a medium so dense and resisting as sea-water!

I have elsewhere[12] described and figured the young of a species of this genus in two of its stages. In the first it may be compared with a prawn, having a lengthened slender body, whose fore part is protected by a prawn-like transparent carapace, with an immensely long straight spine in front, and two hooked ones behind. In the next stage the general figure is acquired, but still the form is more like that of *Porcellana* than of *Galathea*.

Plate XXII

Corkwing Wrasse.

VIII.
August

What eager pursuer of marine animals has not gloated over a rock-pool? On all our rocky coasts we find them more or less developed; but it is on these south-western shores, where the compact limestone juts out into promontories, that we find then in perfection. The burrowing mollusca specially favour the limestone; the *Saxicava*, I think, lives in no other medium; and it is to the operation of this coarse ugly little shell-fish that this rock is indebted for the honeycomb-like excavation which has eroded its surface. Below a few inches this erosion does not extend, for the *Saxicava* is but a small animal, and its siphons must reach the orifice of its burrow; therefore it never goes deeper into the stone than will allow it comfortably to bathe its red nose in the free water, though it is not at all particular about the angle to the surface at which it bores. The myriads and myriads of these auger-holes that have been bored remain, though the feeble animals perish generation after generation; each new-born shell-fish makes a new bore for itself, never appropriating one ready-made, and so there is a perpetual excavation of the living rock with these shallow auger-holes, always of the same width, or nearly; about half-an-inch. The result is what we see; that the surface of the rock knows no such thing as a plane surface, but a surface covered with smooth borings, running in all directions, so as continually to break in on one another; and that so close together, that the interspaces form narrow knife-edges, and sharp angles and projecting points. A particularly interesting circumstance is, that this honeycombed condition is characteristic not only of that level of the rock which is covered by the sea for some portion of every tide, but of that part, to a certain height, which is never covered at all. The Mollusca, it is true, cannot live wholly deprived of sea-water, and, in fact, there are none in this ever-dry portion, though the burrows by thousands testify that they were there once. We must infer that the coast has been generally elevated; perhaps by slow and imperceptible degrees, by an operation still proceeding but unappreciated; perhaps by some sudden convulsion which took place at a remote era, unrecorded and forgotten.

When once raised beyond the level of the highest tide, the eroded surface appears to have a permanency which defies the action of the elements for an undefinable period; for it seems liable to little change. It is probably comparatively unalterable, or alterable slowly, beneath the level of the lowest tide. But between tidemarks, the perpetual change from wetness to dryness and back again, and the incessant wash of the waves, which frequently beat and dash upon the eroded surface with immense violence, are continually grinding down the projecting points and thin walls of stone, and thus creating a new surface, to be bored afresh by new generations of Mollusca.

It has seemed to me that these burrows have played and are playing an important part in the formation of the numberless rocky basins which we call tide-pools, and in which we marine naturalists so much delight. Let us look at the process. About half-tide level there is a mass of bored rock, from whose burrows the tenants are dying out for want of sufficiently long water-covering. A heavy sea is breaking over it, which has snapped off the thin partition beneath two contiguous burrows, breaking it into several sharply angular bits, which fall into the hole. The whirling and eddying of the waves rattle and roll these fragments round and round day after day, week after week, till at last they are ground to nothing: but an equal effect has been produced on the hollow which held them; its cavity has been widened and deepened by the same grinding action. By-and-by a pebble is rolled in, and being almost large enough to fill the cavity, it does not readily wash out, but grinds round and round with the motion of the sea. So the process goes on, perhaps for centuries, perhaps with long intervals of almost sameness; every stone that is washed-in enlarging the work; while, when once the hollow has become only ever so little larger or deeper than those which surround it, the pebbles will have an increasing tendency to roll in and to stay there. So, at length, the basin is formed, tiny at first;—I know scores not so big as a slop-bowl, which yet have their furniture of elegant little sea-weeds, green and purple, and their tenants of worms, and shrimps, and polyps;—but destined by-and-by to become noble reservoirs in which man may pleasantly bathe, and in which little fishes play and shoot to and fro, and hide under the umbrageous fronds of the oar-weed and tangle that droop gracefully into the ample cavity.

In the pleasant sunny afternoons of this season of the year we may find in tolerable abundance the pretty Cork-wing,[1] in such rock-pools as I have been speaking of. In the shallow hollows of the ledges they shoot hither and thither, the swift movement just catching the collector's eye; but here they are difficult to capture, owing to the numerous exits and hiding-places among the stones. Thy deeper basins are pretty sure of containing one or two, and generally of larger size. Here the dip-net can be brought into action, and they are readily taken. But the finest specimens are obtained around the edges of the rocks in the free water, and where there is considerable depth. Here the attentive eye discerns them quietly hovering, some yard or two beneath the surface, deliberately picking their tiny crustacean food from the drooping weeds, or playing to and fro in little parties of half-a-dozen, on motionless or gently undulating fins; a pretty sight to watch. From these seaward edges of the rocks the coarser sea-weeds growing in a thick fringe, when the tide has left them partly exposed, hang their tips in the heaving water; and under this grateful shelter the little Corkwings, as well as other small fishes, their companions, delight to disport themselves, finding copious food in the purple obscurity, and getting many a peep through the latticed leaves at their idler fellows in gamesome play without. If, now, the collector have provided himself with a stiff ring-net, and a long and stout handle, he may sift out, as it were, the tenants of these shades, by collecting, in succession, the drooping weed-tips in the mouth of his net, and lifting it gently through them; when the lovely little emerald fishes will be found, two or three at each dip, struggling and panting and leaping and quivering their helpless fins at the bottom of his bag.

The Corkwing belongs to the great Wrasse family; which, though it chiefly develops itself in the tropical seas, is yet well represented in our own. Yarrell has figured thirteen species, all of them found on our southwestern shores, and a few of them ranging to the north as well. The entire family is remarkable for its bright and gorgeous hues, often taking the form of bands, stripes and spots, well defined, and in vivid contrasts. This little species, which extends to the length of five inches, but is much more commonly taken not more than half that size, is of a rich emerald-green hue, lighter beneath, and generally marked with a conspicuous black spot on each side of the base of the tail. Small individuals are frequently found, of a dark reddish brown, arranged in a minute tessellated pattern on a pale ground; and occasionally of a rich golden bronzed hue. The eyes are usually of the finest vermilion.

They are entertaining inmates of an aquarium; they play slowly up and down in the corners of the tank, exploring every angle and cranny, hanging in every possible attitude, especially at night. They soon become familiar, and may be preserved in health a long time. They are constantly occupied in searching for, and picking off atoms, invisible to us, with their protrusile lips. These organs are remarkably large, thick, and fleshy, whence has been derived the name of the family, *Labridæ* (from *labrum*, a lip); and, in death, they are generally projected in an uncouth and repulsive form. It is a pity that Yarrell's figures have been for the most part copied from specimens in this distorted condition, and are therefore hideous caricatures of the little beauties. His Corkwing is a notable example, presenting but little resemblance to the playful emerald in my tank; while the Gilthead and the Sea-wife are still more horrible. It is matter of regret that so large a portion of our pictorial natural history represents death rather than life; while a herd of slavish compilers, who have never seen the creatures on which they obtrude their teachings, copy such imperfect figures, and copy each other, and go on augmenting the distortions, and straying farther and farther from nature, till all *vraisemblance* is lost in the ludicrous caricature.

In a former work[2] I have narrated the untimely fate of one of these pretty fishes in my possession, through the poison-darts of a Parasitic Anemone.[3] A similar accident befell one lately, which I had kept in my tank for about two months. This individual, about two and a half inches long, active and healthy, made a backward spring, and came in contact with the tentacles of an *Anthea cereus*, which in an instant enveloped its hinder half, clinging round and over it and quite covering that portion. I was looking on, and after a moment's glance to see that the fish was perfectly helpless, I removed it with a stick, so that it was free in about half a minute from its accident. But the effect was manifest; it swam away indeed, but irregularly and fitfully, and presently sank down on the bottom; lay awhile, then struggled up for a few seconds, swimming on one side, as if partly paralysed, and frequently turning over belly-up; then sinking obliquely down and hiding its nose between the stones. The fins were white and ragged, and the skin of the hinder part was ruffled up in parts, and the entire hind-half looked diseased. By night it was not to be seen; but the next morning I. found it, dead and stiff, and with the whole of the parts that had been embraced by the Anthea turned of a pellucid white, the edges of the fins sloughed away and decomposing.

When we consider that the entire period of contact was no more than half a minute, the power of the subtle poison, injected by the *cnidæ* of the Opelet, becomes very manifest; and the accident afforded me another confirmation of what has been fondly denied, the amazing energy of the poison-apparatus in the Actinozoa.

An assiduous searching of these hanging fringes of fuci will be sure to yield a pleasing return of other objects. Neglecting at this moment the Prawns, Æsops, Opossum-shrimps, Spider-crabs, and many other *crustacea*, not to speak of other classes, let us direct our thoughts exclusively to the fishes. You will get probably one or two specimens of that little bull-headed rogue, the Father-lasher,[4] armed at all points, like a knight in the fair time of chivalry. An impudent little rascal he looks, and right villainous; but whether he is in truth guilty of whipping his paternal parent, this deponent saith not. Big-headed, wide-mouthed, staring-eyed, beset on all sides with hard spines as sharp as needles, which he erects with threatening fierceness as he anticipates your touch, this Lucky Proach, as our northern friends name him, may not invite a close acquaintance; and indeed our fishermen generally jerk him energetically out of the net as soon as they see him, thinking themselves "lucky" to be well quit of his prickles.

Yet in truth he makes a funny little tenant of the aquarium. His colours are agreeable; deep rich brown on the upper parts, fantastically patched and clouded with various shades from black to pure white, while the sides and belly are brilliantly silvery or opalescent. His countenance expresses considerable intelligence; and the contrast between his aspect when he is alarmed, and all his spines are laid flat, and when he thinks to carry his point by bullying, and bristles up all his sharp lances, and glares with a threatening goggle, is very amusing. He presently becomes at home; for a day or two he skulks under the rocky ledges, and you see little of him; but soon his characteristic impudence reassures him, and *vires acquirit eundo*; he makes short hasty sallies into the open, and instantly scuttles back to his retreat; presently you see his great head projecting out of some crevice in the rocks, whence he can command a pretty extensive view; and now that is his selected home, and there henceforward you may pretty surely find him, whenever he is not to be seen engaged in predatory forays in some other quarter of the tank. Now he grows very saucy; not a Blenny or Goby or Pipe can come before his castle-gate but Proach must dash out to have a passage-of-arms with him, returning, in all the pride of conquest, when he has driven the routed foe out of sight, to his rocky fortress, and settling himself in the same watchful attitude as before. Every atom of meat that you drop into the water within his range of vision must be his: you perhaps intended the morsel for the Goby or the Blenny, but Proach sees it, and Proach must have it. They indeed may sail up towards the speck, but Proach dashes up, bristling with indignation at their temerity, and snaps the food from before their very noses. Not one of them can get a bit till Proach is satiated; and I have often seen him lie with a morsel projecting from his mouth for some time, absolutely incapable of swallowing more, before he would relinquish the contest. Now he fears nothing; he will even rush to the surface when he sees you approaching, and, with a sudden snap, seize the meat in your fingers, and drag it away.

Mr. R. Q. Couch gives us some interesting particulars of this little fish, or his brother, the Sea-scorpion; for they are so much alike, both in appearance and manners, that some naturalists do not recognise any specific difference between them. "When caught," he says, "it makes a croaking kind of noise; opens its gill-covers, and erects the spines of its head, and stiffens its whole body, as if prepared for a vigorous defence. The spines are covered with a skin or sheath, which the creature has the power of drawing from the points and leaving them bare. This fish will live a long time out of water, provided it be kept slightly wet, but soon dies on immersion in fresh water. Those fish that swim deeply are able to sustain life much longer than those that swim near the surface; and the former are more sluggish in their movements, and require less ærated water for respiration. The more active are surface-swimmers. The immersion in fresh water acts as a poison, death not resulting from any variation in the respirable quality of the water. If a Sea-scorpion, after being taken from the sea, be constantly kept wet with salt water, it will live for a considerable time, the gill-covers acting as if surrounded by water. If the gills be kept wet and the skin dry, the creature gets restless, croaks, the gills move less rapidly than before, and it then dies at an earlier period than when kept altogether moist. If the gills be wetted with fresh water well ærated, life is not so long retained, but the fish seems more active for a time, and dies at last almost in a state of plethora."[5]

According to Yarrell, "this species spawns in January, and the ova at that time are very large and of a fine orange-yellow colour. These are deposited near the sea-shore, frequently in the estuaries, and sometimes even in rivers; the fish having prepared itself for this change by its previous residence in the brackish water, after which it appears to be able to bear either extreme. Its food is small crustaceous animals, and it is said to be particularly partial to feeding on the fry of the Blennies."

Plate XXIII

Father-Lasher. Worm-Pipefish.

On the subject of its instant death, when removed from its native element to fresh water, the same naturalist remarks, alluding to the hypothesis that the speedy death of fishes in general, when removed into the atmosphere, is due to the drying of the delicate membranes of the gills; "the reverse of desiccation takes place in this instance: the gills are bathed with a fluid containing more oxygen than sea-water, and which also yields that oxygen much easier, yet death happens immediately. In this last instance it may be inferred that the fish, unable suddenly to accommodate its respiratory organs to fluids of such different densities as those of pure sea and fresh water, the blood is imperfectly ærated, the brain is affected, convulsions ensue, and if not released it soon dies."[6]

You will pretty certainly find in your net, too, twining and writhing about like little snakes, some of the smaller species of Pipe-fishes, often called Sea-adders, and most abundantly the smallest of them, and the commonest in shallow waters,—the Worm Pipe.[7] The pretty Æquoreal Pipe, or as Mr. Couch appropriately names it, the Painted Sea-adder (from the variegated tints of brown and yellow, wherewith its numerous angular plates are individually adorned), is abundant enough all along our southern coast, in deeper water, affecting the extensive beds of zostera, and of sea-weeds, which in many places clothe the bottom. The eminent Cornish zoologist observes of this species, that "in May and June, and frequently in July, and occasionally in August, these fish rise to the surface of the water, however deep it may be, and bask themselves in the sun. They retain their position at the surface by clasping with their tails the cords and buoys of the crab-pots, sticks, or any other substance they may find floating at the surface. The whole of the caudal portion of the body is coiled round the stick or cord, and the heads lie either horizontally or at right angles to the surface. In some seasons the buoy-ropes of the crab-pots are literally obscured by them from the surface of the water down as far as the eye can penetrate."

The little Worm Pipe may also lay claim to the title of "painted;" for its anterior parts especially are generally marked with spots of pure white bounded by a border of black, while the cheeks and throat are covered with a delicate flush of purple. The habit mentioned by Mr. Couch of curling the tip of the tail around objects in the water is manifested quite as strongly by this more slender and more flexible species, which does not possess any trace of a fin at the tail-tip. This prehensile organ is in a moment whipped round the stem of any sea-weed or similar object with which it comes into contact; and thus moored, the pretty Pipe throws its little body into all sorts of elegant contortions, hanging freely down, or elevating itself almost perpendicularly, at pleasure.[8]

The fins in this genus of fishes are very small and feeble. Some of them have a pair of excessively minute pectorals, an almost invisible anal, and a tiny fan for a caudal. All have a short delicate dorsal, and several have no other fin than this, of which section the Worm Pipe is an example. Yet, according to the Swedish naturalist, Fries, the young of this species possess at their birth both caudal and pectorals, the former extending far up on the body, both on the dorsal and ventral edges. All these are in after life absorbed except sufficient to form the permanent dorsal. This fin, in the whole family, is excessively filmy, and is, during the action of swimming, fluttered with a very rapid screw-like vibration.

Slight as are the organs of motion, they are sufficient for the Pipe-fish's ordinary exigencies; and Mr. Patterson has recorded an interesting example of their capability to achieve movements of an unusual kind. He had captured the finest of our species,[9] which he had committed to a basin of sea-water. "One of the long-bodied crustacea, which are abundant during fine weather, and had been captured at the same time, was placed in the same vessel. It was a species of *Gammarus*, and about an inch in length. The *Gammarus* would seem to have got tired of swimming, and, for a resting-place, it fixed itself on the back of the Pipe-fish, close to the tail. The fish had not been a consenting party to this arrangement, and soon evinced its dissatisfaction, by lashing the tail with great violence on each side, to dislodge the intruder. He, however, kept his hold; and so soon as the fish ceased for a few seconds, he crept a little further up on the back, as if aware that the velocity of movement was less near the centre of the circle. The fish lashed the water again with great violence, but without any good result; and so soon as it stopped, the *Gammarus* crept up a little nearer to the head. The *Gammarus* seemed to be the marine prototype of the old Man of the Mountain, whose pertinacity, in retaining his place on the back of Sinbad the Sailor, is a portion of that lore of our boyhood, that is never afterwards forgotten. The Pipe-fish then changed its tactics. Instead of lashing with its tail, it gave to its whole body the kind of movement it might have had if fixed on a Lilliputian spit, and in the act of being roasted. The body was made to revolve round and round on its longitudinal axis; but the *Gammarus* still held on, and, at each interval of rest, made a few steps further in advance. This was more than once repeated, until, pitying the poor Pipe-fish, we removed the cause of its annoyance to another vessel."[10]

Among these pleasing little fishes some very remarkable deviations from the ordinary economy of animals occur, though not quite unique. In almost all the Mammalia of Australia, as is well known, the female has an external pouch or false belly, into which the young is transferred at a very early period of embryonic life, and there matured. In the *Pipa*, or Surinam Toad, the eggs are laid by the female, and placed on the broad back of the male, cells being then formed in the skin, which receive the eggs till they are hatched.

Somewhat like the latter is the case of the Pipe-fishes, among which it is the male that acts as wet-nurse. Along his belly runs a groove, formed by two flaps of skin, within which the eggs, when laid by the female, are placed, and in which they are safely carried till the birth of the infant fry.

How wondrously diversified are the modes ordained by the Divine Wisdom for maintaining the economy of creation! What a depth is there in that revelation concerning the everlasting Son, "in whom we have redemption," —that "all things were created by Him, and for Him, and He is before all things, and by Him all things *hold together* (συνεστηκε)."[11]

I have taken in similar circumstances a little fish which is considered very rare on our shores, the Butterfly Blenny.[12] The Mediterranean coasts of Europe are its proper home, where it resorts to the tufts of weeds, feeding on minute *Crustacea* and *Mollusca*. Yarrell cites three examples as having been obtained by dredging off South Devon, and one from which his own figure was taken, which was obtained among the rocks of Portland. As he alludes to no other British examples, he probably knew of no more. Mr. R. Q. Couch, in his *Notes on the Fishes of the Land's End*, says, "A single specimen of this fish was taken by a trawl-net in 1845, but the spot on the first dorsal fin was so obscure as scarcely to be noticed."

It is therefore with the more satisfaction that I can record the possession of two specimens, one taken in Weymouth Bay from deep water, the other among the hanging weeds of this shore. Both were in full development and high colour, the spot on the fin from which both the specific and the popular names are derived, strongly marked, so that I am enabled to give a representation of this interesting fish in its vivid hues, as it appears in life and health.

The form is thick-set, as is that of the other more common species of the genus; the forehead is, however, rounded and less abrupt, which imparts to it a different physiognomy. The fins are ample, with the exception of the ventrals, which in all this genus consist of two rays each; the pectorals very large, nearly circular, transparent and colourless, with pearly rays. The dorsal is divided into two portions, of which the first is elevated like a tall sail, the first ray standing up a long way beyond the membrane. Its colour is smoke-brown, deeper at the summit; towards the hind end of this portion there is a large round black spot, surrounded by a well-defined pale ring; very conspicuous, indeed, in my specimens, and strikingly suggestive of the eye-spots in the wings of many butterflies and moths. As if conscious of its beauty, the fish travels *with all sail set*, and thus shows its characteristic mark to advantage.

The body is varied with different hues of brown, black, and grey, the deeper colours forming transverse bands on the upper parts; while along each side run two rows of spots of pearly azure, defined by a dark edge.

Just in front of each eye there is a small appendage which looks like a small horn, with the tip and edge cut into segments; it is but a projection of the skin. Several other species of the genus have similar ornaments on various parts of the face and head: I have no conception of their use in the economy of the tribe.

There is a curious peculiarity in the eye of this fish, which I do not perceive in the Shanny, nor in any other species. On looking cursorily at it, you would suppose that it had a very widely-opened pupil, surrounded by a white line, which appears to be the interior edge of the iris. But on watching it with a lens, the whole of this dark area within the white circle is seen to be prominent, convex, and opaque, of a substance which reflects the richest metallic lustre, sometimes turquoise blue, but changing in other lights to a bronzed or gilded appearance; not, however, as if burnished, but as if dusted with metal filings. In the centre of this area a pupil alternately opens and closes, expanding and contracting circularly, with a regular systole and diastole, a little more quickly than the periodic opening and shutting of the gill-covers, but nearly corresponding therewith. The contraction of this pupil is perfect, so as completely to conceal it, and the expansion is irregular in extent, though regular in time; sometimes it is but just perceptible, when the next opening will be as wide as usual. Occasionally, the motion ceases, the area displaying no trace of a pupil.

Mr. Ross of Topsham, an excellent marine zoologist, has observed a highly curious habit in the commonest of the Blennies. It is the Smooth Shan, Shanny, or Tansy,[13] of our southern shore-bays. I was aware that these little fishes were capable of enduring with impunity a protracted exposure to the air, which would be fatal to many, but I did not suppose that the habit was normal and constant. The facts reported are of great interest.

"A specimen of the fish," says Mr. Ross, "was brought to me on the 3d of June. On placing it in a glass vessel of sea-water, it appeared perfectly quiet for some hours, but at length became restless, and made frequent attempts to throw itself out of the water. It then occurred to me, that on a former occasion, when by the sea-side, I had a Gattoruginous Blenny, in a vessel with some Actiniæ and Serpulæ, which regularly passed a portion of its time on a stone; I therefore placed one in the glass. The *Blennius pholis* immediately leaped on it completely out of the water. It therefore appears that these changes are necessary to its existence. On going to the front of the house, I perceived that it was near low water. Knowing that it would flow till ten o'clock that night, I watched the movements of my little captive, and as the clock struck, had the gratification of seeing it plunge again into its natural element. It has now been more than five months in my possession, and has proved throughout that period a regular and correct tide-indicator. I was well aware that these fish are constantly left by the receding tide on the rocks, remaining concealed in small basins or holes, under the weed, till the returning flood; still I was not prepared to see a fish voluntarily quit the water, and pass so large a portion of its existence in a different element, and by instinct alone time its change of position so exactly."[14]

This is a highly curious observation; but, as to Mr. Ross's inference that "these changes are necessary to its existence," I may remark that I have been in the habit of keeping the Shanny for long periods in my tanks, without any opportunity for such alternations.

I catch at the same time, and at the same place, but under different conditions, a tiny fish of the same family, possessing remarkable delicacy of appearance. It is the Freckled Goby of Yarrell, Spotted Goby of Pennant, *le Boulereau blanc* of the French, the Polewig and the Pollybait of the Thames fisherman.[15] Yarrell tells us that it is most plentiful in the Thames, doubtless coming up with the tide, for I do not think it would live with the admixture of any great quantity of fresh water. It is used for the baiting of the hook in the line-fishing, like most other minute fishes that can be taken in sufficient numbers, and with sufficient certainty, by means of the net.

Here I find it in the wide pools that lie in the hollows of the ledges, with a bottom of sand, and not more than an inch or two of water. Under an August sun this becomes, during the three or four hours that the receding sea of spring-tides leaves it, quite tepid; often standing at blood-heat, or even higher. In these shallows the Freckled Goby lies, companion of the Sand-shrimp, which in size, translucency, and colouring, it closely resembles. It remains quite still, as if conscious of its safety-point, for it is with difficulty visible, even if your eye is resting on the very spot; what little of colour it has being exactly that of the surrounding sand. When danger comes too close, it shoots to another part, and you detect that something indistinct passed rapidly along; it does not, however, habitually seek the shelter of the fringing weeds, as a Prawn would, but suddenly becomes still in the open space, settling close down upon the sand, just as the Shrimps do. It is rather harder to capture than one would suppose; but I find the surest way is to place the mouth of the net obliquely on the bottom, a few inches in front of the fish, without disturbing him; then, approaching him with my hand from behind, he leaps in and is secured. When taken it is a pretty and attractive little species; very pellucid, showing the stomach and intestine quite plainly through the muscles, as a dark mass; and even the brain, which also is darkish, probably from the number and fulness of the blood-vessels which supply that important organ. This apparition of the internal viscera in a vertebrate animal strikes one as something unusual and remarkable.

The entire surface of this translucent and almost colourless body is studded with minute specks of rust-red, and with still smaller ones of opaque pale yellow, which are visible only with the aid of a lens. Nothing can be more sand-like than this aggregation of red and yellow dots, and surely we must look upon it, in conjunction with the habits of the little feeble fish, as a special provision for its safety, ordained by Him whose tender mercies are over *all* His works. The eyes are very prominent, and set in very thick and dark orbits; the pupil is surrounded by a crimson iris. Great size and prominence of the eyes is quite characteristic of the fishes of this family. It may be that their habitual residence in the shallows exposes them peculiarly to the attacks of enemies; and the size of the eye may be connected with a greater power or quickness of sight, indicating a proportionate development of the optic nerve. But this is only a conjecture.

The pectorals, as usual, are large, but quite colourless, and hence can scarcely be discerned, or only like a film of clear talc. The two dorsals are ordinarily carried, when at rest, depressed quite down to the back, but are elevated in swimming. The tail is crossed vertically by bands of red dots. Like most of the sand-loving creatures, the Freckled Goby does not long survive captivity in a tank. Perhaps, however, this may be

Plate XXIV

Freckled Goby. Butterfly Blenny.

because our aquariums are not specially arranged with a view to their instincts. A very wide shallow vessel, with a bottom of sand, and a piece or two of rough rock for shadow, stocked with Freckled Gobies, Weavers, Sand-launces, Shrimps, Venuses, Naticas, etc., might do well. But these will not do with an ordinary collection of rock-loving things.

What Crantz says of the coast of Greenland is not less true of our own rocky sea-margins. "These shores are the best and grandest school for the study of fishes. Here the naturalist may attain a fundamental acquaintance with them, and discover the nature and instincts of each species. It would prove a spacious field of observation for a curious, inquiring mind, which would often fall into a train of profound meditation, as he surveyed the nature and function and relations of the inhabitants of the vast ocean, from the minutest insect, scarce perceptible to the eye, to the monstrous whales, together with the seemingly fabulous great sea-monsters, and the equally inconceivable zoophytes, or" [as then supposed] "half-animal sea productions. Yet, after all, the most speculative and penetrating human mind will never be able to pry so deep into the manifold wisdom of God in his creatures as to search them out to perfection; even the meanest of them, and such as are before every one's eyes. But, for that very reason, because we are so imperfect, we are never satiated with the study of nature, nor weary of rendering that praise to the Lord of Nature which He expects from His creatures."

Plate XXV

Granulate Brittle-Star. Sun-Star.

IX.
September

Good service was done to the cause of science when, some fifteen or twenty years since, Robert Ball of Dublin invented the naturalist's dredge. A huge unwieldy form of the implement has indeed been long in use among fishermen for the obtaining of oysters and scallops; a clumsy affair, of which the frame, furnished only with a single lip, was four or five feet wide, and the bag was formed of iron rings, two inches in diameter,—a loose and open sort of chain-mail. There was an object in this last arrangement; for while the chain-work retained all oysters of a marketable size, the meshes allowed all to escape which were of less dimensions, and so these remained on the ground to grow bigger for another season.

Naturalists did gladly avail themselves of this uncouth apparatus, and many valuable things were scraped from the sea-bottom thereby; but they never could have used it without regret at the thought of the thousands of unknown and unimagined treasures which must have slipped through those huge meshes. No object of less size than two inches in any diameter had a chance of being brought to the surface; and how many precious specimens range below these dimensions we are now beginning to discover.

Yes; I'm glad I have got a Ball's dredge; and this fair autumnal morning I mean to use it; to go out with honest Harvey, and scrape the stony sea-bottom in the offing yonder. It is a nice portable affair, that one hand can manage; eighteen inches by four and a half are the dimensions of the frame; the scraping lips are double, one on each edge, so that, however the dredge falls on the bottom, it is sure to scrape; a double bridle from each side meets in a ring to which the rope is made fast; and the bag, some twenty inches deep, is made of stout twine, well netted, with meshes about half an inch in diameter. Owing to the swelling of the twine in the water, there is scarcely anything of value that will escape such a net.

Harvey has carried down everything to Babbicombe Beach, and now all is on board; dredge, sieve, pans, buckets, jars, bottles, *ad libitum*. And now we run up the mainsail and jib, and with a light westerly breeze and smooth water, lie up for Exmouth, or a little beyond, for about an hour.

Now we have made our offing, and can look well into Teignmouth Harbour, the bluff point of the Ness some four miles distant, scarcely definable now against the land. We pull down sails, set her head for the Orestone Rock, and drift with the tide. The dredge is hove overboard, paying out some forty fathoms of line, for we have about twelve or fourteen fathoms' water here, with a nice rough, rubbly bottom, over which, as we hold the line in hand, we feel the iron lip of the dredge grate and rumble, without catches or jumps. Now and then, for a brief space, it goes smoothly, and the hand feels nothing; that is when a patch of sand is crossed, or a bed of zostera, or close-growing sea-weeds, each a good variation for yielding.

"What d'ye say, Tom? Shall we try it?"

"Ay, ay, sir!"

Up comes the wet line under Tom's strong muscular pulling, and as it leaves his hands, we coil it snug in the bows of the boat. Dimly appears the dredge some yards below the surface, and now it comes to light, and is fairly lifted aboard. "'Tis mortal heavy!" Well it may be, for here is a pretty cargo of huge, rough stones, great oyster-shells, and I know not what. Bright starlets and crimsons and yellows I discern, and many a twinkling movement among the chaos raises our expectations of something good. We pick out the most conspicuous things, and now turn the whole contents bodily on this old shutter, which we have laid across two thwarts. 'Tis done; and now heave the dredge over again, and we are free to work at the mass with all our eyes and fingers.

The first thing that strikes attention from its size and brilliant colours is a great Sun-star.[1] This is a noble example of the Star-fish family, not uncommon off these shores. The disk of this specimen is two inches and a half wide, and the rays, which are here eleven in number (more commonly twelve), are one and three-fourths long, so that the total diameter of this fine creature is six inches. The upper surface is convex and cake-like, but can be plumped up at pleasure. Both disk and rays are studded with small whitish knobs, which seem simple to the eye, but when magnified are seen to be formed of short and close-set spines. They are not regularly arranged on the rays any more than on the disk. Slightly elevated ridges connect the knobs, thus covering the whole surface with a raised network.

The general colour of the disk is a fine rose-pink, deeper on a circular area in the centre; the network is a deeper rose, especially just around the bases of the knobs. The base of each ray is crossed by a broad band of pure white, both knobs and network. The remainder of the rays is of a pale orange-scarlet, becoming more truly scarlet in the middle portion; the network of the same hue, but deeper. Over the entire surface the areas of the net are occupied by series of ovate whitish hollows, from each of which protrudes a minute clear bladder or closed tube, exactly like those we lately saw in the little Starlet. The madreporic plate is seen about midway between the centre and one of the angles, as a tiny cake-shaped white body, grooved exactly like a brain-stone.

Beneath, the rays are ploughed with a deep groove, in which are two rows of sucker-feet; towards the tip, however, their place is supplied by long slender pointed tentacular processes. The avenues are bordered by flat knobs, set like the edging-stones of a garden walk, each of which carries five or six spines radiating like a fan, *lengthwise*. Each set sends off a branch which carries another fan placed *transversely,* of six to ten spines. Then the white satiny skin sends up at the very edge of the ray short stems, each bearing a group of fifteen to twenty spines, having a tendency to a transverse arrangement, but not in a single row. These form the edges of the rays, seen from above and below. At the bases of the rays beneath, the angle terminates in a broad plate, which is cut into a comb of about eighteen flat spines, the whole having a semi-oval outline, projecting towards the mouth. At the tip of each avenue we discern the little scarlet eye, well protected by the crowding rows of fans.

The mouth gapes, and gives an unexpected insight into the diet of this gaily-painted gentleman. We see a bit of an Echinus shell, and on taking hold of it with a pair of pliers, and carefully dragging, lo! forth comes the entire box of a Purple-tipped Urchin, nearly an inch in diameter, empty of course, through the force of Mr. Sun's gastric juice, and denuded of spines. Ugh! the cannibal! to eat his own first cousin!

We put him into a shallow pan of water, where he crawls slowly. He is fond of curling the rays over his back, so as nearly to meet, perhaps to have a look at the new world in which he finds himself. Then he turns himself right over in the shallow water, bathing the under surface in the air, the suckers moving all the time to and fro with great rapidity, and (we fancy) with enjoyment.

Several specimens of the common Cross-fish occur, large and richly coloured, and many of the Urchin just named; but these we can find every day in-shore; so they are contemptuously thrown over the gunwale.

Ha! here is a fine thing! It is the Granulate Brittle-star,[2] a species said to be widely spread, but I never saw it before. It is confined to deep water. It is a very fine imposing species, reminding me (a strange comparison, you will say!) of the great South American hairy Spiders, with a brown body and long bristly legs sprawling over a width of eight or ten inches. Its hues are said to be various, but I will describe this as I see it.

The disk is a plump cushion slightly depressed in the centre, of a light reddish umber, or sand-brown. The base of each ray is rich redbrown, the colour encroaching on the disk with two points, and running down the medial line of the ray. This hue is bordered by velvety black, blending with it; and beyond the middle of the ray, the deepening brown is pretty well lost in the black. The ray is edged with spines standing out at right angles, and set in rows. These spines are black with grey points, and greatly augment the noble aspect of the creature. Each ray is about four and a half inches long, running off to a fine point.

The animal resents being turned over, and refuses to lie in a supine position, unlike the "malus pastor" of the poet. It curls and twists the slender ray-tips, crawls rapidly, and courses round and round the edge of the pan into which we have dropped it.

Let me anticipate here to narrate the after history of my captive. Consigned to a shallow tank at home, after a few days I missed him one morning, and on searching the whole room carefully, found him at length under the edge of the hearth-rug, some yards from the tank, with all his rays broken into many pieces, and only the short stumps remaining. Though dry and apparently dead, I perceived a slight movement in the stumps, which gave me hope of revival, and I replaced the poor maimed thing, sadly shorn of his glory, in the tank. He did revive; and the truncated ends of the ray-stumps enabled me to see the arrangement of the spines. These form about nine rows on each side, radiating fan-like; within the undermost row on each side is a row of flexible bladdery tubes much like the suckers, and like them protruding from orifices in the calcareous skeleton, but not retractile. They are studded with tiny warts, and terminate not in a sucking disk, but in a sort of bifid extremity. They are not used for locomotion, nor are they ordinarily applied to the ground as if tactile, and yet are continually thrown round so that the tip is brought up to the base, and this suddenly and abruptly, and every few seconds, as if something were captured and conveyed to the mouth; but this cannot be, for the mouth is not there, and nothing is seen to be seized. Perhaps some intelligence, in a way unimaginable by us, is thus obtained, of outward things.

The poor maimed creature managed to stump awkwardly about for a few days, but soon died, with no perceptible attempt to renew the self-amputated members.

The Brittle-stars appear to move by means of the flexibility of their long snake-like rays, the spines with which they are furnished enabling these organs to obtain a hold on the surface along which they crawl; and that so secure that even perpendicular and very smooth surfaces present no hindrance to their progression. They have no proper suckers; and the rays are not constituent portions of the body, containing part of the stomach and intestine as in the true Star-fishes, but imperforate appendages to it.

Crouching among the rubbish, with all its long limbs snugly packed together, as if hoping to find safety in being overlooked, we see a strange form of crustacea, the Angled Crab.[3] Vain hope! How can a creature of that bizarre form, and of those conspicuous colours, be concealed from notice by merely lying still? Gently touch him behind, and what an enormous length of limb is suddenly thrown out! If, according to the proverb, "kings have long arms," surely this must be the very monarch of the crabs; and most curiously are they folded when at rest, the fore-arm lying close, throughout its length, upon the upper arm, the elbow projecting far on each side. The carapace is sometimes described as rhomboidal, but this does not give us a correct idea of its form; its outline is rather that of an isosceles triangle, of which the apical half is cut off; the base of this truncate triangle, which is the front side of the shell, runs off into two sharp spines at the angles, and has also a broad projection in the middle, on each side of which are seated the long footstalks of the eyes, and which carries on its front the two pairs of antennæ. The thighs of the true legs are thin and blade-like, so that these limbs all pack one over the other very compactly.

The general colour is a light salmon-red, often with the hinder half of the carapace, and the inner sides of the limbs, of a pale buff. The eyes (not the stalks) and the movable finger of each hand, which is slender and elegantly curved, are polished black.

Not uncommon with us, it is not very often seen even by the naturalist, as it seems to be properly an inhabitant of deep water. Occasionally it is washed ashore on the beach by a heavy sea; but this is accidental. Montagu first ascertained it to be British by finding it at Kingsbridge, near Plymouth. Mr. Couch finds it common on the Cornwall coast, together with an allied, but certainly distinct, species, the *G. rhomboides* of the Mediterranean, to be identified by its lacking a second spine behind each angular one, which is well marked in our species. Though essentially a southern form, it occurs on the Dublin coast, and that in sufficient number to have obtained a popular appellation,—that of "Coffin-crab;" the term "coffin" being possibly a word of the Irish tongue, meaning something very different from that which it suggests to our ears.

Cranch records, as a curious habit of the species, that "they live in excavations formed in the hardened mud, and that their habitations, at the extremities of which they live, are open at both ends." This description implies a habitat above low water, if not above tidemarks; for where else could "hardened mud" be found? or if it were found in the deep water, how could it come under the observer's cognizance? However, I know that many marine creatures are littoral in some localities, which are exclusively deep-water subjects in others.

Several observant naturalists have noticed the frequency with which the species is obtained from the stomachs of the larger ground-feeding fishes, the cod especially. Mr. Ball has taken four at a time from a single cod in Youghal shambles. This is a well-known source for procuring rare specimens of the inhabitants of the deep, particularly Crustacea and the shelled Mollusca; for the fishes are expert and persevering and successful collectors of natural history, and are continually picking up objects for which the naturalist would almost give one of his eyes. Mr. Gordon of Elgin, some years ago, gave a long list of Crustacea, many of them of great rarity, which he had procured from stomachs of cod-fish, "through the agency of Widow Scott and her son John, of the fishing village of Stotfield," on the Moray Firth. His remarks are suggestive, not only to those residing on the coast, but to the denizens of inland towns. "By a small douceur to the fisherman's family, and by the assistance of the fish-curer on the coast, the fishmonger of the large town, or of some acquaintance in the fishing village, it is believed that almost any number of these now useless receptacles [viz., cod-stomachs], could be obtained. It may excite at first a little nausea to open up and examine these omnivorous reservoirs, but this will soon pass off; and were it of longer continuance than it is, the stores to be unfolded would amply compensate for all the disagreeable feeling that may for a time arise. It is not only the crustacean that is thus gathered from the inaccessible depths of the ocean, but often the rare shell, with its still rarer inhabitant. The radiated animal and the curious zoophyte will also be found congregated together there; all of them, no doubt, at times mutilated or partly

Plate XXVI

Nut-Crab. Angled-Crab.

digested, but not unfrequently fresh and complete, as if newly past the voracious jaws."

Two or three specimens of another curious crab are also in our haul. Unlike the *Gonoplax*, the little Nut-crab[4] is not by any means conspicuous in a chaotic heap like this; it requires a sharp eye, and one familiar with the form, to discern him. Remarkably sluggish, he remains motionless; his tiny limbs are almost concealed under the edges of his shell; his body is destitute of sharp angles; its colour is a dull white: in fact the eye might roam over it a dozen times without supposing it anything more than an irregular rubbed quartz pebble.

Yet when you pick it up, it is a pretty little Crab. The form of the body is unlike that of any other of our genera; indeed the type of which it is a representative, though largely developed in the tropical and sub-tropical seas, scarcely reaches to our shores. Some of the allied species in the hotter parts of the globe, are very curious, such as the *Calappa*, a crab in which the very short limbs are so closely packed to the body, and so wholly concealed by the smooth and rounded shell, that the curious sailor often picks it up and pockets it, as a pretty white stone, little suspecting that he has a living Crab in his fob. And there it lies for hours, perhaps, till he pulls out his supposed pebble, which has not ventured all the while to attempt to crawl.

I believe almost all we yet know of the habits of the timid little Nut-crabs is derived from the portrait that I drew of one of them[5] some years ago, from specimens that I obtained at Weymouth. Since then I have repeatedly kept it in captivity for long periods at a time, and indeed I have one or two now. Yet I have little to add to the sketch I then drew of its manners. It is inert, folding its tiny legs on itself when touched, and remaining motionless for some time. It buries itself in the gravel, descending backwards: this is a somewhat slow process, suited to its usual phlegmatic habit. It brings its hindmost pairs of feet on each side together; then thrusting down their united points, opens and expands them, forcing apart the gravel; at the same moment the posterior part of the body is brought down into the hollow thus made, and the action of the feet is repeated. The process is continued until the hinder parts are covered and the muzzle alone is visible, with the two claws. Thus it sits quite still, reminding one of a toad, the broad triangular pedipalps that fit so close occasionally opening, like the folding-doors of a tiny cabinet, and allowing the palpi to be thrust out to wipe the minute eyes. The face, when examined with a lens through the glass walls of the aquarium, has a most funny expression, being singularly like that of an ancient man.

Like many marine animals, *Ebalia* uses the hours of the night as its chief season of activity. As long as the candles are in the room, it remains pretty still, but as soon as darkness reigns, it sets out on its travels. Not indeed with the railway pace of some of its fellows does our little ancient travel; he is but a "slow coach;" but he gropes about among the pebbles, and is usually found the next morning, buried at some distance from the point where the previous evening had left him.[6]

The little specimens before us appear to belong to *Ebalia Bryerii*. It is porcellaneous white, tinged with pale scarlet. The little feet are painted scarlet on a white ground, especially the swollen-jointed claws, which are very gay, and under a lens show a marbled pattern of rich scarlet. This little Crab has an unique appearance, very attractive. Its motions are quick and sudden, mostly lateral, when alarmed; but it is habitually sluggish. Sometimes it appears to sham death; for if pushed, it at first tries to escape by running; but if the annoyance continues, it stiffens its limbs, and allows itself to be pushed without resistance; and when laid on its back in the water, will lie motionless for a minute or more, then suddenly turn over and crawl away.

Hosts of other things we capture in this summary sweeping of the sea-bottom, and by the time we have drifted down towards the Orestone, till we are close enough to make out the noble leaves of the tree-mallows that grow out of its rocky heights, we have accumulated a marvellous store,—almost enough, indeed, to set up a little provincial museum. Brittle-stars and urchins; cucumbers great and small; bivalve and univalve mollusks; swollen ascidians, smooth and warty; active, shuffling, sucking fishes; heaps of mossy *Bryozoa*; long bristling tufts of Hydroid zoophytes; naked worms, twining and writhing amidst the mass, gleaming in purple and pearl; sea-mice "armed in gold," like Virgil's Orion; tangled masses of Serpula-pipes, every one with its scarlet-crowned tenant; these, and multitudes of creatures besides, come up from the teeming sea-floor, and all at once claim our bewildered attention. And there is not one of the host that is not worthy of it; not one that would not be an eloquent witness of its Creator's glory; but we must for the present neglect them all (not without hope of another meeting with some of them at least), in order to devote a few moments to one group of remarkable interest.

It is that unaccountable association of diverse and unrelated creatures, which, if we had not repeatedly seen it, we should not believe; the companionship of the Hermit-crab with the beautiful Cloak-anemone.

Every one is familiar with that impudent and intrusive species of Hermit-crab,[7] which, with its foxy-brown head and legs protruding, rolls over shells and pebbles with rattling patter, on almost every beach. The species I speak of is quite distinct from that homely and amusing subject. Though attaining a size fully equal, its proportions are much slenderer and more elegant; and the colours,—a light fawn, set off with soft tints of azure, lilac, and scarlet,—are far more beautiful than those of its fellow; not to speak of technical characters which abundantly distinguish the two.

The companion of the Cloaklet, which bears the name of Mr. Prideaux of Plymouth, who first made it known, is exclusively a deep-water species. Found on various parts of our coast, it invariably occurs in this association. I believe the Crab in no instance lives without the Anemone, the Anemone in no instance without the Crab. Examples, indeed, do now and then occur, as mentioned by Forbes, in which the one comes up in the dredge without the other; but I believe this is only when the rude action of the dredge has frightened the Crab, and induced it suddenly to vacate the shell and desert its friend. The Bernard is never attended by any such companion.[8]

The history of the tenancy of univalve shells by these curious Crabs is well known; and the comic scenes that take place in the process of flitting from one tenement to another, larger and more commodious, have been so fully narrated by myself and other observers, that I shall assume the reader to be conversant with them.[9] And the rather because the association of the Crab with the Zoophyte is a thing so much more singular, so much more unaccountable, and so much less generally known, that I shall seek to tell the story in some detail.

To premise:—the Cloaklet is an anemone of the *Sagartia* family, beautiful in its colours and remarkable in its form. It is generally reddish-brown on the outer (lower) part of its body, which hue melts into snowy white on the upper parts; the whole studded with rosy-purple spots, and surmounted by a marginal line of pale scarlet. The tentacles and disk are pure white. It attains a rather large size, and has the peculiarity of being not round in its basal outline like other Anemones, but oblong, the base expanding in two lateral directions. It always selects the inner lip of an univalve shell for its place of adhesion, and the two lateral ends of its base gradually extend around the mouth of the shell till they meet on its outer edge, and unite with a suture: thus the outline of the animal forms a ring.

It had often been an interesting speculation with me, in what manner the due relation of size is maintained between the *Adamsia* and the shell, in the progressive growth of the former. There is a manifest proportion between the two, the young Cloaklet occupying a small shell, such as that of a *Littorina* or *Trochus*; the full-grown individual a large one, such as that of a *Natica* or *Buccinum*. The Crab is able to shift from a smaller to a larger shell when he needs enlarged accommodation; and since we know that his congener, *P. Bernhardus*, does this habitually, we naturally conclude that such is the habit of *P. Prideauxii*. Presuming then that this is the case, what becomes of the *Adamsia*?

If the Crab shifts his quarters and leaves the *Adamsia* behind, the association is broken, and we should constantly find *Paguri* without *Adamsiæ*, and *Adamsiæ* without *Paguri*. But we find neither the one nor the other.

On the other hand, if *Adamsia* is able to shift its quarters also, how does it proceed in its search for a new shell? If it forsakes the old tenement at the same time as the Crab, and together with it takes possession of the new one, by what means is unity of will and action secured? What communication of thought takes place from the one to the other? As the *Adamsia* does not adhere to the Crab, but to the shell, that is, as they are independent of each other's movements, who takes the initiative? Who goes to seek the lodging? And at what point of the transaction does the other come in? All these questions I had mused upon with interest; and at length received some light towards their solution.

Plate XXVII

Purple-Hermit Crab. Cloaklet. Common Hermit-Crab.

September

On the 10th of January, 1859, I obtained, by dredging, in Torbay, a specimen of *Adamsia palliata*, about half-grown, on a rather small shell of *Natica monilifera*, tenanted by a *Pagurus Prideauxii*, which seemed already too big for his habitation. Having put them into a well-established tank of large dimensions, the contents of which were in excellent condition, I succeeded in doing what I had never done before, domiciliating both Crab and *Adamsia*. Both continued in the highest health, and became quite at home.

After about three months, however, I noticed that the *Adamsia* was not looking so well. One side or wing had gradually loosed its hold of the shell-lip, so that it hung loosely down beneath the breast of the Crab. Yet in other respects the zoophyte seemed healthy. Latterly, too, the Crab had manifested symptoms of uncomfortable straitness, in the great extrusion of his fore-parts; so great, indeed, as to expose even the front of the soft abdomen. Yet I felt reluctant to present to the Crab a larger shell, fearing that he would, in availing himself of it, desert his zoophyte friend, which would then die, and I should lose the specimen.

At length the desire to solve a problem in science prevailed over this feeling. A fact is better than a specimen. And so (on April 21st) I selected from my cabinet a full-grown *Natica* shell, and placed it on the tank-floor, not far from the disconsolate trio.

The *Pagurus* presently found the new shell, and immediately began to overhaul it. He did not do, however, as his brother Bernhard would have done, at once shift into the new house. Having turned it mouth upward, he took hold of the outer and inner lip, each with a claw, and began to drag it about the tank. Occasionally he relinquished the hold of one claw, and probed the interior in the usual manner, and then resumed his march. I watched the proceedings for an hour or more, when, having other work to do, I left him alone.

The thought did occur to me—Can this delay be intended to make the *Adamsia* cognizant of what is in contemplation, and to prepare it for the change? But I dismissed it as unlikely.

After about an hour's absence I returned to the examination. The *Pagurus* was comfortably lodged in his new abode, and the old one, which now looked small indeed, lay deserted at some little distance. I eagerly turned the latter over, to see what was the condition of the *Adamsia*. Lo! no *Adamsia* was there; and the *Pagurus*, presently approaching the front of the tank, I saw, to my great gratification, that the old association was unbroken. There was the *Adamsia*, with one wing adhering to the lip of the new shell, and apparently the opposite wing also; but, from the position of the group, this I could not be quite certain of. The situation of the zoophyte was quite normal,—the centre immediately below the breast of the Crab, and in contact with the inner lip of the shell, while that wing which I could clearly see was creeping round upon the outer lip.

Examining now more closely the condition of things, with a lens, I saw that the central part of the *Adamsia*'s base was adherent by a small point of its surface to the under side of the thorax of the Crab, between the bases of the legs.

Now this adhesion to the Crab is a circumstance which, so far as I know, never takes place in the ordinary relations of the animals; and therefore I could not but think it an extraordinary and temporary provision for the removal of the *Adamsia* from the old to the new shell, and for the correct adjustment of its position on the latter.

How then can we avoid the conclusion, that, as soon as the Crab had found the new shell to be suitable for exchange, the *Adamsia* also was made cognizant of the same fact; and that, during the two hours which followed, the latter loosened its adhesion to the old shell, and, laying hold of the bosom of its protector, was by him carried to the new house, where immediately it began to secure the like hold to that which it had just relinquished?

Eleven days elapsed after the above observations were made, when I obtained another interesting fact bearing on this strange association. The *Adamsia* had not looked well since the change of residence; its adhesion to the shell had been but partial at the best, some days more, some days less, extensive; but for the most part a considerable portion of the zoophyte was hanging down from the shell. The Crab, on the other hand, was evidently in clover, and showed no inclination to go back to his old lodging.

On the 2d of May I found the *Adamsia* detached, and lying helpless on the bottom of the tank, beneath the Crab, who, when disturbed, walked off, leaving his companion behind. I thought now it was a gone case, and that it was all up with my elegant *protegée*.

An hour or two afterwards, however, how great was my surprise to see the *Adamsia* fairly established again, adhering to the shell by a good broad base, and looking more healthy than I had seen her for many a day! Strangely enough, she was adhering in a false position, having taken hold on the outer lip of the shell, instead of the inner, as usual. Here was a fresh proof of intelligence somewhere; and I at once set myself to find where.

Carefully taking up the shell with the aquarium-tongs, and bringing it close to the surface, but not out of water, I gently dislodged the *Adamsia* with my fingers, and allowed it to fall prone upon the bottom. I then released the shell with its tenant, and drove the latter towards the spot where the zoophyte lay.

No sooner did the Crab touch the *Adamsia* than he took hold of it with his claws, first with one, then with both, and I saw in an instant what he was going to do. In the most orderly and expert manner he proceeded to apply the *Adamsia* to the shell. He found it lying base upward, and therefore the first thing was to turn it quite round. With the alternate grasps of the two pincer-claws, nipping up the flesh of the *Adamsia* rudely enough, as it seemed, he got hold of it so that he could press the base against the proper part of the shell, the inner lip. Then he remained quite still, holding it firmly pressed, for about ten minutes; at the end of which time he cautiously drew away first one claw, and then the other; and, beginning to walk away, I had the pleasure to see that the *Adamsia* was once more fairly adhering, and now in the right place.

Two days after the *Adamsia* was again lost. On searching I discovered it lying in a crevice, whence I plucked it, and laid it on the bottom. Here again the Crab found it, and immediately went through the same process as last described, and again made it adhere. But I saw that the *Adamsia* was unhealthy, for it seemed to have but enfeebled power of retaining its hold. The manifestation of the mode in which the instinctive actings of the two creatures occur is, however, sufficiently clear. The Crab is certainly the more active promoter of the partnership; it is abundantly evident that he values the company of his elegant but very heterogeneous associate. These last observations compel the conclusion that the claws of the Crab are always employed in the transference of the Cloaklet from shell to shell.[10]

But what a series of instincts does this series of facts open to us! The knowledge by the Crab of the qualities of the new shell; the delay of his own satisfaction till his associate is ready; the power of communicating the fact to her; the power in her of apprehending the communication; her immediate obedience to the intimation; her relinquishment of her wonted hold, which for months at least had never been interrupted; her simultaneous taking of a new, unwonted hold, where alone it could have been of any use; the concerted action of both; the removal; her relinquishment of the transitory adhesion as soon as its purpose was accomplished; her simultaneous grasp of the new shell in the proper places;—all these are wonderful to contemplate, wonderful considered singly, far more wonderful in their cumulation. Is there not here much more than what our modern physiologists are prone to call automatic movements, the results of reflex sensorial action? The more I study the lower animals, the more firmly am I persuaded of the existence in them of psychical faculties, such as consciousness, intelligence, will, and choice! and *that*, even in those forms in which as yet no nervous centres have been detected.

Plate XXVIII

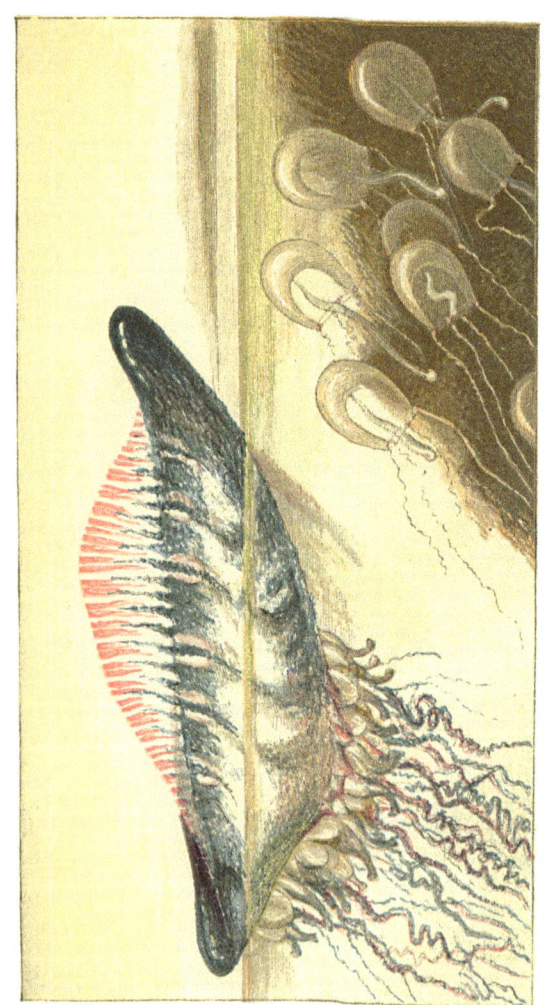

Portuguese Man-of-War. Tongued Sarsia.

X.
October

The naturalist who has occasion to make a voyage over the warmer regions of the ocean, is continually delighted by the sight of numberless forms of animals, principally of the lower invertebrate classes, which either habitually swim at the surface of the sea, or come thither at intervals to enjoy the stimulus of the atmospheric air. Many of these are exceedingly curious and interesting; many totally unlike any forms that occur on the shores of temperate countries; many elegant in contour, and adorned with brilliant colours. Perhaps there is scarcely any that takes a stronger hold on the fancy, certainly none is more familiar, than a little thing that he daily marks floating in the sunlit waves, as the ship glides swiftly by, which the sailors tell him is the Portuguese man-of-war.[1] Perhaps a dead calm has settled over the sea; and the observer, as he leans over the bulwarks of the ship, has opportunities of scrutinizing the ocean-rover at leisure, as it lazily rises and falls on the long sluggish heavings of the glassy surface. Then he sees that the comparison of the stranger to a ship is a felicitous one; for, at a little distance it might well be mistaken for a child's mimic ship, shining in all the gaudy painting in which it came out of the toy-shop; and he is ready to pity the forlorn urchin in tunic and knickerbockers, whose cherished boat has broken her moorings of thread, and drifted with winds and tides far, far out of reach of land.

Not unfrequently does one of the tiny vessels come so close alongside that, by means of the ship's bucket, with a little assistance from a smart fellow, who has jumped into the "chains" with a boat-hook, it is captured, and brought on deck to be subjected to scientific examination. A dozen voices are however lifted, warning you by no means to touch it, for well the experienced seaman knows its terrific powers of defence. It does not now appear so like a ship as when it was at a distance. It is an oblong bladder of tough membrane, varying considerably in shape (and hence no two original figures agree in this respect), and also in size, from less than an inch in length to the size of a man's hat. Once in a voyage to Mobile, when rounding the Florida Reef, I was nearly a whole day passing through a fleet of these little Portuguese men-of-war, which studded the smooth sea as far as the eye could reach, and must have extended for many miles. These were of all sizes within the limits I have mentioned. Generally, there is a conspicuous difference between the two extremities of the bladder, one end being rounded, while the other is more pointed, or is terminated by a small knob-like swelling, or beak-shaped excrescence, where there is a minute orifice. Sometimes, however, no such excrescence is visible, and the orifice cannot be detected.

The bladder is filled with air, and therefore floats almost wholly on the surface. Along the upper side, nearly from end to end, runs a thin ridge of membrane, which is capable of being erected at the will of the animal to a considerable height, fully equal at times to the entire width of the bladder, when it represents an arched fore-and-aft sail, the bladder being the hull. From the bottom of the bladder, near the thickest extremity, where there is a denser portion of the membrane, depends a crowded mass of organs, most of which take the form of very slender, highly contractile, and moveable threads, which hang down into the deep to a depth of many feet, or even occasionally, of several yards.

The colours of this curious creature are very vivid: the bladder, though in some parts transparent and colourless, and in some specimens almost entirely so, is in general painted with the richest blues and purples, mingled with green and crimson to some less extent; these all being, not as sometimes described, iridescent or changeable reflections, but positive colours, independent of the incidence of light, and, for the most part possessing great depth and fulness. The sail-like erectile membrane is transparent, tinted towards the edge with a lovely rose-pink line, the colours arranged in a peculiar fringe-like manner.

When examined anatomically, the bladder is found to be composed of two walls of membrane, which are lined with cilia, and have between them the nutritive fluid which supplies the place of blood. Besides this, the double membrane is turned in, somewhat as the foot of a stocking is inverted, when ready for putting on; and thus there is a bladder within a bladder, both having double walls. The inner (*pneumatocyst*) is much smaller than the outer (*pneumatophore*); and the point where it is turned in is contracted to the almost imperceptible orifice that has been mentioned. The inner bladder sends up closed tubular folds into the crest, which, being invested by the membranous walls of the outer sac, give to the sail that appearance of vertical wrinkles which is conspicuous.

Most formidable are the powers which reside in the long tentacles. Each of these is an excessively slender ribbon of contractile substance, connected at its base with a translucent bag, and carrying at short intervals throughout its length semi-rings of thread-cells (*cnidæ*), similar to those of our Sea-anemones, but of far more deadly virulence. Mr. Bennett, who, for the sake of science, ventured to test their powers, has left us a terrific account of his sufferings. "On one occasion," he says, "I tried the experiment of its stinging powers upon myself, intentionally; when, on seizing it by the bladder portion, it raised the long cables by muscular contraction of the bands situated at the base of the feelers, and, entwining the slender appendages about my hand and finger, inflicted severe and peculiarly pungent pain, adhering most tenaciously at the same time, so as to be extremely difficult of removal. The stinging continued during the whole time that the minutest portion of the tentacula remained adherent to the skin. I soon found that the effects were not merely confined to the acute pungency inflicted, but produced a great degree of constitutional irritation: the pain extended upwards along the arm, increasing not only in extent but in severity, apparently acting along the course of the absorbents, and could only be compared to a severe rheumatic attack; the pulse was accelerated, and a feverish state of the whole system was produced; the muscles of the chest even were affected, the same distressing pain felt on taking a full respiration as obtains in a case of acute rheumatism. The secondary effects were very severe, continuing for nearly three-quarters of an hour; the duration of the pain being probably longer, in consequence of the time and delay occasioned by removing the exciting and virulent tentacula from the skin, as they adhered to it, by the aid of the stinging capsules, with an annoying degree of tenacity. On the whole being removed, the pain began gradually to abate; but during the day a peculiar numbness was felt, accompanied also by an increased temperature in the limb upon which the stings had been inflicted. For some hours afterwards the skin displayed white elevations or wheals on the parts stung, similar to those usually seen resulting from the poison of the stinging-nettle. The intensity of the pain depends in some degree upon the size and consequent power of the creature; and after it has been removed from the water for some time, the stinging property, although still continuing to act, is found to have perceptibly diminished. To remove the irritation, at first cold water was applied, but this, instead of alleviating, increased the evil: an application of vinegar relieved the unpleasant symptoms, and olive oil has produced a similar beneficial effect. I have observed that this irritative power is retained for some weeks after the death of the animal in the vesicles of the cables; and even linen cloth which had been used for wiping off the adhering tentacles, when touched, still retained the pungency, although it had lost the power of producing such violent constitutional irritation."[2]

Among the tentacles there are seen many depending organs, which take somewhat the shape of a claret-bottle, with the mouth a little expanded. These are highly moveable, turning and bending themselves in various directions. They are termed *polypites*, and are the mouths and stomachs of the animal: taking-in and digesting food, much as the protrusile lips of an Anemone do. Mr. Bennett describes the *Physalia* as seizing and benumbing small fishes by means of the tentacles, which are alternately contracted to half-an-inch, and then shot out with amazing velocity to a length of several feet, and which drag the helpless and entangled prey to the sucker-like mouths, the stomach-cavities of which were filled while he looked-on, with atoms of the flesh absorbed.

Dr. Wallich thinks Mr. Bennett must have mistaken what he saw; because he has observed that in a great number of cases the *Physalia* is accompanied by small fishes, which play around and among the depending tentacles without molestation. He has in so many cases seen this, and even witnessed the actual contact of the fishes with the tentacles, with no inconvenience to the former, that he too hastily concludes that "the urticating organs are innocuous." Surely the premises by no means warrant such an inference. There is no antagonism between the two series of facts witnessed by such excellent observers; the venomous virulence of these organs has been abundantly proved by many naturalists, myself among the number, and Mr. Bennett, to his cost, as narrated above. We have only to suppose that the injection of the poison is under the control of the *Physalia*'s will, and the impunity of the bold little fishes is sufficiently accounted for.

That wonderful river that flows with a well-defined course through the midst of the Atlantic,—the Gulf-stream,—brings on its warm waters many of the denizens of the tropical seas, and wafts them to the shores on which its waves impinge. Hence it is that so many of the proper pelagic creatures are from time to time observed on the coasts of Cornwall and Devon. The Portuguese man-of-war is among them, sometimes paying its visits in fleets; more commonly in single stranded hulks. Scarcely a season passes without one or more of these lovely strangers occurring in the vicinity of Torquay; and from one of these I took the opportunity of making the careful drawing with which I illustrate this paper.[3] The fishermen and similar persons who pick them up, always endeavour to make a harvest of their captures, not by the sale, but by the exhibition of them, sometimes carrying the specimen from door to door, sometimes erecting a temporary screen in some place of resort, exaggerating the rarity and value of the specimen outrageously. This summer (1862) I have known of three in this vicinity; and have heard of one at the Isle of Wight, in July, which forms the subject of a memoir and a coloured figure by Mr. Humphreys in the *Intellectual Observer*; also, a fleet of hundreds scattered over both sides of the same island in August, as recorded by Mr. Rogers in the *Zoologist*; and finally, one at Tenby in July, obtained by Mr. Hughes, and recorded in the last-named periodical.

Mr. Hughes in his account mentioned a circumstance as normal, which, being unknown to me, excited my curiosity. His specimen was accompanied by "its attendant satellites, two *Velellæ*." In reply to my inquiries my friend gives me the following information:— "My authority for the association of *Velella* with *Physalia* is Jenkins, the collector at Tenby, who was attending me when they were found.

"The *Physalia* was taken by me first; and, while I was admiring it, I noticed that Jenkins continued searching for something. Immediately afterwards he came up with the *Velella* in his hand, at the same time stating they were generally found with the Portuguese man-of-war. As I had found the man very honest and truthful in his dealings with me (and not previously being familiar with either of the creatures), I accepted the information as correct."

The *Velella* is a creature closely allied to the *Physalia*, having the same essential structure, but differing greatly in form and appearance. It consists of a flat disk of thin cartilaginous shell, of a long rectangular outline, on which stands erect another similar plate somewhat triangular, extending across from corner to corner. One large polypite or mouth hangs down from the centre of the under side, and short tentacles project on all sides from the edges of the horizontal plate. The internal structure is very complex. The whole is enclosed in a thin layer of flesh, which is tinged of a fine blue colour, sometimes varied with purple and green. It is generally about two inches long, and the erect plate rather less in height. As the little creature floats on the waves, this plate forms a sail, and the breeze playing upon it, imparts to the whole animal, according to Mr. Bennett, a rotatory motion.[4]

Both these oceanic forms of the class *Hydrozoa* agree in being quite unprovided with any apparatus for locomotion. Though their parts can be moved among themselves, and sometimes with much vigour, as we have seen in the case of the tentacles of the *Physalia*, yet the whole organism would be absolutely confined for life to one spot, were the elements motionless around it: it is merely passively driven hither and thither by the winds and waves. But there are other members of the class, and even some belonging to the same order, which have express organs of locomotion. A most exquisite example is found in *Stephanomia*, of which a specimen was taken in Kingstown harbour in July 1856, by Mr. Joseph Greene, and described and figured in the "Proceedings of the Dublin University Zoological Association" for that year. The float (*pneumatocyst*) is a small bladder, which is filled with air, and which has the appearance, when alive, of a globule of quicksilver; while the slight inequalities of its surface reflect the light in such a manner that it often looks as if a fine network of crimson veins ramified over its surface. From the end of this oval bladder a long fleshy tube hangs down in the water to the distance of six or seven inches, the upper part of which is surrounded by a number—seven to ten—of little clear transparent bells, looking very much like the blossoms of our common Arbutus, and crowded, like flowers with short footstalks, on the stem. These swimming bells (*nectocalyces*) are true organs of locomotion; for by their contraction they drive out the water contained in their cavities, and by their combined impulse, all acting together, shoot the whole creature forward. This action I will explain more in detail presently.

The long tube or common stem is very irritable, and under stimulus is coiled up in a spiral, then gradually relaxed, and allowed to hang loosely down. Attached to it throughout are the *polypites*, or stomach-mouths, protected by leaf-like organs, which overlap them. Numerous tentacles, too, of exceeding length and tenuity, and throwing off branches, spring from the stem throughout its length, all the extremities of each forming tiny oval knobs of spiral coils, the whole capable of being thrown into the most beautiful and graceful convolutions, now bent at right angles, and again thrown out in a series of light airy-looking arches.

The exquisitely beautiful specimen described was taken in sultry weather, when the sea was perfectly calm. "It lived in a large globe of sea-water for several days, and was a most striking and beautiful object: it generally lay quite upright in the water, the slightest ripple upon the surface of which set it in motion; and immediately coiling up its fishing lines,

Plate XXIX

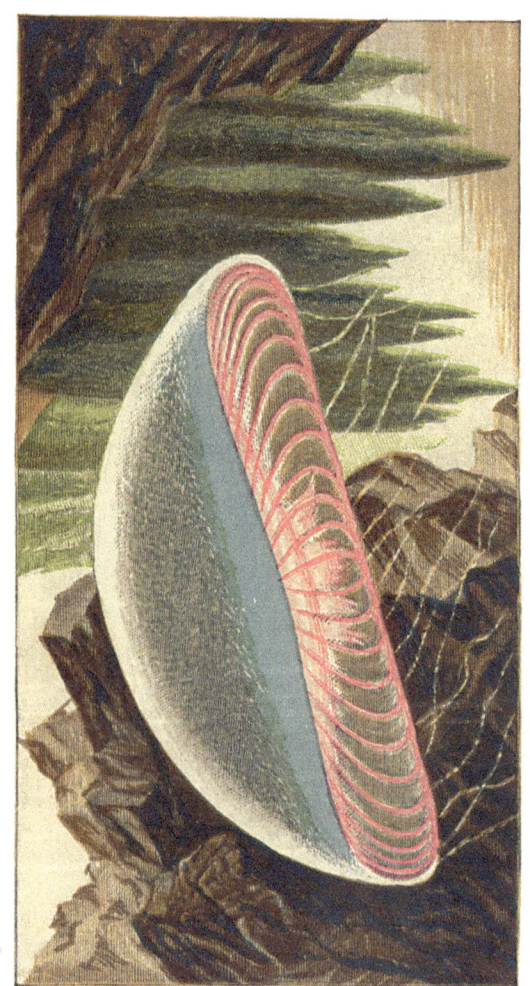

Forbesian Aequorea.

and shortening the length of its stolon by about one-third, it threw its set of little balloons into strong pulsations, until, weary of descending, it submitted to be guided by its brightly glittering head, and soon ascended to the surface. When subjected to examination it soon died, and was not long until it had completely broken itself up."[5]

The *nectocalyx* or swimming-bell is, however, seen in a much more developed condition in the delicate forms which swarm in our harbours and about our rocky coasts in summer and early autumn, and are known by the name of Naked-eyed Medusæ. A common and very characteristic example of this order is the Tongued Sarsia,[6] in which a single swimming-bell forms the greatest portion of the whole creature. It is a tall dome of crystalline colourless flesh, thick at the summit and thinning off at the edges; about half an inch in height. From the interior of this dome hangs the single polypite, exactly as the clapper hangs from the top of a bell. It is long and cylindrical, abruptly attenuated at the upper part into a sort of foot-stalk, and at the extremity enlarging into four fleshy, very protrusile, lips, capable of seizing and sucking in an object much larger than the diameter of the whole polypite. I have seen a Sarsia, in confinement in a tank, lay hold of, and swallow, a newly-hatched fish, notwithstanding the activity of the latter. For hours afterwards the little green-eyed fry was visible, the engulphment being a very slow process; the Medusa, however, never let go its hold; and gradually the tiny fish was sucked into the interior, and passed up the cavity of the polypite, becoming more and more cloudy and indistinct, as digestion in the stomach gradually dissolved its tissues.

These little creatures are endowed with very effective powers of locomotion. In the unbounded freedom of their native sea, and in the limited dimensions of a glass vase, they are alike sprightly. By rapid pump-like contractions of their *nectocalyx*, they dart through the water, and shoot round and round, almost with the force and swiftness of a swimming fish. The summit of the bell always goes foremost, whether the direction of the movement be vertical, horizontal, or, as is most commonly the case, oblique; and the tentacles, and the long white polypite, drag behind in trailing lines. Now and anon, the shooting is suddenly suspended, the bell hangs over and remains awhile motionless, the tentacles are allowed to depend like spiders' webs, or are suddenly drawn up into shrivelled puckers, become mutually entangled and intertwisted, then slowly free themselves, and hang down again. Sometimes the motionless bell itself sinks very gradually, and the tentacle-threads take the most elegant curves and arches in their descent.

The manner in which the strong pulsating movements of the Medusæ are performed depends on the position and action of certain bands of muscular tissue. Four of these radiate from the centre of the dome to the margin. This course is not a straight but a curved one. When, therefore, these bands are simultaneously and forcibly contracted in length, they are drawn from a curved into a straight line, and the cavity, which was bell-shaped, becomes more conical, and its capacity is considerably diminished; a portion of the water which it before held is therefore driven out at the mouth, and by its reaction forces the animal forward with a jerk in the opposite direction. Besides these radiating muscles, there are circular bands which pass round the margin and the interior walls of the dome. These by their contraction diminish the volume of the cavity, and aid the action described above.

The tiny Sarsia has but four tentacles, which spring from as many equidistant points on the margin of the bell. But in the genus *Æquorea*, of the same family, these organs are far more numerous, two species which I first discovered at Ilfracombe having, the one thirty-six, the other about two hundred tentacles. The former of these, which I have honoured with the name of the late Edward Forbes,[7] differs much in general appearance from the little Sarsia, being a cake-shaped segment of a globe, about three or four inches in diameter, and an inch and a half in thickness. The roof of the interior is low and nearly flat, or indeed dropping slightly in the centre.

The polypite is peculiar, and would scarcely be recognised as of the same nature with the lively bottle-shaped organs of the Portuguese man-of-war, or the long nimble tongue of the Sarsia. It forms a very wide circle on the flat roof of the bell, whence the four large triangular lips descend, which are cut into a minutely divided fringe of filaments, that wave loosely in the water. There are about seventy slender vessels which radiate from the polypite circle along the roof to the margin, where they join the circular marginal vessel. I have said that the tentacles are about thirty-six in all; that is, about half as many as the radiating vessels, though the relation of number is not exact.

They hang down in the usual form, to the unassisted eye appearing as excessively slender whitish or flesh-coloured threads, capable of great elongation, or of contraction into ovate spiral masses, hardly perceptible. But by the aid of the microscope we discern that each tentacle consists of a lengthened fleshy tube, on which are set at pretty regular intervals thickened semi-rings, or knobs, very much like the knobs on the horns of an antelope in appearance. They do not quite encircle the tentacle, and thus one side for the entire length is smooth and straight. These thickened swellings are collections of thread-capsules (*cnidæ*), which are packed as close as they can lie in them, and give to the tentacle that power of adhering by a touch to any animal whose tissues are penetrable, and of benumbing and destroying its vitality, in the manner which I have already, on more than one occasion, alluded to.

I have not yet described the colours of this *Æquorea*; they are, however, exceedingly lovely and beautiful. The crystalline translucency of most of these Medusæ, when they are colourless, and of the colourless parts of such as have bright hues, is exquisite in its glass-like purity; in this example the whole of the peripheral portion of the dome is of this hyaline character; but the lower part, which lies just above the flattened roof, is of a lively azure blue, seen to great perfection, when the animal is relieved by a dark background: the colour is gradually lost at about a quarter of an inch from its bottom. Then the radiating vessels are of a bright rose-colour, drawn in lines along the colourless surface of the roof; and the marginal vessel is of the same hue, as are also the four triangular lips of the polypite, with their ciliary fringes. These, as they depend, often extending below the level of the margin, waved about in various directions by the motion of the sea, or by the animal's own movements, add greatly to its elegance.

That strange and at times magnificent and imposing phenomenon, the luminosity of the sea, is certainly due in part to some of the Medusæ. Members of perhaps all the classes of marine invertebrate animals are at one time or other engaged in the illumination, and no doubt the most wide-spread production of spontaneous light, and the most effective, is due to creatures which are individually unrecognisable by the eye. When the ship ploughing through the tropical sea, turns luminous furrows on each side of her prow, and leaves a long wake of curdling light astern, or when the steamer dashes the water of our own estuaries into cascades of fire and showers of coruscating sparks, it is doubtless to the microscopic *Infusoria*, *Annelida*, and *Entomostraca*, that we are mainly indebted for the charming spectacle. Still, many of the Medusæ are conspicuously luminous under certain conditions, generally displaying the phenomenon at the moment of irritation; the light being evolved, not apparently by any proper organs, but either by the whole of the marginal ring, or by the (often coloured) swellings that are seated at the base of the tentacles.

The following appearances proved the luminosity of this beautiful *Æquorea*, on being subjected to experiments in the dark. When with any finger-nail I tapped the glass jar in which two specimens were floating at the surface, instantly each became brilliantly visible as a narrow ring of light, the whole marginal canal becoming luminous. On my touching them with the end of a stick, the light became more vivid, and round spots appeared here and there in the ring, of intense lustre and of a greenish-blue tint. These were, I doubt not, the tentacle-bulbs; and any one of them would be excited to this intensity by my touching that part of the margin with the stick. The luminosity of the ring was not so evanescent as in some species, lasting several seconds, and continuing to be renewed as often as I molested the animal. The two circles of light, two inches or more in diameter, were very beautiful as they moved freely in the water, sinking or rising according as they were touched, now seen in full rotundity, now shrinking to an oval, or to a line, as either turned side-wise to the eye, and reminded me of the *coronæ* of glory in the pictures of the Italian school, round the heads of saints.

Most of the larger Medusæ of our coasts belong to another order, including those which have covered eyes, and some other peculiarities, chiefly connected with reproduction. The *Lucernariæ*, which I have already noticed, formerly associated with the Anemones, are now united with this order. A very familiar example we may see in our harbours and tidal rivers in summer, the common Crimson-ringed Jelly-fish.[8] It is a hemisphere of colourless jelly, some six or eight inches in diameter, which is usually well marked by four imperfect rings of purplish crimson—the reproductive organs—seen through the transparent flesh. The radiating vessels are often tinged with the same colour.

The most interesting circumstances in the history of this large jellyfish are the wonderfully varied phases through which it passes in the earlier stages of its existence. Along the margins of the lengthened flaps of the polypite there are found remarkable pouches, within which the ova are placed, and whence they are hatched in the form of soft flat animalcules, capable of swimming by means of cilia. This has been called a *planula*. After swimming a while, it alters its form to that of a pear, and presently adheres by its slender end to a sea-weed or rock under water, hanging downward. A depression now appears in the larger end, which deepens and forms a mouth and stomach, and the little *planula* has assumed a polype-form. Four tiny warts now spring from the margin of the mouth, which lengthen into tentacles; four more then shoot in the inter-spaces; these eight increase to sixteen, then to thirty-two, all at the same time acquiring great length. In this stage, in which it is very common in our aquaria, it has been supposed a new animal, and has been named *Hydra tuba*. The space between the margin and the mouth has widened into an "umbrella," and the mouth has protruded into a polypite. The whole is of a translucent white hue, and the body without the tentacles is ordinarily about one-sixth of an inch high.

This stage sometimes lasts for years without further change, except that creeping root-threads shoot from the attached base, which send up at intervals buds that grow into Hydræ; and buds break out from different parts of the body itself, which likewise develop themselves, the form in both cases being exactly similar to that of the present *Hydra tuba*. Thus we frequently find numerous colonies of these tiny creatures crowded together.

At length a change takes place. The body enlarges both in length and thickness, and begins to show traces of rings or segments, as if it had been tied tightly round with threads at regular intervals. In this stage it has been described under the name of *Scyphistoma*. These cuts deepen, and the segments thus marked off become hollow; and so they resemble a pile of tiny saucers set one within another, each of which is now divided at its rim into eight teeth. In this stage it has been once more named, as if an independent animal, *Strobila*.

All this time the tentacles have been set around the terminal margin, but now these are absorbed, and a new set rapidly spring from the basal segment. The saucers become very loosely attached; at length the end one breaks away and swims through the sea, as a true Medusa, though no more than a sixth of an inch wide, pumping as it goes in proper parental wise. Others quickly follow, and thus a colony of tiny swimming jellyfishes are shooting hither and thither in the liveliest manner. Strange to say, these little Medusæ, which as to details differ much from their adult form, have been again described, under the name of *Ephydra*; all these appellations indicating the assumptions of various naturalists, who found the little creatures in their respective stages, without knowing their previous history, that each was an independent form of animal life.

As the closer and more severe scrutiny of anatomical structure has induced modern zoologists to separate the *Lucernaria* from its formerly assigned alliance with the Sea-anemones, and to associate it with the Medusæ, it is interesting to remark that the scales of justice have been maintained in equipoise by the like shifting of a member from the Medusæ to the Anemones. The latter animal is one familiar to most haunters of the shore, and invariably admired as one of the most charming of the many lovely forms that throng the summer seas; it is the sweet little *Beröe*, or *Cydippe*.[9] Indeed at first sight you would be little disposed to admit the propriety of the transfer in this case, for certainly the active glittering globule of pure crystal appears to possess much more resemblance to one of the smaller Medusæ, the *Sarsia*, for instance,—than to a daisy or a beadlet. But naturalists look beneath the surface: and they find that, with important peculiarities, the internal economy of the *Cydippe*, and specially its digestive apparatus, are modelled rather on the type of the latter than of the former.

We will not, however, trouble ourselves now with these elaborate matters, but rather look at the exterior and obvious characters of the charming little pet, which is disporting itself in this vase of sea-water on our table. It is a globe of pure colourless jelly, about as big as a small marble, often having a little wart-like swelling at one of its poles, where the mouth is placed. At the other end there are minute orifices; and between the two passes the stomach, of a form which is flat, or wider in one diameter than in the other.

If the stomach be considered as the axis of the globe, and the two extremities as its poles, the meridians of longitude are well represented by eight narrow bands, situated on the surface, which do not, however, reach either pole. Along the course of each of these meridional bands are fixed at close intervals minute square moveable plates, whose outer edges are set with strong cilia, like the teeth of a comb. These are the locomotive organs, and most effective they are. They are used like the paddles of a steamer, the little animal beating the water with them in rapid and regular succession, their minute subdivision causing the rays of light, especially when in the sun, to play along these bands, with the most brilliant prismatic colours; while their vigorous strokes cause the globe to shoot hither and thither through the water with remarkable power.

Within the clear substance of the *Cydippe*, on each side of the stomach, there is excavated a capacious cavity, which communicates by a canal with the surface, near the equator. Within each cavity is fixed a tentacle of great length and slenderness, which the animal can at pleasure shoot out of the orifice, and allow to trail through the water, shortening, lengthening, twisting, or coiling it at will; or, on the other hand, quickly contract it into a tiny ball, and withdraw it wholly within the proper cavity. A peculiarity, which imparts an inexpressible charm to this apparatus, is, that, throughout the length of this attenuate white thread, short

Plate XXX

Cydippe. Common Medusa. Larval Forms.

threadlets are given off at regular intervals, which can be coiled or straightened, lengthened or shortened, individually. They proceed only from one side of the thread-like tentacle, though, from the slight twisting of the axis, they seem now to project on one side, now on another.

It has been well observed that of the grace and beauty which the entire apparatus presents in the living animal, or the marvellous ease and rapidity with which it can be alternately contracted, extended, and bent at an infinite variety of angles, no verbal description can sufficiently treat. Fortunately this little beauty is so common in summer and autumn on all our coasts, that few who use the surface-net can possibly miss its capture. So lovely a creature is worthy of a poet's description: it has received it.

> "Now o'er the stern the fine-mesh'd net-bag fling,
> And from the deep the little Beroë bring;
> Beneath the sunlit wave she swims conceal'd
> By her own brightness;—only now reveal'd
> To sage's eye, that gazes with delight
> On things invisible to vulgar sight.
> When first extracted from her native brine,
> Behold a small round mass of gelatine,
> Or frozen dew-drop, void of life and limb:
> But round the crystal goblet let her swim
> 'Midst her own element; and lo! a sphere
> Banded from pole to pole; a diamond clear,
> Shaped as bard's fancy shapes the small balloon
> To bear some sylph or fay beyond the moon.
> From all her bands see lucid fringes play,
> That glance and sparkle in the solar ray
> With iridescent lines. Now round and round
> She wheels and twirls; now mounts, then sinks profound.
> Now see her like the belted star of Jove,
> Spin on her axis smooth, as if she strove
> To win applause—a thing of conscious sense
> Quivering and thrilling with delight intense.
> Long silvery cords she treasures in her sides,
> By which, uncoil'd at times, she moors and rides:
> From these, as hook-hairs on a fisher's line,
> See feathery fibrils hang in graceful twine,
> Graceful as tendrils of the mantling vine
> These swift as angler by the fishy lake
> Projects his fly the keen-eyed trout to take,
> She shoots with rapid jerk to seize her food,
> The small green creatures of crustaceous brood;
> Soon doom'd herself a ruthless foe to find,
> When in Actinia's arms she lies entwined.
> Here, prison'd by the vase's crystal bound,

Impassable as Styx's nine-fold round,
Quick she projects, as quick retracts again,
Her flexile toils, and tries her arts in vain;
Till languid grown, her fine machinery worn
By rapid friction, and her fringes torn,
Her full round orb wanes lank, and swift decay
Pervades her frame, till all dissolves away.
So wanes the dew conglobed on rose's bud;
So melts the ice-drop in the tepid flood:
Thus, too, shall many a shining orb on high
That studs the broad pavilion of the sky,—
Suns and their systems—fade, dissolve, and die."[10]

XI.
November

If we could roam at pleasure over the bottom of the sea, with the privilege of using all our senses as effectually and as comfortably as in the air, we should doubtless see some wonderful things. We might not, indeed, find all the useful and ornamental articles that drowning Clarence saw in his dream, but doubtless we might substitute for them things that he never dreamed of, things that the eye of man was not as yet cultivated to see. What opportunities for enlarging the bounds of science are possessed by the engineers that have been working many hours a day, for years past, at the great Breakwater in that prolific field of marine life, Weymouth Bay!—working in a capacious diving-bell at the bottom of the sea. But there are many reasons why we can expect nothing in the way of natural history from them. Perhaps not one of them has ever been taught to think upon any of the strange forms that might occur, which do not commonly minister to the pocket of man in the market, as anything but mere rubbish not worth a second glance, or something hurtful or nasty to be crushed beneath the heel. Or if, perchance, an observer of nature's beauties be engaged in such an occupation, his time would be so fully taken up with his urgent duties, as to preclude attention to such amenities. Besides which, the loads of enormous blocks of stone already shot down on the sea-floor, which he is there to arrange and settle, must pretty well have smashed and covered everything which had revelled in dull enjoyment there, before his arrival. Still I fancy I should like to borrow his diving-bell on a holiday, and roam a little beyond those wildernesses of broken stone, picking up treasures here and there such as the scraper of the dredge has never yet been able to gather out of the crevices and crannies of those deep-water rocks.

But such a desire is at present hopeless; and we must be satisfied with such resources as are at our command, thankful that the dredge, and the trawl, and the keer-drag, the fisherman's deep-sea line, the lobster-pot, and the sounding-lead—are all contributing to our acquaintance with the curious, the uncouth, the wondrous, the beautiful, that lurk far down *in profundis*.

Let us then go back to the results of our dredging day that we so much enjoyed a few weeks ago. A portion of its produce yet remains in buckets and pans, waiting for a further overhauling; and it will doubtless yield us some objects worthy of an hour or two's investigation.

Plate XXXI

Pyrgoma on a Coral. Scalpellum. Lobster-Horn. Necked Barnacle. Common Barnacle. Porcate Barnacle.

November

The first thing that our fingers pull up is a great tangled group of Sertularian *Hydrozoa*, of which the finest part consists of some half-dozen stems of *Antennularia*, called, from obvious resemblance, the Lobster-horn Coralline.[1] These are nearly straight, somewhat stiff, unbranched stems, a foot or more in length, with an uniform thickness of about a line, of a buff-yellow hue, closely divided into short joints. Each of the joints gives origin to a whorl of very delicate bristles, giving a hairy appearance to the whole affair, but which under magnifying power are discerned to be colourless, jointed filaments, bearing on the inner shoulder of each joint a tiny glassy cup (*hydrotheca*), within which resides a minute many-tentacled polype. The stems spring in close groups from an obscure root-mass of tangled threads, which cling to stones and shells, and afford a mooring to the Lobster-horn, which in its turn affords support to miniature forests of other *Hydrozoa*, slenderer than the finest hair—*Laomedea, Campanularia*, etc., which crowd together on it, especially around the bottom, and make the investigation of any one specimen very difficult. These have their polype-cups of exquisitely elegant forms, and I see on the latter many of the urn-shaped vessels (now called *gonotheca*), out of which issue what appear to be distinct and independent forms of life, as unlike the parent as can well be imagined, but exactly like the little naked-eyed Medusæ that we lately looked at. This, however, is not properly an animal at all, but only an organ (the *gonophore*) which has the faculty of maintaining a separate existence, and which is destined to give birth to ciliated embryos, like the *planula* of the *Aurelia*, that attach themselves, and develop into new *Campanulariæ*. Most wonderful are the processes and phases of life which have been discovered in these zoophytic forms.[2] A volume might be written on them, full of praise to the all-wise God.

Now, however, we must turn aside to look at other objects. Attached to the base of the Lobster-horn, we find several examples of an interesting Cirripede.[3] It is of a dirty buff, or drab hue, semi-transparent, in outline something like a butcher's cleaver, handle and blade, or still more like a silver butter-knife, but much thicker in proportion; the handle represented by the cartilaginous and flexible stalk, the blade by the compressed valves. These vary much in regularity of form, some being nearly oval, little wider than the stalk, others angular and much wider. The body throws itself vigorously about on the stalk, when disturbed. The valves open, and out comes a widely radiating hand, of brilliantly glassy fingers, the joints and comb-like bristles of which glitter and sparkle as I hold it up in a tumbler of sea-water, examining it with a lens, with a lamp behind. It remains some seconds expanded, as if enjoying contact with the water; or perhaps, if I may draw inferences from some slight twitchings, feeling and testing for the accidental presence of invisible atoms that might serve it for food; then suddenly the fingers close together, and the hand is drawn in with a snap, as if it had taken some prize, though the lens had revealed nothing there. Soon it opens again, and exhibits the same manœuvres. A front view of the hand, the bristle-like fingers radiating in all directions, is a very attractive object for a low magnifying power. There are several tiny ones in another group, the bodies of which are not bigger than hempseed; these make their grasps apparently at random, with regular alternation, much as the commoner Barnacles do.

Of these latter we have no lack, many of the rough shells and small pebbles being incrusted with crowded colonies of the commonest Acorn Barnacle.[4] We see the same species, by tens of thousands, covering roods and roods of the seaward surfaces of our rough rocks between tide-marks. They rarely exceed one-third of an inch in diameter at base; but there is a much more massive kind, rough with ridges and furrows, and hence called *porcate*, occasionally found adhering to the jutting angles of rocks hereabout, and much more commonly on the coast of South Wales, around Tenby.

These Acorn Barnacles have no foot-stalk, but adhere by the whole broad base to the rock or shell, on which a floor either of strong stone, or of thin membrane is formed, and from whose margin the stony plates arise, enclosing a more or less conical chamber, with an orifice at the summit. If we look in at this during the life of the animal, we discern, a little below the rim, some angular valves, which meet with a straight suture, and close the interior. These are moveable, however; and under water they open like folding-doors, and a hand of many fingers, each composed of many joints, modelled on the same plan as that of the *Scalpellum*, but less delicate, protrudes, which makes its cast for prey, and is withdrawn beneath the again-closed valves.

The winds and waves not unfrequently bear into our harbours fragments of spars, old water-casks, or planks, from the hull of some ill-fated ship foundered in the inhospitable ocean, which are teeming with life. Conspicuous on such "flotsam and jetsam," as our ancient maritime law-codes term these relics, we mark the Necked Barnacles,[5] so long believed by our ancestors, with a most implicit credence, to be legitimately descended from, and to be in turn the regular and normal parents of, a certain species of goose, common enough on our northern shores. That myth may, however, be dismissed with a mere recollection.

In this form the neck or stalk is greatly developed, frequently reaching to eight inches and upwards in length, with a thickness of half an inch. Externally it is very tough and leathery, yet it is sufficiently flexible to be jerked vigorously in various directions, and thrown into contorted curves, by means of muscles that run through it. The lower part adheres firmly to the support, which is generally wood, and I believe only in a floating condition. The bottoms of ships in warm climates are generally much infested with these parasites, which acquire a great size in the course of a voyage of only a few months.

The valves resemble delicate shells, and are elegantly painted with various tints of light blue varied with white, the edges of the valves being often rich scarlet or orange. The hand is deep purplish black, the fingers stout and massive; but not differing in their structure or in their mode of use, from those of their sessile fellows.

Perhaps the most interesting of all our native forms of these Cirripedes—for true parasitism is always a subject of peculiar interest—is that little species[6] which invariably selects as its support the stony walls of a coral. Our beautiful Cup-coral, so common at extreme low-water level on both the north and south coasts of Devon and Cornwall, is the favourite species of the *Pyrgoma*. So far as my experience goes, extending over a very extensive series of specimens, I think about one in six of these corals carries the parasite, generally situated either on, or just without, the margin of the cup. I say, "generally," because Mr. Guyon has lately recorded what he thinks an exception to the rule, in two *Pyrgomata* situated on the rock close to the base of the coral. But Mr. Holdsworth, an excellent authority, considers that the exception is more apparent than real.

The number of these little intruders varies from one upwards. I possess specimens, one of which carries nine, the other eleven; the appearance of the ovate barnacles, each with its conspicuous orifice, crowded all round the edge of the coral, is exceedingly curious and novel. Mr. Holdsworth mentions, however, that he has seen fourteen *Pyrgomata* attached to a single *Caryophyllia*, which was dredged in Plymouth Sound.[7]

The transformations of these animals, as investigated by Mr. Darwin, are of great interest. The Cirripede, whatever its genus, and whatever its peculiarities of adult existence, begins its life in a form exactly like that of a young Entomostracous Crustacean, with a broad carapace, a single eye, two pairs of antennæ, three lairs of jointed, branched, and well-bristled legs, and a forked tail. It casts off its skin twice, undergoing, especially at the second moult, a considerable change of figure. At the third moult it has assumed almost the form of a *Cypris*, or *Cythere*, being enclosed in a bivalve shell, in which the front of the head with the antennæ is greatly developed, equalling in bulk all the rest of the body. The single eye has become two, which are very large, and attached to the outer arms of two bent processes like the letters U U, which are seen within the thorax.

In this stage the little animal searches about for some spot suitable for permanent residence; a ship's bottom, a piece of floating timber, the back of a whale or turtle, or the solid rock. When its selection is made, the two antennæ, which project from the shell, pour out a glutinous gum or cement, which hardens in water, and firmly attaches them. Henceforth the animal is a fixture, glued by the front of its head to its support. Another moult now takes place; the bivalve shell is thrown off, with the great eyes, and their U-like processes, and the little Cirripede is seen in its true form. It is now in effect a Stomapod Crustacean, attached by its antennæ, the head greatly lengthened (in *Lepas*, etc.), the carapace composed of several pieces (valves), the legs modified into cirri, and made to execute their grasping movements backwards instead of forwards, and the whole abdomen obliterated, or reduced to an inconspicuous rudiment.

Let us resume our grubbing in the heterogeneous heap of matters with which the dredge has enriched us. The tube-dwelling *Annelida* are

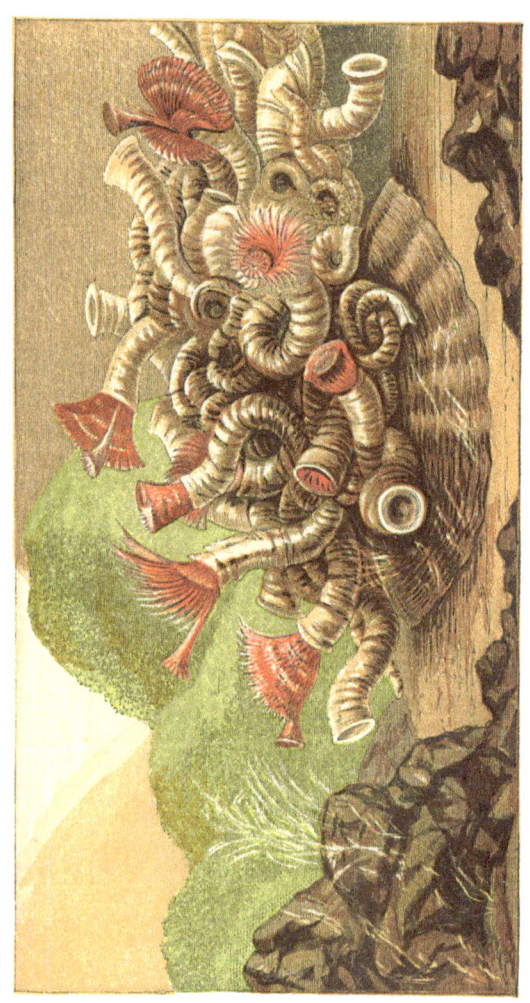

Plate XXXII

Scarlet Serpula.

November

generally prominent in such collections, and accordingly we see conspicuous here great and small heaps of contorted tubes, that look as if a batch of tobacco-pipe stems had become agglutinated together, and strangely twisted in the baking. These are the shelly tubes of the beautiful scarlet Serpula,[8] a general favourite in our aquaria, easily and abundantly procured, and readily maintained in health and beauty for a considerable period. I need scarcely describe the general appearance of an object so commonly kept, and so frequently gazed upon. Many tubes are usually found growing together, adhering to the same shell, bit of broken pottery, or small stone; all much intertwined, and mutually adherent, so that it is practically hopeless to attempt to isolate one. Yet by studying many specimens we are able to ascertain that each individual is at first a very slender tube of white calcareous shell, not thicker than sewing-cotton;[9] this rapidly increases both in thickness and in length, soon rising from its support, to which it at first adhered by the lime deposited in a soft state, and continuing the rest of its growth free, in a direction forming various angles with the ground line, and most irregularly twined and contorted. For the final half of its length, or thereabout, the tube attains a diameter of one-fourth of an inch, the walls being sufficiently thick to be solid, yet leaving an ample cavity for the residence of the industrious mechanic, who thus skilfully builds up his own house.

If we carefully break, by a moderated blow with a hammer, the shelly tube, so as not to crush the tenant, we are able to expose the latter to view. We then see that its length is by no means commensurate with the length of its house, of which indeed it inhabits only the last-made portion, having behind a roomy space into which to retire in case of need. It is not more than an inch or an inch and a quarter long, rather wide in proportion, and flattened, with a well-marked distinction between the corslet and the abdomen. The former carries on each side prominent footwarts, which are vigorously protrusile, and within which bundles of strong bristles are thrust to and fro. On the upper part of each foot, extending half across the back, is a row of microscopic hooks, wielded by long thread-like tendons, which are fixed, on mechanical principles, to the attached end of each hook. By the aid of these, the Serpula so cleverly withdraws with lightning-like rapidity on alarm. By the action of muscles of indescribable delicacy, the hooks are projected to some distance beyond the surface of the body. These organs are formed on the model of a hedger's bill-hook, only that the edge is cut into long teeth. Carefully counting them I have found that each Serpula carries about 1900 such hooks on its corslet, and that each of these being cut into seven teeth, there are between 13,000 and 14,000 teeth employed in catching the lining membrane of the tube, and in drawing the animal back.

The protrusion of the fore parts, which takes place in a much more leisurely manner, is performed by quite another set of instruments, formed on a totally different principle. Their action is a pushing or shoving. The instruments for effecting this are the fine but strong bristles which run through the feet. Each bristle is composed of a strong rigid unyielding shaft, having an expanded shoulder drawn out into a point. On one side of this pointed shoulder may be remarked a double row of fine teeth, admirably calculated to catch against any roughnesses of the surface with which they come into contact, against which they then push with the force of the proper muscles. Acting diagonally backwards, from the two sides of the animal, the result of the combination of the forces is that the animal itself is pushed forwards, and so protruded from the mouth of the tube. The feet on the hinder portion of the body are, according to Dr. Williams,[10] modified in structure with express reference to the duties of mopping, sweeping, scraping, and wiping the inferior closed end of the habitation. I think, however, he has forgotten that this end, formed by the animal in its infant state, must now be very much too strait to be reached by any portion of the body, or by any of its organs.

Dwelling in a tubular house, the Serpula would find its breathing organs scarcely available, if these were placed, as in most *Annelida*, in pairs on the body-segments. They are therefore much modified, and that not only in position but in form. They consist of most elegant comb-like filaments, richly coloured, arranged in two rows around the front extremity, one row on each side of the mouth. They are graduated in length, and are so affixed, that, where the rows meet behind, they can be thrown-in, so that a vertical view of the circular coronet shows a great sinus in it. These brilliant gill-tufts form the most attractive feature in these elegant Worms, and are individually most exquisite examples of mechanical contrivance. Examined under a low microscopic power, they present a most charming spectacle. Each filament consists of a pellucid cartilaginous stem, from one side of which springs a double row of secondary filaments like the teeth of a comb. Within both stem and filaments the red blood may be seen, with beautiful distinctness, driven along the artery, and back by the vein (which are placed close side by side) in ceaseless course, constituting a very striking spectacle.

The exterior of these organs is set with strong cilia, so arranged that the water-current is vigorously driven upward along one side of the filament, and downward along the other. Yet the combined result of all the branchial currents is to bring a powerful vortex into the enclosed funnel, the bottom of which terminates in the mouth. The food which sustains nutrition is thus brought to be swallowed, a large quantity of water being at the same time constantly poured into the body; this is discharged (by the agency of a ciliated lining of the hinder parts) in the form of a strong current, which, impinging against the closed end of the tube, is turned upward, carrying with it all extraneous or fœtal matters, and is ever pouring out of the frontal extremity around the neck of the creature. What a beautiful and effective contrivance is this for constantly keeping in a state of the most unsullied cleanness the interior of the house! It reminds one of the fabled Hercules cleansing the Augean stable by driving the river Peneus through it.

On each side of the mouth there springs a lengthened horny thread, appearing to answer to the antennæ which in other Worms, as well as in

Insects and Crustacea, project from the front of the head. Such seems their true relation considered structurally, but in function and office they are very remarkable and quite peculiar. To these organs is assigned the duty of closing up the tube when the animal has withdrawn its gaily-coloured plumes; and for this end, one of these antennæ is much lengthened, and at the end is expanded into a broad trumpet-shaped club, the extremity of which is somewhat concave, and is delicately marked with radiating grooves. This organ is usually painted with the same brilliant colours as the gill-tufts, and by its length, size, and form, makes a very conspicuous feature in the charming Serpula. Its length is such, that when the gill-filaments are rolled up and withdrawn, the conical club enters after all, and is found accurately to fit the trumpet-like orifice of the tube, just as a cork fits tightly into the mouth of a bottle.

Ordinarily those organs which appear in pairs are formed so as to be the counterparts of each other. But here is an exception. One only, sometimes the right, sometimes the left, indifferently, takes the remarkable form that I have been describing, the other being much shorter, and terminating only in a small knob, like the head of a pin. Why should there be this difference? Why this exception to an all but universal rule? The reason is obvious. Yes, obvious enough when seen and noticed; but it tells an eloquent tale of the Divine forethought and care. If both of the antennæ were furnished with the terminal cone, one would interfere with the other in the performance of their closing, corking-up function; they would jam in the doorway, and the tube would be left open. Hence the one is left undeveloped, yet retaining, as I believe, the latent power of expanding into a cone, if it should ever be needed by the accidental loss of the fellow now so furnished. I thus judge, because experience shows me that the conical club is occasionally thrown off, and quickly renewed, in captivity.

My esteemed friend, the Rev. Sir Christopher Lighton, has indeed put on record an example of a Serpula of this species possessing two equal antennæ, that had replaced the single one accidentally lost. They were both perfectly developed, and joined together near the base. Each was decidedly smaller than the single one that had formerly occupied their place.[11] This exceedingly interesting case can, of course, only be regarded as a monstrosity of redundancy, as children are sometimes born with a superfluous finger. But it is valuable its showing that there is a power of development latent in the crownless antenna. I wish very much that the excellent observer had added a note, telling us to what extent the tube was closed, and how the work was performed without mutual interference.

It has been sometimes brought as an objection to our assigning a certain service to certain organs, that the necessity for such service is a gratuitous supposition, since other creatures similarly formed in most respects, and in which we might infer a like need, have no such supply. We may admit the facts, but refuse the reasoning. There can be no manner of doubt that the conical antenna does act as a stopper to the Serpula, as our eyes can see; and surely it would be most unphilosophical

Plate XXXIII

Sabellae.

to suppose that the function so performed is not serviceable to the creature. Yet its near cousins, the Sabellæ, similarly constructed, and of similar habits of life, and as we should have *à priori* supposed, quite as liable to injury in the same direction, are entirely destitute of this contrivance for protection, and of anything compensating for it, so far as is known. Why the need of one should be met by such a beautiful contrivance, while the same need in the other is wholly unmet, though both are formed by the same Infinite God, is one of those unanswerable questions which, while they leave unimpeached His wisdom, make us deeply conscious of our own ignorance.

We find numerous examples of this genus *Sabella* in our confused heap of tangled life and death. By their vigour and their abundance we have proof enough that their wants *are* supplied, though they do not enjoy this special contrivance: they manage to live and thrive and enjoy themselves, with open doors, taking all risks of insidious robbers,—such, for instance, as that vile burglar, the Longworm,[12] that we found under a stone the other day; which is ever on the watch to insert its snaky head within the unprotected tube, and to tear away with merciless clutch the beauteous gill-tufts.

One species of this genus[13] can by the cursory observer be distinguished from the Serpulæ, only by this absence of the antennal stopper. For it dwells in a shelly tube, essentially resembling those which we have just been examining. It has peculiarities of detail, however. It is never found associated with numbers of its fellows in agglutinated groups, but always, so far as my experience goes, singly. It is more common on shells than on stones, generally attached to the old valve of some cockle or scallop. It is straight or nearly so, never at least contorted. Attached only for a very short portion of its smaller end, perhaps for an inch or so, for which it creeps along the surface, it then rises into a more or less erect position, extending sometimes to a height of seven or eight inches perfectly free. The tube is of about the same diameter as that of the Serpula, but is slighter in structure, or perhaps it appears so, because it is destitute of those expansions which here and there in that species indicate the trumpet-lips of successive stages of development. The extremity of the tube here is simple, not expanding. Slight annular rings, however, do here and there vary the shelly surface of the tube.

The gill-tufts are ample; they are two, considerably infolded, consisting of about forty-five filaments each, which are much longer and slenderer than those of the Serpula, the last filaments of the volutions diminishing rapidly. The secondary filaments, or pinnæ, are very fine and very numerous, so set on the main stem that the two rows form the sides of a narrow groove, facing inwards. The whole is yellowish-white with eight or ten bright scarlet dots set with intervals all along the back or outer side of the stem. When fully protruded, the base of the gills, and even a good deal of the neck, lolls out of the tube. If the animal be removed, the body is seen to be white, elegantly banded with scarlet, and furnished with a broad translucent collar, edged with scarlet: this collar ordinarily lines the mouth of the tube.

From the length and isolation of its shelly tube this is a remarkable species: the great tenuity of its filaments, however, requires a lens to bring out their beauties; but with this aid, the arrangement of the rich scarlet bands and spots on the pale yellow ground cannot fail to evoke admiration.

In general, the Sabellæ inhabit tubes which are not calcareous or shelly; they are composed of a soft flexible substance somewhat resembling wet parchment, made of a secretion from the animal's body, in which the impalpable muddy sediment which the waves agitate, consisting of decomposed organic matter for the most part, is interwoven. The tissue so made is sufficiently tough and enduring, retaining its form long after the animal has died out of it.

In our dredge-hauls we find a pretty little kind[14] common enough, which lives in association, the tubes apparently from half-an-inch to an inch in length, forming dense masses on stones and shells, and projecting in every direction. A dozen or more may be in one group, and when all are alive, one or another protruding or retiring every moment, it makes a pretty object.

The gill-filaments are nine to eleven in each row, of a yellowish white, occasionally patched with dead-white, or red-brown: delicately and densely pinnate. The filaments, in the act of protruding, are closed together like a straight bundle of rods which suddenly fall open at the ends. In this moment of unfolding, their tips are seen to be a little hooked inwards. The tube is about as large as a crow-quill; under a lens it appears speckled, as if the inorganic matter imbedded in it were grains of the finest sand. On carefully removing all the surrounding tubes and other objects so as to isolate one, we see that it is truly about three inches in length, but that two-thirds of the whole are prostrate and adherent; this basal portion is horny and pellucid, no mud entering into its texture. The animal when extracted is an inch in length, of which the gill-tufts form one-third.

Minded with these there are one or two specimens of a much more imposing species, the Hook-plumed Sabella.[15] It grows to a large size, the crown of gill-filaments sometimes attaining a height of an inch, and the same diameter. The two rows are incurved in regular spirals of half a turn, each consisting of about eighteen filaments, which are rather stout, the whole crown sometimes taking the form of a funnel, sometimes that of a cup, often arching inward at the tip. Their pinnæ are long and close, the two rows forming a groove, but nearly parallel. Each primary stem is set along the back with twelve pairs of feather-like processes, hooked downwards;—a very remarkable character, and one by which this species may be in a moment distinguished. Their colour is pale red-brown, mottled irregularly with deep brownish purple and with white; there is a pair of brown specks at the origin of each pair of hooks. The base of the crown is always concealed in the mouth of the tube, but it springs from a narrow frilled membrane of pure white. The body is destitute of a thoracic shield, or conspicuous collar. The tube is largely composed of soft homogeneous mud, usually of a pale purplish hue, of about the thickness of the shelly tube of *S. tubularia*.

The process of building the mud tubes of the Sabellæ is a very interesting one. It is performed, according to my own observations,[16] mainly by means of the gill-filaments and their pinnal grooves. The filaments are bent-over, till the inner or grooved face comes in contact with the soft mud on which the animal is lying, when the sensitive pinnæ close on a minute portion of the mud, taking it up in a pellet, which is then fashioned by the form of the groove; the filament is now erected, and the pellet, passing down the groove to the bottom by means of the cilia, is delivered to the care of two delicate moveable organs, like leaves or flaps, which place it on the edge of the tube, and then shape and mould it, smoothing both surfaces. Doubtless, either from these organs, or from some other part of the circumjacent region, the glutinous secretion is at the same time poured out, which consolidates the mud, and forms the true basis of the tube.

Plate XXXIV

Orange-Spotted Squirter. Four-Angled Squirter. Currant Squirter.

XII.
December

December is here, with its short days, its feeble watery sunshine, its frequent gloom and mist, its hanging leaden skies; in short, as the poet describes it,—

"Sullen and sad, with all his rising train;
Vapours and clouds and storms."

It requires some zeal in the pursuit of scientific lore to leave the glowing fire and the pleasant book, the luxurious arm-chair and the elastic carpet, and to venture down to the wild sea-beach, to poke and peer among the desolate rocks. Yet even now we may find a few bright days, when Nature abroad looks inviting, and when an hour's marine research will prove neither unpleasant nor unsuccessful.

On such a noon, then, calm and quiet, the sun bright and cheerful, if low and feeble, the tide tolerably low and the rocks accessible, we hie down to some one or other of those ledges which have so often already yielded their treasures to our search, and begin our wonted labours at turning over the heavy angular masses. We soon find, attached to the under surfaces of these, what seem to be irregular blobs of coloured jelly of somewhat firm consistence, as if an invalid had been here eating his calves'-foot jelly, whose trembling hand had dropped sundry spoonfuls on the stones. Some appear as flattish shapeless drops, but others take more elevated forms, like sacks set on end, and usually displaying two mouths. One of these is of a pellucid yellowish green, or olive hue, with a cloudy spot of rich orange in the interior. A slight shrinking from the touch, a yet closer contraction of the projecting points, is the only token of life that we can discern in it now; but if we place it in an aquarium,—not forcibly removing it from its attachment, but lifting the shell or stone on which it rests; or, if this be too large, detaching the fragment with a chisel,—and allow it to remain a few hours undisturbed, we shall see evidences of a vitality, indubitable if not very active.

The whole creature is now much plumper and more pellucid; it stands up boldly from its base on the stone; its upper portion is much lengthened, and the two wart-like eminences have become two short tubes with gaping extremities, appearing as if they had been soldered together side by side, of which the one is considerably higher than the other.[1]

We have before us one of the *Tunicata*, an order of molluscous animals which are closely allied to the *Conchifera* or bivalves, but somewhat lower in the scale than they. It has no shell; that is to say, lime is not deposited in the outer investment, so as to give it the hard, rigid, solid texture of shell; but the internal organs, which are essentially similar to those of an Oyster or a Sand-gaper, are enclosed in a tough leathery coat, known as the *test*, which is in fact a closed shell destitute of lime. The eminent physiologist, John Hunter, who had dissected some of these homely Squirters, as they are familiarly called, recognised, with his wonted acumen, the structural similarity of their leathery envelopes to the stony shells of the lower bivalves; and, associating them in a group, called them "soft-shells." The naturalness of this group, since called *Tunicata* by Lamarck, has been recognised by modern zoologists.

If we watch our Ascidia for a few minutes, we perceive that at irregular intervals one or both of the gaping orifices are suddenly closed and contracted, commonly both at the same instant. They are, however, soon opened again; and we may discern, especially if the specimen is in a glass vessel, and we watch it by the aid of a lens, with the light of a window at its back, that a current of the surrounding water flows from all sides to the taller orifice, and pours down its tube; while occasionally we see the ejection of a stream from the orifice of the shorter tube. Thus we have here a receiving and a discharging tube, the exact representatives of the two siphons in such bivalves as *Pholas, Venus*, etc. The former leads down into a capacious sac in the interior, the walls of which constitute the breathing apparatus. The inner surface is marked by regular parallel ridges which run in a horizontal direction; and these are again connected by vertical ridges at right angles, very numerous, enclosing a vast number of oval compartments. The sides of these are richly ciliated; and if the whole apparatus be carefully dissected out, and laid upon the stage of the microscope, the course of the ciliary currents may be distinctly seen, continuing with unabated vigour and with unfaltering precision for a long time after the severance of the organ from the body of the animal. But all this is seen to most advantage, if we select one of the smaller species, which are brilliantly transparent, such as one which grows in groups of elegant tall vases, about an inch in height, around the edges of our rocky pools,[2] or a tiny thing which forms a little heap of transparent globules, like pins' heads, attached to sea-weeds.[3] In either of these, placed in a stage-trough of sea-water, we can watch at leisure the performance of the various vital functions in healthy action, with the knowledge that the little subject has not been martyred to science, but is all the while enjoying its humble life with perhaps as much zest as if it were still environed by the rough walls of its little native basin of rock.

In the tiny pin-head of clear jelly, the microscope displays the branchial sac hanging free in the cavity, like a bag of clear muslin. The oval cavities divided-off by the rectangular ridges are about forty in number, around each of which the ciliary waves incessantly roll, as running spots of black. It is a very charming spectacle to see so many oblong figures set symmetrically all furnished on their inner surface with what look like the cogs or teeth of a mill-wheel, dark and distinct, running round and round with an even, moderately rapid, ceaseless course. These black, well-defined, tooth-like specks are merely an optical effect; they do not represent any actual objects, but only the waves which the cilia make: the cilia themselves being hairs, so fine as to be defined only with high powers. Occasionally we see one or other of the ovals suddenly cease its movement, while the rest go on; and now and then the whole are arrested simultaneously, and presently all start off again together, with a very pleasing effect, as if we were looking at the wheels of a very perfect and complex piece of machinery. These phenomena appear to indicate that the movements are under the control of the animal's will, capable of being suspended or continued, wholly, or in any degree, at pleasure; which is not the case in the higher animals; our own respiratory movement, for example, as well as the pulsations of the heart, going on without the concurrence of our will, and even without our consciousness.

The action of the heart in these transparent creatures is equally visible. Below the muslin curtain with its living chambers, down at the very bottom of the body-cavity, there is a transparent sac of membrane, which takes the appearance of a long bag, pointed at each end, but not closed, and strangely twisted on its long axis, so as to make three turns. This is the heart; and within it are seen many colourless globules, floating freely in a clear fluid, which answers to the blood. This circulates throughout the system in the following manner:—We see a spasmodic contraction at one end of the bag, which drives forward the globules contained there; the contraction in an instant passes onward along the three twists of the vessel, the part behind expanding immediately as the movement passes on, and the globules are forcibly expelled through the narrow but open extremity. Meanwhile the free globules surrounding the commencing end have rushed in as soon as that part resumed its usual width, and are in their turn driven forward by the periodic repetition of the pulsation. The fluid, with its globules thus put in motion, is then driven along through the interstices of the various organs of the body, not through a system of closed blood-vessels, some finding their way along the transverse lines that separate the rows of gill-ovals, until they sooner or later arrive at the point where they entered the heart, to take the same course over again.

As in the kindred forms of animal life, the same orifice, the same cilia, the same currents are subservient to breathing and to the reception of food; the stomach digesting the microscopic animalcules which are poured with the entering stream through the receiving siphon. At some distance within the interior of this orifice there are a series of thread-shaped tentacles, affixed in a ring, which we may suppose to exercise some kind of superintendence, by touch or other perception, over the atoms which indiscriminately enter upon the stream, accepting or rejecting. Probably it is in the exercise of the latter discretion that those irregular regurgitations of the current take place, accompanied by a momentary closing of the mouth, that we frequently notice.

Still further ancillary to the protection of the stomach from the intrusion of inimical matters, we may safely suppose certain eye-like specks which are placed at the very vestibule. In the larger species, as this red-clouded green Squirter, there are seated in special fissures at the very margin of the expanded siphon-orifices, red dots,—eight around the receiving, six around the ejecting, siphon. Each dot seems ascertained to be an eye of very rudimentary structure, seated on a mass of orange pigment. We should probably do wrong if we attributed any higher vision to these organs than a low degree of sensibility to the general stimulus of the light.

Some species have the orifices of the siphons four-cornered, whereas the sort I have been describing have them circular; there are differences also in the breathing sac, which in the square-mouthed species is folded lengthwise, while in the round-mouthed it is plain. Hence the former have been separated from the *Ascidiæ*, as a distinct genus, named *Cynthia*; both including a large number of species.

We have a pretty attractive little *Cynthia* in our dredging,—the Currant Squirter.[4] It is not uncommon in deep water off this coast, and in Weymouth Bay; frequently occurring in family groups crowded together on old shells. Generally there is one of superior dimensions to the rest, the venerable parent of the colony; and, surrounding him, others of varying size, and (doubtless) age, down to very minute infants. The full size is about that of half a small cherry; but it is more usual to see them not exceeding that of half a red currant. These comparisons will also give a fair idea of their shape and colour, especially in a state of contraction, as when lifted from the water: for they are little hemispheres of a brilliant, scarcely pellucid, crimson hue, seated on the shell by the whole broad base. Under water, and at ease, the form becomes more conical, rising into a point; whence, in full expansion, the two siphons protrude, slightly divergent, and the one a little superior to the other, each opening by a distinctly quadrangular orifice.

Contrasting with this neat and pretty little family, we have here another species of the genus,—the Four-angled Squirter.[5] You would hardly suppose this to be an animal at all, if uninitiated; but might readily pass it over as a rude stone, or a bit of wood roughly bruised and worn by the waves beating it among the rocks, so uncouth and coarse and shapeless it is. It forms a great mass, some two inches high, rudely four-sided, of a dull yellowish-olive hue, rising into two blunt eminences, which individually retain the quadrangular shape, and in activity open by symmetrically quadrangular orifices. It is a sluggish, unattractive lump of flesh, somewhat between leather and jelly in texture, coarsely pellucid, but not transparent, and its exterior is usually distinguished by various extraneous matters imbedded in the test, as well as by forests of tangled zoophytes which creep over it and root in it as on the rock. The surface itself, moreover, is much corrugated by an irregular network of depressions, marking off angular warty areas.

On the other hand, the little Currant is a pleasing inhabitant of the aquarium. Of manners, to be sure, it has not much, good or bad, but the form and colour are agreeable; as is also the effect produced by the grouping of the brilliant drops of jelly. Little of change takes place, beyond the occasional contraction and re-protrusion of the orifices; but sometimes you may see, as I have seen, at certain times, the laying of eggs by this species, which is an interesting phenomenon. These are perfectly globular, about the size of small shot or pins' heads, of a rich scarlet-crimson hue: they are deposited in a singular manner. The oviduct does not extend to the exterior of the body, but discharges the eggs into a large cavity formed by the mouth, of which the discharging siphon is the outlet. From this orifice, then, they are expelled, shot out perpendicularly with considerable force, so that they describe arched courses through the water, like bombs shot from a mortar, rising to a height ten times that of the animal. I have observed a dozen or more eggs thus discharged in quick succession, which then fall to the bottom around the parent, destined to constitute one of those family groups in which we usually find the species.

I have not been successful in rearing these eggs to maturity. The development of the *Tunicata* has, however, been observed by various naturalists, and by none more thoroughly than by the late Sir John Dalyell, whose elaborate and costly works, profusely illustrated, are such a mine of information respecting the lower forms of marine life.

The young escapes from the egg in a form as unlike the parent as can be imagined. It is a flat ovate body with a long flat tail, altogether presenting a curious resemblance to the tadpole of a frog. In this condition I have found the larva of the *Clavelina*, and have followed it to the development of the *Ascidia* form. By means of the rapid vibrations of the powerful tail, the little tadpole swims for short distances through the water, with more effort than effect. After a while, it rests; swims again, and again rests; till at last it moves no more. A coloured eye-speck is visible on the surface, destined to be absorbed; the tail is beginning to disappear (in some cases it is separated by a spontaneous constriction at its junction with the body, in others it appears to be gradually absorbed); one or more warts are seen budding from the opposite extremity of the body. These last secrete a cement by which the animal is finally attached to its support,— shell, stone, or seaweed, either growing out into creeping and adherent root-threads, or enlarging into a broad base, from which the body begins to grow upward. After a while the two orifices are formed; first within, on the mantle, before the exterior test is pierced; then the internal organs, the gill-sac, and the pulsating heart, if it be one of the transparent species, become recognisable; the single eye-speck, a temporary organ, pales and disappears; and the permanent circles of visual organs are formed around the siphonal orifices. And thus the Ascidian is developed.

The genera *Ascidia* and *Cynthia* consist of isolated distinct individuals; the *Clavelina* and the *Perophora* exist in the form of groups, composed of distinct individuals associated by a common branching root-thread, whence they irregularly bud forth. There are, however, other genera, in which the compound life is more prominently manifest, the individual being recognisable only by carefully dissecting it out from the common

Plate XXXV

Botrylli.

mass. To this form belong many gelatinous masses which occur on our rocky coasts; one in particular,[6] conspicuous for its rich scarlet and orange colours, which forms irregular pear-shaped lumps, that hang from low-lying ledges, and that look not unlike strawberries. This is extremely abundant. More attractive still are the *Botrylli*,[7] which doubtless many persons have gazed on with admiration, wondering what they can be,— animal, vegetable, or what. They look as if small quantities of jelly had been spilt, sometimes on a stone, sometimes on the broad leaf of a tangle, sometimes on a shrubby sea weed, entangling the twigs and leaves in the gelatinous mass. When we look closely at such an object, we see that it is studded with little starry systems of oblong specks, of some bright colour contrasting with the ground-tint;—perhaps the stars are bright orange on a warm brown, or pale straw-colour on, a chocolate ground, or green on an iron-grey. The stars vary in outline, often being angular, often oval, or circular: they vary, too, in dimensions, and in number of the constituent specks; some may be a sixth of an inch in diameter, and contain a dozen or more; others may be less than half that size, and have no more than two or three; or even a single speck may be seen here and there, which has not yet begun to develop the starry form.

Each bright speck in these radiating star-like systems is an animal essentially of the Ascidian form, with the following peculiarities. All have budded from one primary individual, which was produced as a tiny tadpole, from an egg: the manner and direction in which the buds were put forth determining the starry arrangement. There is a common gelatinous envelope, in which the whole are imbedded, and which ever extends as the individuals and systems multiply, and which seems to have the power of developing isolated individuals which have not budded in the ordinary way, but which then produce others by budding, and so become the commencing points of other systems. In each individual the siphonal orifices are remote from each other, the receiving one being placed on the circumference of the ring or system, while the ejecting one is placed at the opposite end, opening, in common with the discharging siphons of all of that system, into a central main orifice, which rises out of the level with a circular rim, and forms the dark centre of the system.

In the open ocean there are forms of *Tunicata* which are not attached, but swim freely; and, what is surprising, even compound forms are thus found, progressing by a combined action. One of the most curious is the genus *Pyrosoma*, which consists of long-bodied Ascidians, so united in rings as to constitute a long, free cylindrical tube, closed at one end and open at the other. By the rhythmical contractions and dilatations of the multitude, this great cylinder slowly swims through the open sea. But the most interesting circumstance in its history is that it is intensely luminous, lighting up the midnight ocean with flashes of vivid light, or seen gliding through the dark water like glowing sticks of fire. So it is described by some voyagers, perhaps with a little exaggeration, for Mr. Bennett, to whom we are indebted for many valuable remarks on oceanic zoology, speaks in more subdued tones of it. His account of this and other pelagic phosphorescence is very interesting:—

"On the 8th of June," he observes, "being then in lat. 30° S., and long. 27° 5' W., having fine weather and a fresh south-easterly tradewind, and the range of the thermometer being from 78° to 84°, late at night, the mate of the watch came and called me to witness a very unusual appearance in the water, which he, on first seeing it, considered to be breakers. On arriving upon deck, this was found to be a very broad and extensive sheet of phosphorescence, extending in a direction from east to west, as far as the eye could reach. The luminosity was confined to the range of animals in this shoal, for there was no similar light in any other direction. I immediately cast the towing-net over the stern of the ship, as we approached nearer the luminous streak, to ascertain the cause of this extraordinary and so limited phenomenon. The ship soon cleaved through the brilliant mass, from which, by the disturbance, strong flashes of light were emitted; and the shoal, judging from the time the vessel took in passing through the mass, may have been a mile in breadth. The passage of the vessel through them increased the light around to a far stronger degree, illuminating the ship. On taking in the towing-net, it was found half filled with *Pyrosoma* (*Atlanticum*?), which shone with a beautiful pale-greenish light; and there were also a few shell-fish in the net at the same time. After the mass had been passed through, the light was still seen astern, until it became invisible in the distance; and the whole of the ocean then became hidden in the darkness as before this took place. The scene was as novel as beautiful and interesting; more so from my having ascertained, by capturing luminous animals, the cause of the phenomenon.

"The second occasion of my meeting these creatures was not exactly similar to the preceding; but though also limited, was curious, as occurring in a high latitude, during the winter season. It was on the 19th of August, the weather dark and gloomy, with light breezes from northnorth-east, in lat. 40° 30' S., and long. 138° 3' E., being then distant about 368 miles from King's Island (at the western entrance of Bass's Straits). It was about eight o'clock p.m. when the ship's wake was perceived to be luminous; and scintillations of the same light were also abundant around. As this was unusual, and had not been seen before, and it occasionally, also, appeared in larger and smaller detached masses, giving out a high degree of brilliancy,—to ascertain the cause, so unusual in high latitudes during the winter season, I threw the towing-net overboard, and in twenty minutes succeeded in capturing several *Pyrosomata*, giving out their usual pale-green light; and it was, no doubt, detached groups of these animals that were the occasion of the light in question. The beautiful light given out by these molluscous animals soon ceased to be seen emitted from every part of their bodies; but by moving them about it could be reproduced for some length of time after. As long as the luminosity of the ocean was visible (which continued most part of the night), a number of *Pyrosoma Atlanticum*, two species of *Phyllosoma*, an animal apparently allied to *Leptocephalus*, as well as several crustaceous animals (all of which I had before considered as intertropical species), were caught and preserved. At half-past ten p.m the temperature of the atmosphere on deck was 52°, and that of the water 51 1/2°. The luminosity of the water gradually decreased during the night, and towards morning was no longer seen, nor on any subsequent night."[8]

Let us come back from the wide world of waters, with its nightly illuminations, and its other ten thousand marvels, to our own homely and quiet beach. A tribe of existences is awaiting our notice, which we have as yet neglected; which yet we cannot fail to observe whenever we peep beneath these boulders, and look at these rocky ledges, just left exposed by the lowest retiring tides. They are the Sponges; the most debatable forms of life, long denied a right to stand in the animal ranks at all, and even still admitted there doubtingly and grudgingly by some excellent naturalists. Yet such they certainly are, established beyond reasonable controversy as true and proper examples of animal life, and therefore having a rightful claim to be painted and described in this series of essays. However, as they are the lowest, so shall they be the last; for, with a few notes on some of our species, I shall dismiss my kind and courteous readers.

The inferior surface of this huge slab of limestone, supported at one end by a boulder, while the other end is imbedded in the mud or concealed by the smaller fragments that are thrown in confusion around, is densely studded with organisms. It is only at very low tides that this arch is exposed, though now we can creep in and work with no great discomfort, though with some defilement of our garments from the mud and slime. The absence of direct light is favourable to the growth of marine productions, and thus we have another congenial element in the obscurity. With some of the smaller sea-weeds, chiefly of the filamentous kinds, as *Cladophora*, *Conferva*, some of the minuter *Callithamnia*, etc., the majority of the forms that crowd and cover the rock so densely are animals: indeed there are large areas where the animate forms struggle so perseveringly for standing-room, that not a filament or frond of vegetation can be seen, and you could not thrust the point of a penknife down to the rock in any spot without wounding some or other of the incrusting creatures. *Polyzoa* are here, chiefly of the tufted species; *Hydrozoa*, too, hang down; Anemones, but not in abundance, may be seen; *Saxicavæ* push their crimson siphons through, here and there; *Botrylli* are spread in patches, and *Amœrœcia* are suspended like a plentiful crop of tempting strawberries; but Sponges constitute the staple of the crop; it is a veritable field of Sponge.

I have on other occasions described some of the more characteristic phenomena of this class of creatures;—the volcanic eruptions of the Crumb-of-bread Sponge, the hills and poles and webs of the Rosy Crumb, the protrusile bladders of the Sanguine, the starry spicula of the Flat-Sack.[9] These I shall assume as known, and shall confine myself to the enumeration and description of a few other species which are found congregated on this rocky roof.

One of the first to catch the eye, by its gorgeous colour, is a rather thin, soft, spreading patch, of the richest vermilion hue.[10] It is of close substance, the surface covered with shallow irregular sinuous channels and minute orifices. It rarely exceeds an inch in diameter, but throws out slender clinging processes to some length. The flesh is dense. Under the microscope it contains three-rayed spicula, which are for the most part somewhat blunt, but some are very sharp. After death it rapidly loses its brilliant hue, and dries of a dull oak-brown.

Another occurs in the form of low irregular spreading patches of a greyish black, very smooth and shiny, more plump than the former, and a little larger.[11] There are no visible orifices on the surface. The substance is yellowish grey, compact, with a distinct demarcation from the thin black tough skin. The spicula of the flesh have three rays in one plane, and one standing up from it; very stout, sharp-pointed, with a distinct canal running through the centre of each ray of the larger ones. There are a few rods abruptly hooked at the tip; a few very long, straight, and slender, with pin-like heads; and a few simple needles, long, slender, pointed at one or at both ends.

Some largish rounded masses occur, several inches in diameter, and rising to a thickness of three-fourths of an inch.[12] The surface is undulate, the summits slightly ridged, covered with shallow sinuous channels having sharp edges, not very confluent: large round mouth-orifices (*oscula*) generally mark the summits of the ridges. The colour of this fine species is a deep buff, and its appearance is much like that of our Turkey Sponge, with something of the same feel, but much firmer. The interior is full of channels. The spicula here are very varied and interesting, comprising some curious and unusual forms. Some, indeed, are simple needles, nearly straight, pointed at one end rather abruptly. The following are minute. There are a number of rings interrupted at one side, like the letter C, some thicker and more elliptical, others slender and rounder, C. A few take the form of the letter S, but having one lobe much more developed than the other. Some of the C form have both the extremities bifid, and the points widely diverging; and some of these have the back straight, instead of curved, and these with their bifid points, look, when viewed in front, like double anchors. All are, as usual, spun out of the most brilliant glass.

Then we have in some abundance a sort[13] with firm cartilaginous walls, about one-eighth of an inch thick, standing up to the height of three-fourths, with rounded summits, running in irregular sinuations and convolutions, not unlike the cartilage of the human ear, enclosing deep hollows. The colour is opaque white, tinged with red, probably from the red mud, which is prevalent here. When cut with a knife this sponge has a sharp, crisp, gritty feel, and when a little is crushed between glass plates we distinctly hear a creaking sound.

These phenomena depend on the circumstance that it is almost wholly composed of great stout three-rayed spicula, solid throughout, together with a multitude of excessively slender needles, straight, long, pointed at one end; and many others as slender, but very short; no longer, indeed, than the thickness of one of the three-rayed.[14]

Equally numerous with these, and possessing a certain amount of resemblance to them, are some thick, compact, sack-shaped masses, with angular edges and blunt points: sometimes they are flattened and dilated, like a sack when empty; sometimes rounded, like a sack when full. In the former condition several perforations occur along the terminal ridge, in the latter there is generally but one. The colour is white, slightly tinted, just as in the preceding. It stands up boldly and stiffly (or rather *hangs* in the natural state) from its rather narrow base to the height of about two-thirds of an inch, and the flattened specimens are as wide as this. It is nearly made up of three-rayed spicula, some of large size, but more rather small. A transverse section shows no obvious arrangement, except that of the great central channel, into which the points of the spicula project; but a longitudinal section shows the spicula built up one on another in many courses, so nearly symmetrical that hexagonal canals are formed, whose axes run transversely to the axis of the sponge; *i.e.*, horizontally. There is very little fleshy or gelatinous matter.[15]

Again we see a showy species,[16] making soft, spongy patches of an orange or red-lead colour, an inch or more in diameter, rising into ridges a quarter of an inch high, and forming low peaks, whose apices are perforate. Its substance contains simple needles, long, nearly or quite straight, pointed at one end; these are found in great numbers in close array, the points mostly projecting from the surface. Some of them are twice as thick as others.

Now we notice another peculiar form:[17] creeping, worm-like masses of orange-yellow or buff hue, soft and spongy in texture, which throw up one or more free, erect, processes, irregularly curved, an inch or more long, and about one-eighth thick on an average, but frequently swollen and contracted by turns. These are not tubular, and the tips are rounded. The general surface under a magnifier appears slightly channelled. Within we find simple needles, long, nearly straight, pointed at both ends, moderately numerous, enveloped in much yellow granular flesh.

Then there are some imposing masses of a globose form,[18] some of which attain a foot or more in diameter, though others are not more than an inch. The surface is compact and smooth, of a delicate purplish-grey hue, with a few minute orifices, each surrounded by a small paler area.

The spicula in this noble species are various:—simple rods, straight, thick, long, slightly spindle-shaped, blunt at both ends, with a linear axis; three-rayed, large, stout, very unequal angled, without any central channel; a number of very small five- and six-rayed stars, the rays projecting in different planes. They are set in a dense, yellow, gelatinous flesh, in which we may at all times discover many gemmules, or eggs; the smaller (or younger) are nearly round, bristling with points in all directions like sea-urchins, changing as they grow larger to a more oval form, beset with rounded warts, instead of points. These are discharged, when mature, with the currents of water, through the orifices, and find their way to

Plate XXXVI

Sponges. Chiton.

some suitable spot, where they develop themselves into the parent form.

Finally, here is a sort[19] whose colour is a pale Indian red; occurring in masses which take the form of thick, plump bands, about half-an-inch in width, but alternately swelling and contracting, which creep over the rock, meeting and uniting, and then separating, so as to leave hollow open interstices, which, however, in some specimens are gradually filled up. The swellings form pointed hillocks, the apices of which are pierced with from one to three orifices. Irregular shallow channels cover the hillocks, and converge to the apices. It contains simple needles, slender, straight (or slightly curved), pointed at each end, not very numerous, thickly invested with granular flesh. This Sponge shrivels much, and becomes shapeless in drying, but changes little in colour. It is abundant.[20]

Thus the praise of the all-glorious God lies latent in all his creatures, whether man educe it or not. Too often, when we observe the wondrous variety, the incomparable delicacy, elegance, beauty, the transcendent fitness and perfection of every organ and structure, we are more occupied with our own pleasure or our own glory than with the praise of God: our own pleasure in acquiring new knowledge, or in admiring unexpected beauties; our own glory in opening up new stores of science;—these are our motives to study, and we withhold from, or feebly and grudgingly give to, the Blessed Creator and Fashioner, the honour, of which every atom, every combination, every exquisite contrivance, is eloquently discoursing to us the while. Forgive, O Thou, who hast created all things, and for whose pleasure they are, and were created, that we so often touch with irreverent hand Thy glorious works; that we so often walk with silent tongues on this holy ground!

I cannot conclude this volume without recording my solemn and deliberate protest against the infidelity with which, to a very painful extent, modern physical science is associated. I allude not only to the ground which the conclusions of modern geologists take, in opposition to the veracity of the "God which cannot lie," though the distinct statements which He has made to us concerning Creation are now, as if by common consent, put aside, with silent contempt, as effete fables, unworthy of a moment's thought, and this too before vast assemblages of persons, not one of whom lifts his voice for the truth of God. These assaults are at least open and unmasked. But there is in our scientific literature, and specially in that which takes a popular form, a tone equally dangerous and more insidious. It altogether ignores the awful truths of God's revelation, that all mankind are guilty and condemned and spiritually dead in Adam; that we are by nature children of wrath; that the whole world lieth in the wicked one; and that the wrath of God abideth on it: it ignores the glorious facts of atonement by the precious blood of Christ, and of acceptance in Him. It substitutes for these a mere sentimental admiration of nature, and teaches that the love of the beautiful makes man acceptable to God, and secures His favour. How often do we see quoted and be-praised, as if it were an indisputable axiom, the sentiment of a poet who ought to have known better,

> "He prayeth best who loveth best
> All things, both great and small;"—

a sentiment as silly as it is unscriptural; for what connexion can there be between the love of the inferior creatures, and the acceptableness of a sinner praying to the Holy God? It is the intervention of Christ Jesus, the anointed Priest, which alone gives prayer acceptance.

There is no sentimental or scientific road to heaven. There is absolutely nothing in the study of created things, however single, however intense, which will admit sinful man into the presence of God, or fit him to enjoy it. If there were, what need was there that the glorious Son, the everlasting Word, should be made flesh, and give His life a ransom for many?

If I have come to God as a guilty sinner, and have found acceptance, and reconciliation, and sonship, in the blood of His only-begotten Son, then I may come down from that elevation, and study creation with advantage and profit; but to attempt to scale heaven with the ladder of natural history, is nothing else than Cain's religion; it is the presentation of the fruit of the earth, instead of the blood of the Lamb.

This will be, in all probability, the last occasion of my coming in literary guise before the public: how can I better take my leave than with the solemn testimony of the Spirit of God, which I affectionately commend to my readers,—

> There is No Way into the Holiest
> but by the Blood of Jesus.

Finis.

Footnotes

Chapter I

[1] *Trochus ziziphinus*, which the reader will see figured in the upper right corner of Plate I.
[2] *Phasianella pullus*.
[3] *Conch. Syst.* ii. 252.
[4] *Leç. Elém.* 188.
[5] *Nassa incrassata*.
[6] *Nassa reticulata*. A figure of this species is seen in the lower left corner of Plate I.
[7] *Aporrhais pes-pelicani*, which the reader will see figured in the centre of Plate I.
[8] *Cypræa Europæa*, which is delineated in the lower right corner of Plate 1.
[9] *Pecten opercularis*, of which see a group in Plate II.
[10] Parnell's "Hermit."
[11] For a description of the mode in which this action is performed, see *Devonshire Coast*, p. 50, *et seq*.
[12] Quin died in 1766. Montagu, in 1803, says of this Pecten, that "it is known by the name of Frills or Queens," with no allusion to the actor. The term "frill" obviously refers to the form of the shell.
[13] The principal figure in Plate III. represents this species (*Pentacta pentactes*) in the expanded condition described in the text.
[14] *Sipunculus punctatissimus*, figured in Plate III., to the left.
[15] *Sipunculus Bernhardus*.

Chapter II

[1] *Triopa clavigera*.
[2] *Doris tuberculata*, which the reader will see figured in Plate IV., in the centre of the foreground.
[3] *Eolis coronata*, figured in the upper part of Plate IV., above the Sea Lemon.
[4] Both these are depicted in Plate IV. That on the right of the picture is the spawn of *Doris tuberculata*; that on the left is the spawn of *Eolis coronata*.
[5] Alder and Hancock (Doris).
[6] *Purpura lapillus*, sometimes known as the Dog-winkle. Three individuals, representing the varieties of colour, are seen in the middle of Plate V., and a cluster of their egg-capsules in the lower left corner.
[7] See *Devonshire Coast*, p. 60.
[8] *Trans. Micr. Soc.* (Ser. II.), vol. iii. p. 17.
[9] *Patella vulgata*, represented by two examples in Plate V., at the left side of the picture.
[10] *Emarginula reticulata*, of which a figure appears in the right-hand corner of Plate V.
[11] *Fissurella reticulata*.
[12] *Pholas dactylus*; the principal figure in Plate VI., represented as exposed in its burrow by the splitting off of a portion of the limestone rock.
[13] *Zoologist*, p. 7819.
[14] *Nat. Hist. of Brighton*, p. 185.

[15] *Zoologist*, p. 6541.
[16] *Saxicava rugosa*; represented by the smaller figure in Plate VI.

Chapter III

[1] *Actinia mesembryanthemum*, represented in Plate VII., at the lower right-hand corner.
[2] *Anthea cereus*, var. *smaragdina*, represented at the right hand of Plate IX.
[3] M. Coste has lately communicated a paper to the Academy of Sciences on the progress of his artificial oyster-beds on the western coast of France. Several thousands of the inhabitants of the island of Ré have been for the last four years engaged in cleansing their muddy coast of the sediments which prevented oysters from congregating there; and as the work advances the seed wafted over from Nieulle and other oyster localities settles in the new beds, and, added to that transplanted, peoples the coast, so that 72,000,000 of oysters, from one to four years old, and nearly all marketable, is the lowest average per annum registered by the local administration, representing, at the rate of from 25 to 30 francs per thousand, which is the current price in the locality, a suns of about two millions of francs, the produce of an extremely limited surface. That the waves or currents carry the seed of oysters is a well-known fact, since the walls of sluices newly erected are often covered with them. In the island of Ré, the existence of the oyster-beds, however, no longer depends upon this contingency, they being now in a state of permanent self-reproduction. The distinction of oyster-beds into those of collection and those of reproduction is quite unnecessary, since the property of reproduction belongs to them all. In some localities it is sufficient to prepare the emerging banks for collection to see them soon covered with seed; but in other places nothing would be obtained without transplanting proper subjects, an operation which by no means impairs their reproductive qualities. The concession of emerging banks is anxiously applied for by the inhabitants of the coast; the more so as improvements in the working of this branch of trade are of daily occurrence. Thus, Dr. Kemmerer, of Ré, covers a number of tiles with a coating of a kind of mastic, brittle enough to enable him to detach the small oysters from it. When this coating is well covered with seed he gets it off all in one piece, which he carries to the place where the seed is to grow. The same tile he coats a second time, and so on as long as the seed will deposit upon it. In short, wherever the violence of the currents and the instability of the bottom do not present irresistible obstacles the cultivation of the oysters has become a lucrative business.
[4] *Alcyonium digitatum*, for which see Plate VII. It is the white object near the middle of the picture, partly concealed by the intervening leaf of green *Ulva*.
[5] *Sagartia rosea*, of which a specimen, only partially open, is delineated in the centre foreground of Plate VII.
[6] *Sagartia miniata*.
[7] *Sagartia nivea*; two of this species, one closed, the other partially opened, are seen at the left corner of the foreground in Plate VII.
[8] *Sagartia venusta*, a group of which occupies the right-hand side of Plate IX., including both expanded and closed individuals.
[9] *Sag. bellis, sphyrodeta, troglodytes, pura*.
[10] See my *History of the British Sea-anemones*.

[11] *Actinoloba dianthus.*

[12] For a fuller account of these organs and their offensive function, which constitute an apparatus not exceeded in interest by any that I know of in the whole realm of natural history, I beg to refer the reader to my *Naturalist's Rambles on the Devon-shire Coast*, and my *Actinologia Britannica, passim*.

[13] *Tealia crassicornis*, which forms the subject of Plate VIII.

[14] *Lucernaria campanulata* is represented in the upper right-hand corner of Plate VII.

Chapter IV

[1] *Cardium rusticum*, figured at the left hand of Plate X., with the foot thrust out and pushing.

[2] *Cardium edule.*

[3] *Highlands and Islands of Scotland*, vol. iii. p. 349.

[4] *Voyage round Scotland*, vol. i. p. 460.

[5] *Venus fasciata*, of which a figure is given in the midst of the foreground of Plate X.

[6] *Palæmon serratus*, represented in the upper figure in Plate XI., resting, as described, on a leaf of *Iridæa edulis.*

[7] *Crangon vulgaris*, a figure of which may be seen in the lower part of Plate XI.

[8] *British Stalk-eyed Crustacea*, p. 257.

[9] *Solea vulgaris*, and *S. pegusa.*

[10] *British Fishes*, vol. ii. p. 298.

[11] *Rhombus punctatus*, delineated at the right-hand side of Plate XII., adhering to a flat stone.

[12] *Ammodytes lancea*, for which see the centre of Plate XII.

Chapter V

[1] *Trachinus vipera*, represented by the lower figure in Plate XIII.

[2] So old Drayton, in his "Polyolbion" sings, quaintly enough, and with a noble defiance of grammar:—
"The Weever, which, although his prickles venom be,
By fishers cut away, which buyers seldom see,
Yet for the fish he bears, 'tis not accounted bad."

[3] Since the above was written, the question has been set at rest, by Dr. Günther's and Mr. Byerley's actual discovery of poison-glands in connexion with these spines.

[4] *Gasterosteus spinachia*, represented by the upper figure in Plate XIII.

[5] It is depicted in Plate XIV.

[6] Jones's *Animal Kingdom*, p. 90.

[7] This species, together with the following, is represented on Plate XV.; the latter coiled among the stones, and preparing to attack a *Serpula.*

[8] *Glaucus*, p. 103.

Chapter VI

[1] *Aplysia punctata*, of which two specimens, one viewed sidewise, and the other mounting an angle of rock, showing the front of its head, are depicted in Plate XVI. Sowerby applied the name of "*hybrida*" to the species, and Forbes and Hanley have adopted it; but even the inflexible law of priority does not warrant the perpetuation of a name which is glaringly absurd, and expresses a manifest contradiction; for if the creature were a hybrid, it would not be a species, and not be entitled to a specific name.

[2] *Outlines of Comp. Anatomy*, p. 371.

[3] *De Anim. Maria.*, quoted in Johnston's *Introd. to Conchology*, p. 18.

[4] This animal will be described in a subsequent chapter.

[5] *Journal of Researches*, chap. i.

[6] Johnston.
[7] *Dentalium entalis*, represented at the right-hand corner of the foreground in Plate XVII.
[8] *Pileopsis Hungaricus*, of which a specimen is represented in the attitude of life, adhering to the dark rock, in Plate XVII.
[9] *Litt. de la France*, i. 133.
[10] *Gammarus locusta*.
[11] Bate and Westwood's *Crustacea*, p. 382.
[12] Bate and Westwood, p. 380.
[13] Bate and Westwood, p. 391.
[14] It is named *Ligia oceanica*, and is represented in Plate XVII., in the centre of the picture.
[15] *Phyllodoce viridis*.
[16] *P. laminosa*, represented in the middle and right of Plate XVIII.
[17] *Litt. de la France*, ii. 223.
[18] *Nereis margaritacea*, of which the head and fore parts of the body crawling over a stone are depicted at the left-hand corner of Plate XVIII.
[19] *Polynœ cirrata*.
[20] Dr. Williams, *On the British Annelida*, p. 219.

Chapter VII

[1] *Lepidogaster bimaculatus*, of which individuals of different varieties of colour, and in different attitudes, are represented in Plate XIX.
[2] Let me refer my readers to an excellent and most interesting paper on this little fish, by my friend, Mr. W. R. Hughes, in the *Zoologist* for July 1864.
[3] *Asterina gibbosa*, figured in the right-hand foreground of Plate XX.
[4] *Echinus miliaris*, a specimen of which may be seen delineated in Plate XX., in the upper left-hand corner.
[5] *Comatula rosacea*; a fine specimen of which, taken by myself in a little cove near Torquay, I have delineated in the centre of Plate XX.

[6] *Porcellana longicornis*.
[7] *Porcellana platycheles*, represented by the central figure in Plate XXI.
[8] *The Aquarium*: 2d Ed. pp. 37-45.
[9] *Galathea squamifera*, represented in Plate XXI., at the left hand, in the act of shooting backward.
[10] *G. nexa*, for which see the right-hand corner of the same plate.
[11] *G. strigosa*.
[12] *Tenby*, p. 169, Plates VII and VIII.

Chapter VIII

[1] *Crenilabrus Cornubicus*, of which a group, in several varieties of colour, size, and position, are represented in Plate XXII.
[2] *Aquarium* (2d Ed.), p. 108.
[3] *Sagartia parasitica*.
[4] *Cottus bubalis*, two specimens of which are figured in the centre and left corner of Plate XXIII.
[5] *Zoologist*, p. 1403.
[6] *British Fishes* (2d Ed.), pp. 79, 81.
[7] *Syngnathus lumbriciformis*, represented in its favourite attitude, on a tuft of *Chondrus*, at the right side of Plate XXIII.
[8] In a paper read before the Zoological Society on June 11th, 1861, Dr. J. E. Gray describes as new to naturalists these and other habits of the Pipe-fishes, which he had observed when watching specimens kept in the tanks of the gardens in Regent Park. And he takes occasion to lecture other "persons who have leisure and opportunity" for not giving more particulars of the manners of fishes. But the habits in question had been described in minute detail by myself nine years before (see my *Devonshire Coast*, p. 180, *et seq.*), together with many other interesting points in the economy of these curious fishes. The still earlier observations of Mr. Couch are also thus cavalierly ignored.

Footnotes

[9] *Syngnathus acus.*
[10] *Zoology for Schools*, p. 221.
[11] Col. i. 16, 17.
[12] *Blennius ocellaris*: it is the principal figure in Plate XXIV.
[13] *Blennius pholis.*
[14] Originally communicated to a Monmouthshire newspaper in Oct. 1847.
[15] *Gobius minutus* of zoologists, represented in the centre of Plate XXIV., partly overshadowed by the Butterfly Blenny.

Chapter IX

[1] *Solaster papposa*, represented, about one-third of the natural size, by the right-hand figure on Plate XXV.
[2] *Ophiocoma granulata*, seen in the upper left-hand corner of Plate XXV.
[3] *Gonoplax angulatus*, the principal figure in Plate XXVI., occupying the foreground.
[4] *Ebalia*; a male specimen of *E. Bryerii* is represented in Plate XXVI., clinging to the stem of an aged tangle, in the upper left-hand corner.
[5] *E. Pennantii.*
[6] *Aquarium* (2d Ed.), p. 154.
[7] *Pagurus Bernhardus*; so called, I presume, from Bernard, the monk, in allusion to its passing its life in its cell: whence also "Hermit-crab."
[8] In Plate XXVII. both species are represented. In the foreground is a full-grown *Pagurus Prideauxii* tenanting a whelk-shell, which carries a fine specimen of the Cloak Anemone (*Adamsia palliata*). In the distance is seen *P. Bernhardus*, inhabiting a shell of *Natica*.
[9] See my *Aquarium*, p. 156, *et seq.*
[10] These facts were originally published in the *Zoologist* for 1859 (p. 6580). In the *Quarterly Journal of Science* for January 1864, some observations of Colonel Stuart Wortley are cited, confirmatory of mine, which, however, are wholly ignored by the Editors.

Chapter X

[1] *Physalia pelagica*, of which a representation is given in the centre of Plate XXVIII. Some naturalists make two or three other species, but I do not think that their distinctive characters can as yet be depended on.
[2] *Gatherings of a Naturalist*, p. 7.
[3] I ought to say that, as usual in these stranded examples, the tentacles and suckers were so mutilated by washing on the shore, that I have been compelled to aid my observation by the figures of Eschscholtz and Huxley, on whose correctness I could depend.
[4] See his *Gatherings in Australasia*, for much interesting information on both these animals.
[5] *Op. cit.*
[6] *Sarsia tubulosa*; a group is represented of the size of life, in the lower right-hand corner of Plate XXVIII.
[7] *Æquorea Forbesiana*; this fine species forms the subject of Plate XXIX.
[8] *Aurelia aurita*, represented (about one-fourth of the natural size) in Plate XXX. On the extreme right and left are seen the young, in the stages of *Hydra*, *Strobila*, and *Ephydra.*
[9] *Cydippe pileus*, seen, of the size of life, near the upper left-hand corner of Plate XXX.
[10] Dr. Drummond, in *Trans. Roy. Irish Acad. for* 1839.

Chapter XI

[1] *Antennularia antennina*, figured in Plate XXXI., springing from the

lower left corner. It will be easily recognised from the description.
2 For details and figures of these developments, I beg to refer the reader to my *Naturalist's Rambles on the Devonshire Coast.*
3 *Scalpellum vulgare*, seen in Plate XXXI., in the position described in the text.
4 *Balanus balanoides*, of which a group is seen in the extreme left of the foreground in Plate XXXI.; *B. porcatus*, a single specimen, is a little to the right.
5 *Lepas anatifera.* A group, the size of life, is seen depending in the upper right-hand corner of Plate XXXI.
6 *Pyrgoma Anglicum*, of which three specimens are seen attached to a *Caryophyllia Smithii*, at the left side of Plate XXXI.
7 *Zoologist*, pp. 7054, 7111.
8 *Serpula contortuplicata*, a mass of which forms the subject of Plate XXII., mingled with *S. triquetra.*
9 Some in this infant state are seen in Plate XXXIII.
10 Brit. Annelida. in *Rep. Brit. Assoc.*, 1851.
11 *Zoologist*, p. 5976.
12 *Vide supra*, p. 75.
13 *Sabella tubularia*, represented as occupying the foreground and the left-hand side of Plate XXXIII.
14 I have figured a group in the centre of Plate XXXIII. I cannot satisfactorily identify it with any species described in Grube's *Fam. der Anneliden.* It has some affinities with the *Sabella penicillus* of Müller; and still more with *S. gracilis* of Grube. This latter is defined, however, as wanting the two naked threads by the mouth, which in my little species are sufficiently conspicuous. I must leave it undetermined.
15 *Sabella bombyx*, represented in Plate XXXIII., towards the right hand, springing out of a group of Serpula tubes.
16 *Intellectual Observer*, vol. iii. p. 77.

Chapter XII

1 Ascidia —?; perhaps *A. prunum*; but much uncertainty rests on the names of the *Tunicata*. The species is represented in Plate XXXIV: two specimens on the right hand.
2 *Clavelina lepadiformis.*
3 *Perophora Listeri.* For magnified figures of these animals the reader is referred to my *Tenby*, Plate V., and *Devonshire Coast*, Plate XV.
4 *Cynthia grossularia*; of which a group is depicted in Plate XXXIV, seated on an old cockle valve, to the right of the foreground.
5 *Cynthia quadrangularis*, represented in the background of Plate XXXIV, rising above the cockle shell which supports the Currants.
6 *Amœrœcium proliferum.*
7 Two familiar kinds of *Botryllus* are represented in Plate XXXV; of which I cannot with certainty indicate the specific names.
8 *Wanderings in New South Wales*, etc., vol. i.
9 *Tenby.*—The systematic appellations of these four species are *Halichondria panicea*, *Halichondria rosea*, *Halichondria sanguinea*, and *Grantia compressa.*
10 *Grantia coriacea.*
11 *Halina Bucklandi.*
12 *Halichondria incrustans.*
13 *Leuconia nivea.*
14 It is possible that these may be fragments of the longer needles; but from their bluntly-pointed ends, and general agreement *inter se*, I do not think so.
15 *Leuconia Gossei* (Bowerbank MS.). Dr. Bowerbank, to whom I have communicated this species, thinks that it may have been confounded by former observers with the preceding. "The broad specific difference between them is that *L. nivea* has very large triradiate spicula at

its surface, and *L. Gossei* has not, but has in lieu of them very large acerate ones at right angles to the surface." (Bowerb. *in litt.*)

[16] *Hymeniacidon caruncula.*
[17] *Hymeniacidon albescens.*
[18] *Pachymatisma Johnstoni.*
[19] *Microciona carnosa.*
[20] I have been minute in the descriptions of these species, because the student of marine zoology has so little to aid him in the identification of our Sponges. This South Devon coast is peculiarly rich in these productions; and several of these, though common here, are considered, as Dr. Bowerbank tells me, quite rare. The figures, which I have drawn from the life with great care, will, I trust, leave no difficulty in the identification.

Plate XXXVI. is devoted to the above species of Sponges. Beginning from the upper right corner, we have *Halichondria panicea*, greenish yellow, with perforated hillocks: it occurs also in other parts of the picture. The scarlet one next below is *Grantia coriacea*. The black one to the right is *Halina Bucklandi*. The plump buff one under the scarlet is *Halichondria incrustans*. Below this is the contorted *Leuconia nivea*. Then follows, below, and a little to the left, *Hymeniacidon caruncula*. Below this are two specimens of *Leuconia Gossei*, and on the left, yellow, with a slender serpent-like projection, *Hymeniacidon albescens*. Behind this is the grey globular *Pachymatisma Johnstoni*, and below, to the left, the pale red *Microciona carnosa*.

www.ingramcontent.com/pod-product-compliance
Ingram Content Group UK Ltd.
Pitfield, Milton Keynes, MK11 3LW, UK
UKHW061222180426
11947UKWH00026B/1965